The Horn of Africa

THE HORN OF AFRICA

Intra-State and Inter-State Conflicts and Security

Edited by
Redie Bereketeab

PLUTO PRESS Nordiska Afrikainstitutet
The Nordic Africa Institute

First published 2013 by Pluto Press
345 Archway Road, London N6 5AA

www.plutobooks.com

In cooperation with the Nordic Africa Institute
P.O. Box 1703, SE-751 47 Uppsala, Sweden

www.nai.uu.se

British Library Cataloguing in Publication Data
A catalogue record for this book is available from the British Library

ISBN   978 0 7453 3312 0   Hardback
ISBN   978 0 7453 3311 3   Paperback
ISBN   978 1 8496 4823 3   PDF eBook
ISBN   978 1 8496 4825 7   Kindle eBook
ISBN   978 1 8496 4824 0   EPUB eBook

Library of Congress Cataloging in Publication Data applied for

This book is printed on paper suitable for recycling and made from fully
managed and sustained forest sources. Logging, pulping and manufacturing
processes are expected to conform to the environmental standards of the
country of origin.

10   9   8   7   6   5   4   3   2   1

Typeset from disk by Stanford DTP Services, Northampton, England
Printed and bound by CPI Group (UK) Ltd, Croydon, CR0 4YY

Contents

Maps and Figures

Abbreviations

ABC	Abyei Boundaries Commission
ABY	Abyei
ADF	Allied Democratic Forces
AFP	Agence France Presse
AIAI	Al-Ittihad Al-Islamiya
AL	Arab League
AMIS	African Union Mission in Sudan
AMISOM	African Union Mission to Somalia
ARDU/F	Afar Revolutionary Democratic Union/Front
ARPCT	Alliance for the Restoration of Peace and Counter-Terrorism
ARS	Alliance for the Re-Liberation of Somalia
ATP	Abyei Territory Puzzle
AU	African Union
BLB	Borderline Belt
BNR	Blue Nile River
BNS	Blue Nile State
CAR	Central African Republic
CDO	Closed Districts Ordinance
CEWARN	Conflict Early Warning and Response Mechanism
CPA	Comprehensive Peace Agreement
DMLK	Democratic Movement for the Liberation of Kunama
DoP	Declaration of Principles
DPA	Darfur Peace Agreement
DUP	Democratic Unionist Party
EBBC	Ethiopia–Eritrea Boundary Commission
ECOWAS	Economic Community of West African States
EDU	Ethiopian Democratic Union
EEZ	exclusive economic zone
ELF	Eritrea Liberation Front
EPDM	Ethiopian People's Democratic Movement
EPLF	Eritrean People's Liberation Front
EPPF	Ethiopian People's Patriotic Front
EPRDF	Ethiopian People's Revolutionary Democratic Front
EPRP	Ethiopian People's Revolutionary Party
ESPA	Eastern Sudan Peace Agreement

EU	European Union
FRUD	Front for the Restoration of Unity and Democracy
GNU	Government of National Unity
GoSS	Government of South Sudan
ICU	Islamic Courts' Union
IGAD	Inter-Governmental Authority on Development
IGDD	Inter-Governmental Authority on Drought and Development
ICPAT	IGAD Capacity Building Programme against Terrorism
IDPs	internally displaced persons
IPF	IGAD Partners' Forum
JEM	Justice and Equality Movement
JIUs	joint integrated units
LJM	Liberation and Justice Movement
LRA	Lord's Resistance Army
NBI	Nile Basin Initiative
NCP	National Congress Party
NDA	National Democratic Alliance
NFD	Northern Frontier Districts
NSDB	North Sudan Dragon Belt
OAU	Organization of African Unity
OIC	Organization of the Islamic Conference
OLF	Oromo Liberation Front
ONLF	Ogaden National Liberation Front
PCA	Permanent Court of Arbitration
PFDJ	People's Front for Democracy and Justice
PRP	People's Rally for Progress
RSADO	Red Sea Afar Democratic Organization
RSS	Republic of South Sudan
SADC	Southern African Development Community
SAF	Sudan Armed Forces
SDS	South Darfur State
SINS	Sinnar State
SKS	South Kordofan State
SLM	Sudan Liberation Movement
SNM	Somali National Movement
SPLA	Sudan People's Liberation Army
SPLM/A	Sudan People's Liberation Movement/Army
SRC	Supreme Revolutionary Council
SRRC	Somalia Reconciliation and Restoration Council
SSDF	Somali Salvation Democratic Front

SYL	Somali Youth League
TAP	Two Areas Protocol
TBC	Technical Border Committee
TFG	Transitional Federal Government
TFI	Transitional Federal Institutions
TFP	Transitional Federal Parliament
TNG	Transitional Government
TPLF	Tigray People's Liberation Front
TRS	The Republic of Sudan
TTAs	Three Transitional Areas
UIC	Union of Islamic Courts
UN	United Nations
UNAMID	United Nations African Mission in Darfur
UNMID	United Nations Mission in Darfur
UNS	Upper Nile State
UNSC	United Nations Security Council
UP	Umma Party
UPDA	Uganda People's Democratic Army
USC	United Somali Congress
UWSLF	United Western Somali Liberation Front
WNR	White Nile River
WNS	White Nile State
WNSB	White Nile Sugar Bowl
WSLF	Western Somali Liberation Front

Selected Chronology

SUDAN

1955	Emergence of Anyanya I
1956	Independence of Sudan
1958	Military coup by General Aboud
1964	Popular uprising, General Aboud deposed, civilian government
1969	Military coup by General Ghaffar El Nimeiri
1972	Addis Ababa Agreement, end of first civil war
1983	Collapse of Addis Ababa Agreement, second civil war, SPLM/A
1985	General El Nimeiri deposed by popular uprising
1986	Introduction of civilian government
1989	Military coup supported by National Islamic Front
2003	Darfur war breaks out
2005	Signing of the Comprehensive Peace Agreement
2011	9 January, referendum in South Sudan
2011	9 July, South Sudan independence

SOMALIA

1941	Defeat of Italy, Four Powers to decide fate of Somalia
1948	Four Powers refer Somalia to UN
1950	Italy and Somali Trusteeship
1960	Somalia becomes independent
1964	War between Ethiopia and Somalia
1969	Military coup by General Siad Barre
1977–78	War between Ethiopia and Somalia
1981	Outbreak of civil war
1991	Collapse of the Siad Barre regime
1991	Somaliland declares independence
2000	Formation Transitional National Government
2004	Formation Transitional Federal Government

ETHIOPIA

1935	Italian invasion
1941	Return of the emperor from exile

1973   Foundation of OLF
1974   Fall of the monarchy
1975   Foundation of the TPLF
1977   The Dergue allies itself with the Soviet Union
1984   Foundation of the ONLF
1989   Foundation of the EPRDF
1991   Demise of the Dergue. EPRDF takes power
1992   OLF second armed struggle

ERITREA

1890   Colonized by Italy
1941   Defeat of Italy, Four Powers take over
1950   UN decides to federate Eritrea with Ethiopia
1952   Federation begins
1961   Launching of armed struggle by the ELF
1962   Eritrea Annexed by Ethiopia
1970   Formation of the EPLF
1972–74 First civil war
1980–81 Second civil war
1991   Eritrea gains independence
1998   War breaks out between Eritrea and Ethiopia

DJIBOUTI

1977   Djibouti becomes independent
1991   Foundation of FRUD
1994   Peace agreement with faction of FRUD
2001   Peace agreement with remaining faction of FRUD
2008   Conflict with Eritrea
2010   FRUD launches armed rebellion

Foreword

The Horn of Africa continues to hold the attention of many strategic thinkers and commentators, leaders, scholars, policy makers and citizens of the countries in the region. While some note that it has remained one of Africa's most conflicted and unstable regions, others draw attention to the emergence of some unique experiments in managing diversity, state formation and governance, and forms of engagement with outside cultures and influences. Whether seen from the perspective of state, intra-state and inter-state conflicts, the absence of peace in the Horn has its roots in a long and complex history, political economy, state formation processes and struggles, international intervention, identity conflicts and environmental change. Untangling the complex web of conflicts, understanding the connections at the local, sub-national, national, regional and global levels, engaging in deeper reflections and proffering viable options for promoting participatory, sustainable people-centred peace and development in the Horn remain compelling challenges.

In the days of the East–West Cold War, the Horn was one of the spaces within Africa where the superpowers fought proxy wars which were always to the detriment of the peoples of their client-states and neighbouring regions. The end of the Cold War and the impact of global transformations on the Horn have been as complex as they are far-reaching. Intra-state wars have mutated either in response to the collapse of central authority as in the case of Somalia, or to the survival, splintering or emergence of rebel groups, leading to immense suffering, international intervention and the emergence of new conflict actors. It has also contributed to the birth of new states such as Eritrea, and most recently South Sudan, and the unrecognized states of Somaliland and Puntland. The brief war between Ethiopia and Eritrea reminds us of earlier cases of inter-state conflict in the Horn, but it is important to note that beyond being conflict actors or sites of conflict within national borders, states can be conflict actors in intra-state conflicts in other countries. However, the conflict dynamics in the Horn have not been limited to within state borders or limited to state actors, but have drawn in non-state actors. Non-state actors, such as militias, rebel groups and armed bands, have proliferated in some of the countries, operating within and across borders, with violent conflict assuming cross-border and regional dimensions. This scenario is further complicated by the involvement of diasporas, trans-territorial actors and the world's established and emerging powers in the festering conflicts.

As this study of the Horn aptly demonstrates, the local, sub-national, state and inter-state levels of the conflicts in the Horn are feeding the securitization of the region and higher levels of international intervention and indeed military presence, driven by the 'new international scramble for markets and natural resources', the global war on terror and the war on piracy in the coastal waters of the Horn. The emerging paradox is a scenario of growing concern about the risks and insecurities that the higher stakes portend, as well as a lingering hope that peace and development lie somewhere beyond the war-scarred horizon, regional-institutional responses and the conflicting interests of hegemonic national, regional and global interests.

In a region and continent where the stirrings of an Arab Spring and episodic outbursts of various 'Springs' sit cheek by jowl with the challenges of everyday survival, the contributors to this compelling volume challenge us to imagine that the people of the Horn as sovereign actors can, through everyday struggles, in the future negotiate a new social contract with the states and regional institutions, and perhaps open up radical pathways to peace and development in a highly conflicted region.

Cyril Obi
Social Science Research Council
New York, 2012

Part I
Causes of Conflicts

1
Introduction

Redie Bereketeab

This book explores perspectives on intra-state and inter-state conflicts in the Horn of Africa. Comprising Djibouti, Eritrea, Ethiopia, Somalia and Sudan, this is the most conflicted region in the African continent. The recent major expressions of these virulent conflicts are manifested in the second North–South civil war (1983–2005) in Sudan and the intra-state war in Darfur (Johnson 2003; Deng 2010; Barltrop 2011); as well as the inter-state Ethiopian–Eritrean war of 1998–2000, which devastated the region (Jacquin-Berdal and Plaut 2004). Since 9/11, the region also has become one of the theatres of the global war on terror, driven principally by factors related to the collapse of the Somali state and the emergence of al-Shabaab, and the escalation of piracy off the Somali coast.

The conflicts ravaging the region are underpinned by historical, socio-economic and environmental issues and can be classified into two categories: intra-state and inter-state. Furthermore, they have been compounded by intra-regional and international intervention. Ostensibly, such interventions have been driven by competing national interests and a multitude of factors – economic, political, security-related and strategic – linked to the war on terror and international alarm about piracy (Sörenson 2008; Zeleza 2008). International interventions, therefore, have contributed to the intractability of the conflicts and insecurity of the Horn (Cliffe 2004; Woodward 2006).

The strategic importance of its location has always attracted outside interest, notably the proximity of the Horn of Africa to the highly sensitive region of the Middle East, where two factors – oil and the Arab–Israeli conflict – interface. In addition, Bal el Mandeb and the Red Sea are the main shipping route for goods from the Middle East and the Far East to Europe and the Americas (Sörenson 2008: 8). The discovery of natural resources, highly coveted by transnational corporations and states alike, also makes the region of strategic interest to external actors, with the result that the global war on terror and the recent explosion of piracy have seen naval forces converging off the coast of the Horn.

All these factors feed into the crisis of the state, which has become a characteristic of the region. Equally, the crisis of the state feeds into the conflicts and insecurities there. All these factors require more scientific and critical studies of the conflicts and their regional dynamics. This volume seeks to contribute to the provision of tools that scholars, policy makers and concerned actors need in their search of scientific and critical, context-sensitive studies, relevant and well-formulated policies and regional outlook, making concerted and rigorous efforts to find viable and durable solutions to these extensive and intractable conflicts and insecurities.

The intra- and inter-state conflicts besetting the Horn of Africa are intimately connected. Intra-state conflicts very easily spill across international boundaries triggering conflict between states, resulting in inter-state conflicts. Inter-state conflicts also tend to spawn national cleavages, that is to say intra-state conflicts. In recent decades inter-state conflicts have been steadily waning, while intra-state conflicts have increased (Goor et al. 1996, Fearon and Laitin 2003; Smith 2004; Zeleza 2008).

The contributors to this volume reflect on and analyse various dimensions and cases of intra-state and inter-state conflicts and security in the Horn of Africa. They examine a variety of aspects that exacerbate conflict situations. A focus on conflicts and security is the integrating theme. The problem of intra- and inter-state conflicts and security and how to promote peace, stability, security and development are addressed. This first chapter offers an overview of the chapters by focusing on the types and forms of the conflicts, and international intervention and politics of conflict resolution.

DEFINING INTRA-STATE AND INTER-STATE CONFLICTS

Conflict as a social phenomenon is widely perceived to be part of daily life (Axt et al. 2006: 19). Its manifestation, however, varies, contingent on a number of factors – contestation, the actors involved, duration, accessibility to conflict-sustaining technology, and so on. Concerning the origin of conflicts two approaches are provided (Axt et al. 2006): the subjective and the objective. While the objective approach traces the origin of conflict to the socio-political fabric and structure of society, the subjective approach attributes the origin of conflicts to the perceived incompatibility of goals and differences (Deutsch 1991). According to the latter approach it is incompatible differences that engender conflict. Underlying this understanding is that in order for conflict to exist there should be position difference or interest opposition between groups over certain values (Axt et al. 2006: 6). What we are dealing with here, of course, is political conflict.

Conflicts are broadly categorized into two groups, the violent and the non-violent. More specifically, five types of conflicts are described: latent conflict, manifest conflict, crisis, severe crisis and war. The first two are assumed to be non-violent, the others are classified as engaging in violence (Axt et al. 2006). War is violent conflict. A further distinction is made between intra-state and inter-state conflicts: 'inter-state wars, fought between two or more state members of the inter-state system; (2) civil wars, fought within the "metropole" of a member state of the system by forces of the regime against an insurgent group' (Sarkees et al. 2003: 58). This definition rests on the political status of the combatants. If they are recognized members of the international state system, then the conflict is defined as inter-state, whereas if one of the combatants is not a recognized member of the international state system but is located within a recognized state, the conflict is defined as intra-state or civil. Concerning intra-state conflicts Sarkees et al. (2003: 59) note:

> Intra-state wars are now those between or among two or more groups within the internationally recognized territory of the state. They include civil wars (involving the state government and a non-state actor) and inter-communal conflicts (involving two or more groups, none of which is the state government).

A further distinction is made in that intra-state conflict can be divided into strife to control the central government and strife over local issues, which may include secession (Sarkees et al. 2003: 59). Accordingly, 'A civil war, therefore, is simply a war over the state itself. Either a new regime replaces an old regime or a new regime (and state) is created by secession. A war across states is something different. It is a war about the state' (Hentz 2010: 91). Yet another distinction divides intra-state war into six types: secessionist, irredentist, wars of devolution, wars of regime change, wars of social banditry and armed inter-communal insurrections (Zeleza 2008: 6).

For the last 50 years the Horn of Africa has suffered protracted, chronic and complex intra- and inter-state conflicts (Cliffe 2004:

151). These conflicts fall into three categories: state–society; state–state; and society–society. While state–society conflicts relate to civil wars (communities with legitimate grievances challenge the state), state–state are conflicts between sovereign states. The third type, society–society, concerns communal strife (intra-communal and inter-communal), under the shadow of the state. What all types of conflict have in common is that the underpinning source is the state. A fragile state or state in crisis in the Horn of Africa has become the source of conflicts and insecurity.

CAUSES OF CONFLICTS

It is no exaggeration to state that conflicts the world over are characterized by myriad causes. Further, they are embedded in the socio-economic, politico-cultural, historical, identity constructions and experiences of the societies, the societies' relation with intra-regional and international actors; and local, national and regional configurations. This multiple context of causality shows that there is no single explanation to the conflicts in the Horn of Africa. To complicate matters, conflict causalities are categorized into root, proximate and tertiary causes.

Some of the commonly alluded to causes are: territory, ideology, religion, language, ethnicity, self-determination, access to resources, markets, dominance, equality and revenge (Singer 1996). In reference to inter-state conflict, Pfetsch and Rohloff (2000) identify nine items, which they call commodities, which historically constituted the cause of conflicts between states. These are: territory (border), secession, decolonization, autonomy, system (ideology), national power, regional predominance, international power and resources. Nonetheless, there seems to be a broad consensus among scholars that the classic cause of conflict is territory (Axt et al. 2006: 12). Relative deprivation theory (Gurr 1970) also attributes conflicts to a group's expected or actual access to prosperity and power. Relative deprivation theory is closely connected to group entitlement theory (Horowitz 1985), which attributes conflicts to ethnic identification (Smith 2004: 5). Other theories that seek causes of conflicts include: poor economic conditions theory, repressive political system theory and environmental degradation theory (Smith 2004: 7). Injustice and marginalization theories locate the causes of conflict in social relations in which certain groups are subjected to grave injustices and chronic marginalization. People, therefore, engage in conflict not only because they see it as just, but because they see no alternative to alleviate their plight.

The drivers of conflicts are internal as much as they are external as they entail international, regional, national and local actors and networks which are at the same time social, economic, political and military (Zeleza 2008: 15). It is noted that 'We need to incorporate in our analyses the interplay of historical and contemporary processes, and the role played by the state, capital and civil society; material forces and popular discourses institutional conditions and symbolic constructs structure and reproduce conflicts' (Zeleza 2008: 16).

The causes of the conflicts in the Horn of Africa are many. Here I will mention some of those most commonly referred to. These are:

- Livelihood-based resources (land, water, grazing, pasture).
- Culture (ethnicity, language, religion).
- Politics (power, inequality, domination, discrimination, marginalization and alienation).
- External intervention (colonial, Cold War, regional, the war on terror and piracy).
- Socio-economic (poverty, illiteracy, endemic health problems, unemployment, draught, environmental degradation).
- Lifestyle (peasantry, sedentary, pastoral, nomadic, highland, lowland).
- Dysfunctional governance practices (absence democracy, accountability, transparency; tyranny; dictatorship; sham and/or unrepresentative electoral practices; alienation and marginalization of local indigenous institutions and practices, state legitimacy deficiency).
- Underdevelopment (lack of industrialization, investment; agricultural, pastoral and agro-pastoral economy; primary goods export, pre-capitalist economic dominance).

Combinations of some or all of these explain the conflicts the Horn of Africa is experiencing. If we take the Darfur conflict as an example, we can easily see that a combination of livelihood-based resource competition, culture, political, socio-economic and lifestyle factors underpin it. The inter-state conflict between Eritrea and Ethiopia (1998) also involves culture, politics, external intervention, socio-economics and dysfunctional governance practices.

In order to highlight and map the focal points of conflicts I will now examine intra-state conflicts. This will be followed by an examination of inter-state conflicts. It is also worthwhile to note that structures, levels, objectives and agencies may influence the causes as well as the effects of conflicts. Local (community), national (intra-state) and international (inter-state) (McGinnis 1999) arenas are where the conflicts are played out. While local conflicts are often between identity-based groups and are driven by resources, national conflicts occur as contestants vie for state power. International conflicts take place between sovereign states and differ in their political, military, diplomatic and economic objectives and dynamics. They are also discernible by their practices and the war technology involved.

MAPPING INTRA-STATE CONFLICTS IN THE HORN OF AFRICA

The Sudan suffers complex and multiple society–society and society–state conflicts. Marginalization, alienation and discrimination by the centre against the peripheries have plunged Sudan into a perpetual state of conflict since independence in 1956 (Johnson 2003; Ahmed 2010; Deng 2010). The North–South divide has the characteristics of both society–society and state–society conflicts. It is in the society–society category because it is between 'African Christian animists' (South) and 'Arab Moslems' (North). It also has a state–society dimension because the state is dominated by the 'Arab Moslem' community and that gives it the sense of a state waging war against a section of society.

The seeds of the first intra-state conflict in Sudan were sown on the eve of independence. The mutiny of a Southern unit of the Sudanese army in Torit, Equatoria on 18 August 1955 marked the onset of the first civil war in the Sudan (Ahmed 2010: 4). The war ended with the signing of the Addis Ababa Accord in 1972 which gave the South self-rule. This though was rescinded by the military leader Ghaffar al Nimeiri in 1983 (Johnson 2003; Deng 2010). The division of the South into three provinces, coupled with the introduction of shari'a law, sparked the second civil war, which ended after 22 years with the signing of the Comprehensive Peace Agreement (CPA) on 9 January 2005 under strong external pressure (Ahmed 2008; Deng 2010; Barltrop 2011). The main provision of the Agreement allowed the people of the South, at the end of a six-year period, to decide their future in referendum. That took place on 9 January 2011. The outcome was that the South became an independent state on 9 July 2011.

The seeds of secession are embedded in the provisions of the CPA, which was designed so that the Sudan People's Liberation

Movement/Army (SPLM/A) would represent the people of the South, while the rest of the population was left to the National Congress Party (NCP). Therefore, the idea of New Sudan was that it was orchestrated to serve as a negotiating position for the SPLM/A to achieve its objectives, though there are those who believe that John Garang (former leader of the Sudanese Liberation Army and first vice president of Sudan who was killed in a helicopter crash one month after taking office) was committed to the vision of New Sudan and that the idea died with him (Grawert 2010). The mediators, not least the United States, also seem to have accepted the notion of separate states. The problems of the Sudan were reduced to the North/South dichotomy in the CPA. It should be borne in mind that the South was never properly integrated and the colonial and post-colonial state of Sudan facilitated the realization of the notion of separate statehood. The British ruled the South as part of their East African colonies and they had plans to merge the South with Uganda (El Mahdi 1965; Johnson 2003; Deng 2010). Following independence successive power holders in the capital, Khartoum, made no serious attempt to integrate it in the emerging nation state. Nevertheless, the secession faced daunting challenges – border demarcation, wealth sharing, the national debt, citizenship and relocation (Ahmed 2010) – all of which seriously undermined the construction of the new state. This may plunge the Sudan into inter-state conflict.

The Sudan is also mired in intra-state conflicts in the eastern, western and northern parts of the country (Ahmed 2010: 4). In the east, the Beja people live with the reality of remaining at the margins of central power, which is located in Khartoum, power that has stubbornly proved to be discriminatory, exploitative and repressive. As an expression of their dissatisfaction with the emergent power arrangement, and in seeking their rightful place in the post-colonial state, they launched the Beja Congress in 1958 (Young 2007: 11). Since its formation the Beja Congress has intermittently engaged in the national political realm, advocating improvement of the plight of the Beja people from their alienation, marginalization, underdevelopment and neglect under northern Muslim-Arab elite domination. Successive leaders in Khartoum have periodically banned the Beja Congress, yet it keeps re-emerging (Young 2007; Ahmed and Manger 2009). By the early 1990s the conflict had developed into full-blown war between the NCP and the Eastern Front, the latter formed by two resistance movements, the Beja Congress and the Rashaida Free Lions, in 2005 (Ahmed and Manger 2009: 8). Until the signing of the Eastern Sudan Peace Agreement (ESPA) following the Asmara Agreement in October 2006, the Beja Congress, with the help of SPLM/A, carried out several operations in eastern Sudan. The ESPA allowed the Eastern Front to join the Government of National Unity as a junior partner. Shortly after the signing of the ESPA, however, the Eastern Front disintegrated into four factions. Darfur exploded in 2003 just as Sudan was closing one chapter of its bloody conflicts in the South. In response to rebel attacks the NCP unleashed a militia known as the Janjeweed whose systematic, concerted attacks laid waste to Darfur. The rebel movement in Darfur comprises the Justice and Equality Movement (JEM), the Sudan Liberation Movement (SLM) and the Liberation and Justice Movement (LJM). Negotiations between the government and rebel groups to resolve the conflict were initiated. The Abuja Initiative, and later the Doha Process, are two mediation efforts to resolve the conflict. Opposition groups to the NCP have attempted on various occasions to form a united front. In 1995, through the Asmara Declaration, the Democratic Unionist Party (DUP), Umma Party (UP), SPLM/A and Beja Congress formed the National Democratic Alliance (NDA). Great hope was invested in the NDA to challenge the NCP. The signing of the CPA between the SPLM/A and NCP, however, put the NDA into disarray. In spite of several agreements – the CPA, ESPA and the Darfur Peace Agreement (DPA) – (Ahmed 2008, Deng 2010) peace eludes the Sudan.

Low-intensity conflicts against the North intermittently emerge in many other regions too. These include the Southern Blue Nile, South Kordofan and Nubia which complicates the picture. These conflicts gained momentum following the independence of the South in July 2011.

Ethiopia's claim on the former Italian colony of Eritrea sowed the seeds of intra-state conflict in that country. The UN-sponsored federal arrangement which came into force in 1952 was from the outset subjected to systematic violations. Over its ten-year life-span, the provisions of the federal arrangement were dismantled, engendering serious political grievances that ultimately descended into intra-state war in Ethiopia. The Eritrea–Ethiopia conflict is sometimes classified as an inter-state conflict, since Eritrea is considered an autonomous state created by the former colonial power (Mengisteab 2010). The annexation of Eritrea in 1962 drove the final nail in the coffin and ignited the 30-year war which only ended in 1991 with the fall of the military regime (Habte Selassie 1980; Gebre-Medhin 1989; Iyob 1995; Bereketeab 2007). The war of liberation in Eritrea was later joined by ethnic movements such as the Oromos, the Somalis and Tigrayans seeking to revise the political arrangement which they saw as the source of their alienation and marginalization. Non-ethnic groups poised to change the political system and informed by leftist ideologies also came on board (Berhe 2009; Zewde 2010).

On the eve of the fall of the monarchy political tensions in Ethiopia were high, but it was the deposing of Emperor Haile Selassie in February 1974 and his replacement by a military junta (commonly known as the Dergue, which means committee in Amharic) that set in motion the proliferation of liberation movements poised to transform the Ethiopian state. The Tigray People's Liberation Front (TPLF), formed on 18 February 1975 (Berhe 2009: 38), had a confused objective. The TPLF entertained overtly or covertly the idea of establishing a democratic republic of Tigray. Towards the end of the Dergue's rule, however, it played a dominant role in the creation of a multi-ethnic coalition, the Ethiopian People's Revolution Democratic Front (EPRDF), which was formed in 1989. In the post-Dergue era the TPLF remained the dominant force in EPRDF-ruled Ethiopia.

Another ethno-national liberation that joined the struggle for the creation of a new Ethiopia was the Oromo Liberation Front (OLF), founded in 1973. The OLF championed the right of self-determination up to and including secession of the Oromo people. The OLF joined the EPRDF coalition as a junior partner and participated in the EPRDF-led transitional government in 1991, but due to fundamental policy differences with the TPLF, it withdrew from the coalition in 1992. Since then it has been engaged in armed struggle. The other ethno-national movement is the Ogaden National Liberation Front (ONLF), which represents ethnic Somalis in Ethiopia; it was founded in 1984. Since then (with brief interruptions) it has been involved in armed struggle with the aim of separating the ethnic Somali people from the Ethiopian state.

The non-ethno-national movements were offshoots of the student movement inside as well as outside Ethiopia. The two major parties that crystallized from the student movement were the Me'ison (All Ethiopia Socialist Movement) and the Ethiopian People's Revolutionary Party (EPRP) (Zewde 2010: 8). Bitter rivalry between the Me'ison and EPRP opened the way for the military to hijack the popular uprising. First, using Me'ison, the Dergue destroyed EPRP, and later turned against Me'ison itself. The rump of the EPRP joined the armed liberation movements. This brought the EPRP into conflict with the TPLF. The TPLF defeated the EPRP and drove it into the Sudan in 1978. Later, a faction of the EPRP was reorganized as the Ethiopian People's Democratic Movement (EPDM) and returned to Ethiopia as an armed insurgent group. The EPDM entered the coalition that formed the EPRDF and subsequently joined the government (Berhe 2009).

While for the various ethno-nationalist movements Ethiopia's predicament concerned marginalization, alienation and exclusion of ethnic communities, the analysis of the non-ethnic or multi-ethnic movements focused on democratization, power-sharing and resources, and to certain extent on the issues of nationalities (Zewde 2010). The cumulative efforts and momentum of all these movements changed the political landscape in 1991. The military regime was deposed and the liberation movements took state power. This opened the way for the radical restructuring of the state. The EPRDF convened a national conference in 1992 where a transitional National Charter by which the new Ethiopia was to be governed was agreed. The main provisions of the Charter covered the restructuring of the state on the basis of ethnic identity. Hence state reconfiguration took the form of ethnic-based federalism. At first this bold undertaking received immense praise and was perceived as offering a durable solution to the entrenched culture of conflict.

Nonetheless, there were many who warned that an ethnic-based federal state would lead to the disintegration of the Ethiopian state (Habtu 2003; Teshome and Zohrik 2008) and it did not take long before things began to go wrong. Although the downfall of the Dergue regime seemed to have paved the way for a new social contract in the relations between the various ethnic groups in Ethiopia, another round of intra-state conflict unravelled, thereby perpetuating the culture of war. It was hoped that the ethnic-based federal arrangement in Ethiopia would provide a lasting solution to fractious ethnic relations thereby changing the tainted image of Ethiopia, described by some as a 'prison of nations' (Gudina 2003; Berhe 2009). The Charter was endorsed by the main ethnic liberation movements that had ousted the Dergue and was signed by the movements representing the main ethnic groups: the Oromo Liberation Front (OLF), the Ethiopian People's Democratic Movement (EPDM), Tigray People's Liberation Front (TPLF), Ogaden National Liberation Front (ONLF). However, the Charter soon ran into considerable legal, political and implementation obstacles. As a result the OLF felt compelled to withdraw in order to achieve their objectives. Subsequently, the ONLF, Ethiopian People's

Patriotic Front (EPPF) and other supra-ethnic-based movements revisited the now well-known armed liberation struggle launching Ethiopia back into a series of intra-state wars.

Somalia gained independence on 1 July 1960. It comprised British Somaliland (today's Somaliland) and Italian Somaliland, which were unified four days after British Somaliland was granted formal independence on 26 June 1960 (Samatar and Samatar 2002: 31). From the outset, however, Somalia was beset with tensions that led to both intra-state and inter-state conflicts. The integration of British Somaliland and Italian Somaliland, perhaps due to their diverse colonial legacies, soon proved to be disadvantageous to the Somali state (Lewis 2002). The clan-based division of post-colonial leaders and parties culminated in political chaos and tension in 1968. Exploiting the chaos that accompanied the 1969 election, a coup headed by General Siad Barre, staged in October 1969, ended the brief era of multi-party civilian government with the imposition of a military junta. This, compounded by Cold War interventions, geo-regional and clan politics, precipitated the collapse of the Somali state in 1991 (Lewis 2002; Samatar and Samatar 2002; Möller 2008).

Mobilization and the arming of clans produced clan-based organizations such as the Somali Salvation Democratic Front (SSDF, Mijerteen), the Somali National Movement (SNM, Isaaq) and the United Somali Congress (USC, Hawiye), which finally deposed the Siad Barre regime in 1991 (Jhazbhay 2008: 61; Möller 2008: 102–3). But their victory proved to be an impossible task to control and configure into a national project. The apportioning of Somalia as a reward to the rival movements pursuant to the fall of the regime produced the following entities: Somaliland, dominated by Isaaq; Puntland, dominated by Mijerteen; and central and southern Somalia, dominated by Hawiye. An inevitable consequence of all this is that Somali society is submerged in a seemingly intractable war. While central and southern Somalia are suffering from extremism and the 'global war on terror' as a consequence of regional and international interventions, the two breakaway regions, and particularly Somaliland, have established peaceful, stable and relatively democratic political systems.

The tiny territory of French Somaliland gained independence in 1977. The territory, which in 1967 was renamed Issa and Afar, was later named Djibouti. It comprises two major ethnic groups: the Issa Somalis and the Afars. Djibouti's independence was marred by conflict between the majority Somalis and minority Afars and civil war and low-intensity intra-state conflict have been going on for decades. The minority Afars feel excluded and discriminated against by the majority Issa and have mounted resistance. Nevertheless, Djibouti is, relatively speaking, considered stable in a region where stability is rare.

The Front for the Restoration of Unity and Democracy (FRUD), representing the Afar people, launched an armed insurgency in November 1991 (Abdallah 2008: 276). A main faction of FRUD signed a power-sharing accord with the ruling People's Rally for Progress (PRP) on 26 December 1994. Nevertheless, a faction led by Ahmed Dini (Prime Minister, 1977–78) rejected the accord and continued a low-intensity war. The government signed a peace agreement with this group on 12 May 2001, thereby ending the decade-long intra-state war. Yet in 2010 the intra-state conflict again erupted (AFP, May 2010). Some associate this with the recent conflict between Djibouti and Eritrea.

The last nation to gain independence, Eritrea, is also embroiled in intra-state conflicts. Eritrea represents a classic example of an abortive decolonization process when it was transferred, through a UN-sponsored federal decision, from Italian colonial rule to Ethiopian rule after the former's defeat in the Second World War (Gebre-Medhin 1989; Habte Selassie 1989; Iyob 1995). Ten years of deliberation on how to dispose of the ex-Italian territory culminated in the decision to tie Eritrea with Ethiopia through federation (Ellingson 1977; Pool 1979). This flawed federal arrangement was arbitrarily revoked in 1962 and this led to a 30-year independence struggle which finally came to an end in 1991 (Habte Selassie 1989; Iyob 1995).

During the liberation struggle, the liberation movement was engaged in two armed conflicts. The Eritrean Liberation Front (ELF) and Eritrean People's Liberation Front (EPLF) fought each other in 1972–74 and again in 1980–81, with the ELF ultimately defeated. The various factions of the ELF continued their struggle against the EPLF from their diaspora. Following independence the various ELF factions continued their politics of resistance because they were not permitted to return to the country as an organized force. Since the outbreak of the second Ethiopia–Eritrea war, however, different groups, mainly based in Ethiopia, have been carrying out sporadic violent actions to depose the regime in Asmara.

The new state of South Sudan is already experiencing intra-state conflicts with some dissident officers challenging the Government of South Sudan (GoSS).

MAPPING INTER-STATE CONFLICTS IN THE HORN OF AFRICA

The history of inter-state conflicts in the Horn of Africa can be traced to the 1960s when intra-state conflicts entered the emerging polity of the countries. There seems to be a clear connection between intra-state and inter-state conflicts. Intra-state conflicts somehow find their way across international geo-political boundaries. In other words, they easily spill over into inter-state conflicts. The mechanisms of any spill-over assume a range of forms. Migration, border ethnic groups, poorly defined and contested boundaries and proxy wars are some of the factors that mediate these inter-state conflicts. In terms of proxy wars, for instance, both Sudan and Ethiopia have supported rebel groups in the other's country. Sudan gave sanctuary to the Eritrean liberation fighters and other Ethiopian opposition groups; in tit-for-tat actions, Ethiopia supported Sudanese opposition groups which locked the two countries into inter-state conflicts (Cliffe 2004). Although it could not be said that Ethiopia and Sudan have descended into overt inter-state wars, they have experienced the longest history of inter-state proxy wars in the Horn of Africa due to their history of intra-state conflicts.

The relations between Somalia and Ethiopia have been characterized by conflicts, mainly due to the presence of the Somali ethnic population in Ethiopia. Post-independence nationalist leaders of Somalia have made clear their strong ambition to unite the five units of the Somali nation which were divided by colonialism. This set them on a collision course with both Kenya and Ethiopia. Hence Somalia went to war on two occasions (1964 and 1977) with Ethiopia (Lewis 2002; Kusow 2004; Möller 2008). The first inter-state war in the Horn of Africa therefore took place in 1964 between the new post-colonial Somali state and the oldest established state of Ethiopia. The largest in scale, duration and devastation, however, was fought in 1977–78 when the swift penetration and occupation of south-western Ethiopia by Somalia was only halted by massive Soviet and Cuban involvement (Adam 1994: 118; Greenfield 1994: 108). The crushing defeat of Somalia in this war was seen as the beginning of the collapse of the state of Somalia (Samatar 2004: 1136).

Eritrea has been involved in inter-state conflicts with all its neighbours. The post-liberation Eritrean state came into being in a highly volatile and conflicted region, which may explain its political behaviour (ICG 2010). A border skirmish between Eritrea and Ethiopia along their common borders led to outright war in

1998–2000 (Bereketeab 2009). Although the border dispute was settled by the Permanent Court of Arbitration verdict on 13 April 2002, peace and normalization remain as remote as ever. Therefore, not only is there a real danger of the prevailing no war/no peace situation easily turning into a hot war, but it has also given rise to proxy wars. While it is largely believed that Eritrea and Ethiopia have shifted their war to Somalia, internally they are actively engaged in supporting opposition groups to destabilize each other. The youngest nation state, South Sudan, which came into being in July 2011, faces serious challenges in its relations with the North. Another dimension of the proxy war in the Horn of Africa is often expressed in the form of geo-strategic, interest-driven interventions. Western powers in effect use other governments to promote their geo-strategic interests by pitching states against each other with devastating consequence for the region.

A FRAMEWORK FOR SECURITY ANALYSIS IN THE HORN OF AFRICA

One of the implications of the conflicts relates to security. These intractable intra- and inter-state conflicts have rendered the region the most insecure place in the world. The notion of security has undergone a huge metamorphosis in recent years. It has come a long way from its classic meaning and definition, in the legacy of the Westphalia Convention, where it traditionally focused on the security and sovereignty of the state (Koponen 2010).

Security, for the current purpose, takes multidimensional forms: regional, national, human and environmental. The regional dimension refers to the security and well-being of the region as a whole. In this sense, the Horn of Africa, as an integrated security complex, stands to gain from collectively designing, deciding and implementing its own security architecture, grounded in free will, mutual interest and respect for other states and societies without manipulative, geo-strategic-driven foreign interventions. This is of current importance due to the intensity of the militarization and securitization of the region as a result of the global war on terror and piracy off the coasts of Somalia, which together adversely affect both intra- and inter-state conflicts.

National security concerns the integrity and stability of individual nation states. National security is in line with the classic definition of security of the state. Human security essentially means the individual's right to life, liberty and livelihood. It also means freedom from want and fear; protection of democratic and human rights and promotion of human development (Adekanye 1999: 107; Koponen 2010). Quite often individual rights are counterpoised against collective or state rights. Yet, these two rights are not inherently incompatible. Environmental security concerns maintaining a life-sustaining environment. The environment, as the life supporter *par excellence*, must be restored, maintained and sustained (Tvedt 1999). This is of great significance in the Horn of Africa, because for the last several decades the region has been characterized by droughts, soil erosion, desertification, deforestation and environmental degradation, leading to recurrent famine. Insecurities produced by environmental degradation, which relate to food insecurity, shortage of drinking water and shrinking of grazing and arable land, constitute great threat to life. In addition, they are increasingly becoming sources of conflicts. Tackling environmental insecurity will therefore contribute to peace, security and development.

In all these dimensions, security is a scarce commodity in the Horn of Africa. Moreover, these insecurities feed into intra- and inter-state conflicts, which add to the volatility and fragility of the state.

In light of all these, the challenge scholars and concerned others face is how to deal effectively with these complex problems. To date they have met without success. One of the reasons for this is to do with the tools we use in understanding and analysing the conflicts and insecurities in the Horn of Africa. The tools we have been employing have revealed a serious deficiency. This volume attempts to redress that.

INTERNATIONAL INTERVENTION, CONFLICTS AND THE POLITICS OF CONFLICT RESOLUTION

The Horn of Africa has a long history of international intervention. Colonialism, the Cold War and more recently the war on terror and against piracy are some of the international interventions which have resulted in dire consequences for the stability, security and development of the region. The cumulative outcomes of these interventions are political divisions, economic distortions, protracted conflicts, environmental degradation and corrupt state-building.

The gravity of these problems has generated intense international involvement by peace brokers, well-wishers and other interested actors. Yet despite all their efforts to bring about peace, security, stability, democracy and development, no meaningful peace has been realized. The crucial question is, why not? A number of reasons can be given. And one has to do with the methodology of conflict analysis and conflict resolution.

The methodology of conflict resolution and international mediation intervention put in place functionally and structurally has proved to be deficient in meeting the complex configurations and challenges the Horn of Africa is facing, notably its politicization. The politics of conflict resolution, as interpreted and acted on by international actors, places great emphasis on geo-strategic, security, political and economic interests. Consequently, local initiatives perceived to be at odds with global interests are either discouraged or actively opposed. Another shortcoming is the emphasis on dealing with one conflict at a time. The piecemeal, isolated approaches to the various conflicts thus seem to have brought at best partial success and at worst have been a complete failure. For instance, the single approach in Sudan which led to the signing of the CPA with the SPLM/A, the DPA reached with some Darfur rebels and the ESPA (Ahmed 2008: 1; 2010) signed with the Eastern Sudan Movement failed in bringing a comprehensive solution to the problems of that country. To begin with, the CPA signed between Khartoum and SPLM/A was not as comprehensive as it was portrayed. On the contrary, it was so narrow that it further marginalized the conflicts in eastern Sudan, Darfur, Nuba Mountain and Kordofan, a marginalization that only aggravated the situation (Barltrop 2011; ICG 2011).

Similarly, efforts to resolve inter-state conflicts in isolation have not borne fruit. Researchers, think tanks and research institutes have suggested that the international community should adopt a regional approach and mechanism of conflict resolution in the Horn of Africa if international intervention is going to have any bearing. One such effort might focus on the epicentre of the overall conflict configuration in the Horn of Africa – the Eritrea–Ethiopia conflict (ICG 2008; Reid 2009). For the quest for a lasting resolution to the Somali problem, the Djibouti–Eritrea conflict and internal problems within Sudan, Eritrea and Ethiopia would benefit greatly by addressing the Eritrea–Ethiopia conflict at the same time. Nonetheless, geo-strategic-driven expediency precludes pursuing a regional approach, which would necessarily mean putting pressure on states that are in alliance with the crusaders of the global war on terror.

The Horn of Africa is probably the region of Africa most burdened by external interventions. Successive external interventions, including colonialism, the Cold War, the war on terror and piracy, have skewed the developmental, democratization, peace and security processes. A successful international intervention thus should focus on three dimensions: (1) it should put at the centre the concerned country's situation and interest, not self-serving geo-political strategy and security interests; (2) it should pursue balanced and even-handed interventions; and (3) it has to develop an historicized and contextualized approach, that is to say, it needs to be sensitive to history and local situations. The selective enforcement of international laws and conventions and selective international interventions that characterize engagement in the Horn of Africa are part of the problem.

The strategy of demarcating the states in the region as moderates/extremists, friendly/hostile, which results frequently in isolation of some while favouring others, has far-reaching consequences in inter-state relations. While those labelled hostile are sanctioned harshly, those considered friendly are allowed to get away with serious breaches of international law and violation of human rights. This complicates relations, negotiations and peaceful resolutions of both intra- and inter-state conflicts. Rather than taming so-called unfriendly states, it turns them into pariahs. A skewed geo-strategic security and interest-oriented policy therefore produces failed states. It also highlights the distorted aspect of the methodology of the politics of conflict resolution and international intervention.

This would enable us to conclude that the interconnected conflicts and insecurities ravaging the region require holistic, multidisciplinary, multidimensional, regional approaches and mechanisms. It is this realization that motivated the Nordic Africa Institute to organize the workshop where scholars from the region and international scholars renowned for their work on the region met and deliberated on the complexity of the conflicts and insecurities and suggested ways of resolving them. Some of the papers that were presented at the workshop and others are presented in this volume.

THE THEME OF THE BOOK

The central theme the contributors address is conflicts – intra-state and inter-state conflicts. The authors broach the theme of conflicts and security from different angles. The primary coordinating theme is the interplay of intra- and inter-state conflicts. The second theme is the focus on the regional dimension and regional perspective. A third theme that runs through the chapters is the role of external actors driven by geo-strategic security and other interests. A fourth theme the chapters interrogate is the role of leadership in the dynamics of the conflicts. Further issues of border demarcation, democratic deficit, the crisis of nation- and state-building, the role of traditional authorities and environmental degradation are analysed, with the aim of explaining the intractable nature of the conflicts in the Horn of Africa, and seeking possible and sustainable ways of resolving them.

The contributors highlight the factors, structures and forces that generate intra- and inter-state conflicts and the effects these have on the security, development and well-being of the region. What distinguishes this volume from others (other than being the only volume to appear in the last decade or so that analyses the interconnectedness of conflicts in the region) is its multidisciplinary, multidimensional, regional perspectives and approaches.

Each contributor deals with one or more issues and cases of intra- and inter-state conflicts and security in the Horn of Africa, and seeks to explore the challenges the region is facing. The book is arranged in three parts. Part I deals with the causes of conflicts, highlighting the complex and interlinked factors such as poverty, inequality, identity and the role of leadership. Part II analyses the dynamics of conflicts and seeks to address their nature. It analyses the conflicts in the Horn of Africa, their implication for regional security, border changes in Sudan, regional dynamics and the politics of violence. Part III is concerned with regional and international interventions. It examines the role external interventions play in intra- and inter-state conflicts and security, the role IGAD plays in regional relations and the phenomena of militias and piracy.

Each part has three chapters. These thematic chapters deal with specific aspects that implicitly or explicitly contribute to understanding and analyses of intra- and inter-state conflicts and insecurity in the Horn of Africa, their possible root causes, the actors involved and the role of local, regional and international actors. Together, the thematic chapters highlight the measures that need to be taken.

The contributors seek to establish an adequate framework for understanding the concepts of 'conflict', 'war', 'security', the nature of various actors, how intra-state conflicts feed into each other and the challenges posed by problems related to the durability and quality of peace agreements. They also take note of the problems of inherited and disputed borders, which split ethnic communities among neighbouring countries and became a critical factor in intra- and inter-state conflicts in the Horn of Africa.

The contributors also discuss the transnational nature of the wars in the Horn of Africa, and the roles of the political leadership, traditional authorities, the state and civil society in promoting sustainable democracy, peace and development. The focus is turned to inter-communal conflicts over land, water and livestock, exploring the possible link between climate change, conflict and peace in the Horn; and international piracy off the coast of Somalia. International intervention in the pursuit of geo-strategic, security and economic interests is identified as one of the drivers of the conflicts in the region.

CONCLUSION

The complexity and interconnectedness of intra- and inter-state conflicts and the concomitant pervasive insecurity ravaging the region make the Horn of Africa the most conflict-ridden region in the African continent. This has rendered the task of building durable and meaningful peace and security in the region and beyond extremely difficult. At the root of these intra- and inter-state conflicts and insecurity is the crisis of the state. The precarious state-building process has rendered the state crisis-stricken. State crisis in turn gives rise to conflicts and insecurity.

Underpinning these bitter conflicts and insecurities are historical, socio-economic, domestic, intra-regional and international factors and underdevelopment. External interventions, driven by competing national, economic, political, security and strategic-linked interests connected to the war on terror and concern about piracy, render the conflicts intractable. In spite of the engagement of many local, national, regional and international actors in the attempt to mitigate the conflicts, so far no significant results have been achieved. The methodology of international intervention and the politics of conflict resolution, which stress global strategic, security, political and economic interests, has not only proved lacking, but has also skewed the process of state-, peace- and security-building. The piecemeal approach to conflict resolution quite often emanating from geo-strategic expediency is another factor that perpetuates conflict in the Horn of Africa. Interlinked conflicts and insecurities demand holistic, historicized, multidimensional and multidisciplinary analyses, regional approaches and mechanisms.

REFERENCES

Abdallah, Abdo A. (2008). 'State Building, Independence and Post-Conflict Reconstruction in Djibouti', in Ulf Johansson Dahre (ed.), *Post-Conflict Peace-Building in the Horn of Africa*, Research Report in Social Anthropology 2008: 1, Lund: Lund University.

Adam, M. Hussein (1994). 'Somalia: Federalism and Self-Determination', in Peter Woodward and Murray Forsyth (eds.), *Conflict and Peace in the Horn of Africa: Federalism and its Alternatives*, Aldershot, Brookfield, WI, Singapore and Sydney: Dartmouth.

Adekanye, J. Bayo (1999). 'Conflict Prevention and Early-Warning Systems', in Lennart Wohlgemuth et al. (eds.), *Common Security and Civil Society in Africa*, Uppsala: Nordisk Afrikainstitutet.

Agende France Presse (AFP) (2010). 'Djibouti Rebels Claim to Kill Three Soldiers', 31 May.

Ahmed, Abdel Ghaffar Mohamed (2008). *One Against All: The National Islamic Front (NIF) and Sudanese Sectarian and Secular Parties*, SWP 2008: 6, Bergen: Chr. Michelsen Institute.

Ahmed, Abdel Ghaffar Mohamed (2010). *Sudan Peace Agreements: Current Challenges and Future Prospects*, SWP 2010: 1, Bergen: Chr Michelsen Institute.

Ahmed, Abdel Ghaffar Mohamed and Manger, Leif (2009). *Peace in Eastern Sudan: Some Important Aspects for Consideration*, Bergen: University of Bergen.

Axt, Heinz-Jurgen et al. (2006). *Conflict: A Literature Review*, Duisburg: Jean Monnet Group, 23 February.

Barltrop, Richard (2011). *Darfur and the International Community: The Challenges of Conflict Resolution in Sudan*, London and New York: I. B. Tauris.

Bereketeab, Redie (2007). *Eritrea: The Making of a Nation, 1890–1991*, Trenton, NJ and Asmara: Red Sea Press.

Bereketeab, Redie (2009). 'The Eritrea–Ethiopia Conflict and the Algiers Agreement: Eritreans' Road to Isolation', in Richard Reid (ed.), *Eritrea's External Relations: Understanding its Regional Role and Foreign Policy*, London: Chatham House.

Berhe, Aregawi (2009). *A Political History of the Tigray People's Liberation Front (1975–1991): Revolt, Ideology, and Mobilisation in Ethiopia*. Los Angeles, CA: Tsehai Publishers.

Cliffe, Lionel (2004). 'Regional Impact of the Eritrea–Ethiopia War', in Dominique Jacquin-Berdal and Martin Plaut (eds.), *Unfinished Business: Ethiopia and Eritrea at War*, Trenton, NJ: Red Sea Press.

Deng, Francis M. (ed.) (2010). *New Sudan in the Making? Essays on a Nation in Painful Search of Itself*, Trenton, NJ and Asmara: Red Sea Press.

Deutsch, Morton (1991). 'Subjective Features of Conflict Resolution: Psychological, Social and Cultural Influences', in Raimo Väyrynen (ed.), *New Direction in Conflict Theory: Conflict Resolution and Conflict Transformation*, London, Thousand Oaks, CA and New Delhi: Sage.

El Mahdi, Mandour (1956). *A Short History of the Sudan*, London, Ibadan, Nairobi and Accra: Oxford University Press.

Ellingson, Lloyd (1977). 'The Emergence of Political Parties in Eritrea, 1941–1950', *Journal of African History*, vol. XVIII, no. 2: 261–81.

Fearon, James D. and Laitin, David D. (2003). 'Ethnicity, Insurgency, and Civil War', *American Political Science Review*, vol. 97, no. 1: 75–90.

Gebre-Medhin, Jordan (1989). *Peasant and Nationalism in Eritrea: A Critique of Ethiopian Studies*, Trenton, NJ: Red Sea Press.

Goor, Luc van de et al. (1996). *Between Development and Destruction: An Enquiry into the Causes of Conflict in the Post-Colonial States*, London: Macmillan.

Grawert, Elke (ed.) (2010). *After the Comprehensive Peace Agreement in Sudan*. Oxford: James Currey

Greenfield, Richard (1994). 'Towards an Understanding of the Somali Factors', in Peter Woodward and Murray Forsyth (eds.), *Conflict and Peace in the Horn of Africa: Federalism and its Alternatives*, Aldershot, Brookfield, WI, Singapore and Sydney: Dartmouth.

Gudina, Merera (2003). *Ethiopia: Competing Ethnic Nationalisms and the Quest for Democracy, 1960-2000*. Addis Ababa: Shaker Publication.

Gurr, Ted Robert (1970). *When Men Rebel*. Princeton, NJ: Princeton University Press.

Habte Selassie, Bereket (1989). *Eritrea and the United Nations*. Lawrenceville, NJ: Red Sea Press.

Habtu, Alem (2003). 'Ethnic Federalism in Ethiopia: Background, Presentation and Future Prospects', paper submitted to the 2nd EAG International Symposium on Contemporary Development Issues in Ethiopia, 11–12 July.

Hentz, James (2010). 'War across States and State Collapse in Africa', in Muna Ndulo and Margaret Brieco (eds.), *Failed and Failing States: The Challenges to African Recognition*, Cambridge: Cambridge Scholar.

Horowitz, Donald L. (1985). *Ethnic Groups in Conflict*. Berkeley, CA: University of California Press.

International Crisis Group (ICG) (2008). *Beyond Fragile Peace between Ethiopia and Eritrea: Averting New War*, Africa Report No. 141, 17 June.

International Crisis Group (ICG) (2010). *Eritrea: The Siege State*, African Report No. 163-21, September.

International Crisis Group (ICG) (2011). *Division in Sudan's Ruling Party and the Threat to the Country's Future Stability*. African Report No. 174-4, May.

Iyob, Ruth (1995). *Eritrean Struggle for Independence: Domination, Resistance, Nationalism*, Cambridge: Cambridge University Press.

Jacquin-Berdal, Dominique and Plaut, Martin (eds.) (2004). *Unfinished Business: Ethiopia and Eritrea at War.*,Trenton, NJ and Asmara: Red Sea Press.

Jhazbhay, Igbal (2008). 'Somaliland's Post-war Reconstruction: Rubble to Rebuilding', *International Journal of African Renaissance Studies*, vol. 3, no. 1: 59–93.

Johnson, Douglas H. (2003). *The Root Causes of Sudan's Civil Wars*, Oxford, Bloomington, IN, Indianapolis and Kampala: James Currey, Indiana University Press and Fountain Publishers.

Koponen, Juhani (2010). 'The Security–Development Nexus, State Fragility and State Building: A Beginner's Guide to Discussion and Some Suggestions for Orientation', in Henni Alava (ed.), *Exploring the Security–Development Nexus: Perspectives from Nepal, Northern Uganda and 'Sugango'*, Helsinki: Ministry of Foreign Affairs.

Kusow, Abdi (2004). 'Contested Narratives and the Crisis of the Nation-State in Somalia: A Prolegomenon', in Abdi Kusow (ed.), *Putting the Cart Before the Horse: Contested Nationalism and the Crisis of the Nation-State in Somalia*, Trenton, NJ: Red Sea Press.

Lewis, I. M. (2002). *A Modern History of the Somali: Nation and State in the Horn of Africa* (4th edition). Oxford, Hargeisa and Athens, OH: James Currey, Btec Books and Ohio University Press.

McGinnis, Michael D. (1999). 'Conflict Dynamics in a Three-Level Game: Local, National, and International Conflict in the Horn of Africa', paper presented at the 33rd North American Meeting of Peace and Science Society, University of Michigan, Ann Arbor, MI, 8–9 October.

Mengisteab, Kidane (2010). 'Critical Factors in the Horn of Africa's Ravaging Conflict', paper presented at the International Workshop on Intra-State and Inter-State Conflicts and Security in Horn of Africa, The Nordic Africa Institute, Uppsala.

Möller, Björn (2008). 'The Horn of Africa and the US "War on Terror" with a Special Focus on Somalia', in Ulf Johansson Dahre (ed.), *Post-Conflict Peace-Building in the Horn of Africa*, Research Report in Social Anthropology 2008:1. Lund: Lund University.

Pfetsch, Frank R. and Rohloff, Christoph (2000). *National and International Conflicts, 1945–1994: New Empirical and Theoretical Approaches*, London: Routledge.

Pool, David (1979). *Eritrea: Africa's Longest War*, London: Anti-Slavery Society.

Reid, Richard (ed.) (2009). *Eritrea's External Relations: Understanding its Regional Role and Foreign Policy*, London: Chatham House.

Samatar, Abdi Ismail (2004). 'Ethiopian Federalism: Autonomy versus Control in the Somali Region', *Third World Quarterly*, vol. 25, no. 6: 1131–54.

Samatar, Abdi Ismail (2008). 'Ethiopian Occupation and American Terror in Somalia', in Ulf Johansson (ed.), *Post-Conflict Peace-Building in the Horn of Africa*, Research Report in Social Anthropology, Lund: Lund University and Somali International Rehabilitation Centre.

Samatar, Abdi Ismail and Samatar, Ahmed Ismail (2002). 'Somalis as Africa's First Democrats: Premier Abdirazak H. Hussein and President Aden A. Osman', *Buldhaan, An International Journal of Somali Studies*, vol. 2.

Sarkees, Meredith Reid et al. (2003). 'Inter-State, Intra-State, and Extra-State Wars: A Comprehensive Look at Their Distribution over Time, 1816–1997', *International Studies Quarterly*, vol. 47: 49–70.

Singer, D, Joel (1996). 'Armed Conflicts in the Former Colonial Regions: From Classification to Explanation', in Luc van de Goor, Kumar Rupesighe and Paul Sciarone (eds.), *Between Development and Destruction: An Enquiry into the Causes of Conflict in Post-Colonial States*, London: Macmillan.

Smith, Dan 2004. 'Trends and Causes of Armed Conflicts', *Berghof Research Centre for Constructive Conflict Management*, www.berghof-handbook-net.

Sörenson, Karl (2008). *State Failure on the High Seas: Reviewing the Somali Piracy*. FOI Somalia Paper: Report 3.

Teshome, Wondwosen B. and Zahorik, Jan (2008). 'Federalism in Africa: The Case of Ethnic-based Federalism in Ethiopia', *International Journal of Human Sciences*, vol. 5, no. 2, np.

Tvedt, Terje (ed.) (1993). *Conflicts in the Horn of Africa: Human and Ecological Consequences of Warfare*, Uppsala: Uppsala University.

Woodward, Peter (2006). *US Foreign Policy and the Horn of Africa*, Aldershot and Burlington, VT: Ashgate.

Young, Crawford (2007). 'Nation, Ethnicity, and Citizenship: Dilemmas of Democracy and Civil Order in Africa', in Sara Dorman et al. (eds.), *Making Nations, Creating Strangers: States and Citizenship in Africa.* Leiden: Brill.

Zeleza, Paul Tiyambe (2008). 'Introduction: The Causes and Costs of War in Africa, from Liberation Struggles to the "War on Terror"', in Alfred Nhema and Paul Tiyambe Zeleza (eds.), *The Roots of African Conflicts: The Causes and Costs*, Addis Ababa, Oxford, Athens and Pretoria: OSSREA, James Currey, Ohio University Press, Unisa Press.

Zewde, Bahru (ed.) (2010). *Documenting the Ethiopian Student Movement: An Exercise in Oral History.* Addis Ababa: Forum for Social Studies.

2
Poverty, Inequality, State Identity and Chronic Inter-State Conflicts in the Horn of Africa

Kidane Mengisteab

INTRODUCTION: CHRONIC CONFLICTS IN THE HORN OF AFRICA

The Horn of Africa is a region heavily impacted by wars and conflicts. In the post-colonial era, from the late 1950s to the present, the region has experienced several devastating inter-state wars, including the Ethiopian–Somali wars (1964, 1977–78, 2006–9), the Kenyan–Somali war (1963), the Ugandan–Tanzanian war (1978–79) and the Ethiopian–Eritrean border war (1998–2000). It has also witnessed destructive cross-border communal conflicts often triggered by environmental degradation and facilitated by porous borders, which are not always respected or even recognized by pastoral communities, especially those who belong to ethnic groups split across national boundaries. Armed gangs in the eastern Equatoria region of southern Sudan, for example, are said to have carried out raids in Gambela state in south-western Ethiopia. According to the Conflict Early Warning and Response Mechanism (CEWARN) of the Inter-Governmental Authority on Development (IGAD), such cross-border conflicts resulted in casualties numbering about 517 in Ethiopia, 1,072 in Kenya and 2,852 in Uganda between 2003 and 2009 (Wulf and Debiel 2009).

The region's most devastating conflicts, however, are intra-state, which conceptually are of three types, although in reality they are often hard to distinguish. The first are inter-communal conflicts, which are fought among ethnic, clan and occupational groups (e.g. pastoralists vs. sedentary farmers). These conflicts are generally fought by communities over land, water and livestock (in the form of cattle rustling) and are often provoked by resource scarcity, resulting from a rapidly deteriorating environment and fast-growing populations.[1] The second type is the one-sided conflict, which entails atrocities perpetrated by governments and rebel groups against unarmed civilian populations for a variety of reasons. The third and perhaps the most devastating type of intra-state conflict the region has experienced consists of 'civil wars' and chronic strife between the state and organized political groups, which are mostly ethnic- or region-based.

The repercussions of the various conflicts that the region has endured are not well documented. There is little doubt, however, that they have had devastating impacts. From anecdotal evidence it also seems that the civil wars, which are more numerous than the inter-state wars, have had much greater effects. Rough estimates of casualty figures from Darfur, Southern Sudan and the various conflicts in Ethiopia, Somalia and Uganda seem to support this assertion.[2]

The economic impacts are also barely documented. However, Mwaura, Baechler and Kiplagat's (2002) claim that the conflicts are the single greatest barrier to socio-economic development seems highly plausible. The Horn of Africa is one of the poorest regions of the world. All the countries of the region fall within the bottom 20 per cent of UNDP's Human Development Index. There is little doubt that the alarming number of human casualties, the vast sums some of the governments spend on security,[3] the destruction of property, the disruption of economic activity by the large refugee outflows and internal displacements, and the removal of significant portions of the workforce from productive economic activity into the war effort are, no doubt, major factors contributing to the region's general misery.

The objective of this chapter is to examine some of the key factors that engender civil wars and chronic strife between states and ethnic and region-based groups in the region. A more specific focus, however, is to explore the impact of socio-economic inequality, poverty and identity of the state on civil wars and chronic strife in the Greater Horn of Africa. The chapter is organized into three sections. The first briefly raises some problems with the way in which civil war is conceptualized in the literature. The second reviews the existing theories of civil war and assesses their appropriateness in explaining the conflicts in the Greater Horn. The third suggests some modifications to these theories in order to make them more relevant to the conflicts in the countries of the Horn of Africa and other African countries. A brief conclusion attempts to explore the policy implications of the modified explanation.

ISSUES OF CONCEPTUALIZATION

The conceptualization of civil wars in much of the literature is problematic. Generally, the literature defines a civil war as one where the parties to the conflict are the state or militia groups created by the state on the one side, and an armed political group or groups, such as ethnic, regional, religious or other political organizations, on the other. At least two problems arise from this. One relates to the disputed identity of the state, which blurs the boundaries between inter- and intra-state conflicts. The Ethiopian–Somali wars and the Ogaden insurgencies were, for example, hard to distinguish in the 1960s and 1970s. The Shifta wars in Kenya and the Somali–Kenyan wars were also indistinguishable. Whether or not Eritrea's war of independence constituted a civil war is also a contentious issue. Ethiopia viewed it as a civil war while Eritrean nationalists perceived it as a war against colonial occupation.

To distinguish civil wars from one-sided wars, the literature suggests that opponents should be able to inflict at least 100 casualties a year on the government's side (Sambanis 2002; Cramer 2006). One problem with this classification is that the states in the Horn of Africa rarely report their casualty figures when engaged in conflict against insurgents. Both governments and insurgency groups also tend to exaggerate the number of casualties they inflict on the enemy. Accurate casualty figures are, thus, rarely known and, in the absence of reliable data, cannot provide a good criterion for distinguishing civil wars from one-sided wars.

In addition, the conflicts between states and ethnic- or region-based insurgency groups tend to last a long time with fluctuating levels of violence. Adherence to the criteria of civil wars, which are based on casualty figures, may lead to focusing on the peaks of these conflicts, while neglecting the periods of low intensity, which may then be viewed as absence of civil war when in fact they are gestation periods for the next cycle of more intense violence. The ongoing Ogaden problem in Ethiopia, for example, goes back to the early 1960s, although over the years the level of violence has fluctuated and the insurgency has been led by different organizations. Yet it remains essentially the same war fought for more or less the same reasons. Conceptualization of civil wars on the basis of casualty figures will only register certain periods of this chronic conflict.

Third, ethnic- and region-based wars in the Horn of Africa are essentially reflections of the challenges of state-building and nation-building processes and looking only at the periods of high-intensity violence may not identify the underlying causes of chronic conflicts. In order to avoid some of these conceptual problems this chapter treats periods of high-intensity violence (civil wars) and periods of low-intensity conflict of the same chronic strife as a single conflict whatever the intensity of violence.

EXISTING EXPLANATIONS OF INTRA-STATE CONFLICTS

A number of explanations of civil wars and models attempt to predict them are available (see Wulf and Debiel 2009). Most can, however, be collapsed into one of two widely debated theories. One broad explanation is generally referred to as the relative deprivation (or 'grievance and justice-seeking') model. According to this approach, collective violence is driven by relative deprivation, defined as the gap between what a social group believes it deserves and what it actually gets (Gurr 1970). The conflict, according to this theory, is between social forces who want either to improve their disadvantaged socioeconomic position or to preserve their privileged position and the state, which may support one side or the other. A number of studies (Auvinen and Nafziger 1999; Stewart 2000; Nafziger 2002) find a positive relationship between income inequality and the occurrence of civil war. Stewart makes the very strong contention that 'if there is group conflict, we should expect sharp economic differences between conflicting groups associated (or believed to be associated) with differences in political control' (Stewart, 2000: 248).

One example of the relative deprivation thesis is the Political Instability Taskforce model, which relies on regime types, deprived neighbourhoods, infant mortality and the presence/absence of state-led discrimination as its key variables in predicting conflict. The Failed State Index is another model that relies on social, economic and political indicators to explain and predict conflicts. The key variables of this model include demographic pressure and displacements, unequal economic development, the de-legitimization of the state, human rights violations, deterioration of public service delivery and external intervention.

A rival explanation contends that measures of socio-economic or political grievances, such as income inequality, do not systematically affect the likelihood of conflict and that the measures of grievance, to the extent that they factor in at all, amount to little more than a rebel discourse used to mask and justify their predatory activities among those whose support they seek (Collier and Hoeffler 2000).

This theory, which is generally referred to as 'greed/opportunity' ('greed and loot-seeking' or 'acquisitive desire'), claims that greed or economic motivations and opportunities rather than ethnic, socioeconomic or political grievances explain the onset and continuance of conflict (Collier and Hoeffler 2000; 2004).

The two theories complement each other in many respects and have contributed useful insights that expand our understanding of civil wars and intra-state conflicts. However, both have serious limitations. The greed/opportunity theory is said to be relevant in explaining the conflicts in Liberia, Sierra Leone, the Democratic Republic of the Congo and Angola, although it is debatable that greed for resources and wealth was the primary source of the conflicts in all those cases. Ambition for power rather than greed seems to be the greater motivator for the wars by Savimbi-led UNITA, for instance.

More importantly for our purposes, the theory hardly corresponds with the specific characteristics of the conflicts in the Horn of Africa. Eritrea's war of independence could not have been motivated by greed and resources, since during its armed struggle Eritrea had very few known resources, which the country's liberation fronts might have wanted to control. If anything, the view at the time was that the country would not be economically viable if it gained independence. Nor can the Ogaden wars in Ethiopia be explained by greed. Although it is claimed that the Ogaden has oil deposits, there is little indication that oil wealth was a factor when the wars started in the early 1960s. The civil wars in Somalia, led by various groups including the Somali Salvation Democratic Front (SSDF), the Somali National Movement and the United Somali Congress (USC), were also hardly motivated by greed and resources. Rather, they were waged to overthrow the regime of Siad Barre, which they considered to be not only repressive but also favouring some clans over others in order to remain in power. It is also difficult to attribute Somaliland's declaration of independence from the rest of Somalia to any known resource wealth. There are also no known resources that could have motivated the insurgency of the 'shifta' wars of the 1960s in Kenya's North-East Province. Similarly, there is no obvious resource base that sustained or motivated the chronic Afar–Issa conflicts in Djibouti. Southern Sudan's war is perhaps the only conflict in the region that can be related to a major resource – oil. Yet even in this case, the onset of the conflict pre-dates the discovery of oil by more than two decades.[4]

Several other weaknesses, both substantive and methodological, have been associated with the greed/opportunity model (see Ballentine and Nizschke 2003, 2005; Berdal 2005). One of the major shortcomings of the model is its neglect of the role and behaviour of the state and the problems of governance and diversity management at the outset of civil wars. The theory thus reduces the many facets of the politics of civil wars to the politics of greed, even though greed for economic and political power plays a significant role in many conflicts. Moreover, the greed is mostly attributed to rebel groups when communities in resource-rich areas are often subjected to evictions and severe environmental degradation, as in the case of the Niger Delta.

In the case of the Horn of Africa, the relative deprivation (the 'grievance and justice-seeking') theory, which incorporates political, economic and cultural marginalization as explanatory factors, seems to be more apposite. As Table 2.1 shows, every country in the region has experienced at least one civil war or ethnic-based rebellion during the post-independence era. In most cases the countries have fought multiple civil wars and experienced chronic strife. Most have also witnessed one-sided violence of varying magnitude, from states and rebel groups alike. Uganda's Idi Amin and Ethiopia's Mengistu Hailemariam were perhaps the most notorious in this regard. Yet, most of the regimes in the region have engaged in one-sided violence when confronted with insurgencies and expressions of opposition. Most of the areas of conflict have also experienced various forms of relative deprivation. Although reliable data on comparable indicators of deprivation are not available for all the countries of the region, the data in Tables 2.2–2.7 give a good indication that the areas of conflict in most cases suffer from marginalization. Table 2.1, though not exhaustive, identifies the most important civil wars and rebel group activities in the countries of the region.

Ethnic and regional conflicts in Sudan are many but the most important are those between the government and insurgency groups in southern Sudan, Darfur, the Beja in the east and the Nuba mountains in the central parts of the country. As Table 2.2 shows, all these areas are marginalized in terms of access to political power. Table 2.3 shows that the regions of conflict are also relatively deprived in terms of per capita expenditures as well as social indicators, such as access to health and education.

The relationship between inequality and civil wars and conflicts in Ethiopia is a little challenging to establish because of the changes in administrative regions following the institution of the largely ethnic-based federal system in 1994. Before then data were reported on the basis of the old administrative provinces. Another reason is the marked improvement in access to resources, especially health and education, in some formerly marginalized areas of the country since the change of government in 1991.

Table 2.1   The Most Important Ethnic- and Region-based Civil Wars and Rebellions in the Horn of Africa

Country	Civil war
Djibouti	Issa-dominated People's Rally for Progress (government) vs. an Afar organization, The Front for the Restoration of Unity and Democracy, 1991–94 (1994–2001 low-intensity)
Eritrea	The Red Sea Afar Democratic Organization (RSADO) and the Democratic Movement for the Liberation of Kunama (DMLK).*
Ethiopia	Eritrea war of independence, 1961–91; Government vs. TPLF, 1975–91; Government. vs. various Somali Ogaden rebels (WSLF, the Somali Abo Liberation Front, 1975–89; Ogaden National Liberation Front). Government vs. Afar Liberation Front, 1975–97; Government vs. the Afar Revolutionary Democratic Union/Front (ARDU/F) 1993–present; Government. vs. OLF, 1975–present.
Kenya	Shifta wars (1963–67); post-election crisis, 2007–8.
Somalia	Somali Salvation Democratic Front (SSDF), the Somali National Movement and the United Somali Congress (USC) vs. the government of Siad Barre, 1989–91; civil war (warlords), 1991–2006; Puntland vs. State of Somalia, 2004; ICU vs. ARPCT, 2006; TFG vs. UIC, 2005–6; TFG vs. Shebaab and Hizbul Islam, 2009–present.
Sudan	North–South 1955–72; North–South 1983–2005; Darfur conflict, 2003–present; government vs. the Nuba Mt; government vs. the Beja Lions.
Uganda	Government vs. Uganda People's Democratic Army (UPDA), 1986–88; government. vs. the Allied Democratic Forces (ADF), 1996–present: government vs. the Lord's Resistance Army (LRA), 1987–present.

*On the basis of the casualty threshold, the activities of these rebel groups do not constitute civil wars.

Nevertheless, it is clear that the conflict areas of Somali (Ogaden) and Afar states are among the most deprived regions of the country. In the case of Afar, Table 2.4 shows that the state ranks well below the national average in terms of urbanization, access to health facilities (medical doctors) and school enrolments. The Somali state similarly ranks well below the national average in access to health facilities (medical doctors) and school enrolments. Tigray was one of the centres of civil war (1975–91). It was also one of the marginalized and impoverished provinces at the time. The

Table 2.2   Regional Distribution of Political Power in Sudan

Region	Eastern*	Northern	Central	West	South†
Population per cent of total, 1986	11.8	5.4	26.5	32.6	23.7
Ministerial positions, 1954–64 per cent of total	1.4	79	2.8	0	16
Ministerial positions, 1969–85, per cent of total	2.5	68.7	16.5	3.5	7.8
National Council for Distribution of Resources, per cent	4	76	4	4	12

*Eastern region includes Kassala, Gadharif, and Red Sea Provinces.

† Southern region includes Upper Nile, Bahr Alghazal and Equatorial.

Source: 'Seekers of Truth and Justice. The Black Book: Imbalances of Power and Wealth in Sudan, Part 1', in Salah M. Hassan and Carina E. Ray (eds.), *Darfur and the Crisis of Governance in Sudan*, Ithaca, NY and London: Cornell University Press, 2006, pp. 406–34.

Table 2.3   Regional Distribution of Social Indicators in Sudan

	North	East	Centre, Excluding Khartoum	South	West*	Darfur region
Population distribution, 2001	4.7	11.7	21.4	16	30.6	–
Gross primary school enrolment, 2002	82.4	42.5	70.4	11.6	44.2	–
Total expenditure/per capita as per cent of North, 1996–2000	100	73.7	60.6	-	44.1	
Hospitals per 100,000 people	3.9	–	–	1	–	0.4
Doctors per 100,000 people	13.4	–	–	2.8	–	1.5

*Includes Darfur and Kordofan.

Source: Alex Cobham (2005). *Causes of Conflict in Sudan: Testing the Black Book*, QEH Working Paper No. 121, January; Abdullahi Osman El-Tom (2006). 'Darfur People: Too Black for the Arab-Islamic Project', In Salah M. Hassan and Carina E. Ray (eds.), *Darfur and the Crisis of Governance in Sudan*, Ithaca, NY and London: Cornell University Press, pp. 84–102.

number of people per doctor in 1982 in Tigray was, for example, 258,137 compared to Shewa Province, where the ratio was 176,639 people per doctor. With respect to school enrolments in Tigray it was 0.03 per cent of the province's total population compared to Shewa's 0.08 per cent (Ethiopia Statistical Abstract 1982). Relative to other regions, access to education and health care have improved in Tigray, Benishangul-Gumuz and Gambela since 1991. Oromia, the largest state, with the biggest single ethnic group, hosts the Oromo Liberation Front. Oromia, however, does not show marked deprivation relative to the other large states, Amhara and Southern Nations, in terms of urbanization, school enrolments and access to health facilities. Lack of political power at the federal level reflective of its size is one of the matters of contention.

Table 2.4　Regional Inequalities in Ethiopia

State/Region	Urbanization per cent of population, 2004	No. of people per medical doctor, 2004	Primary and secondary school enrolments per cent of population, 2004
Tigray	18.1	44,706	16.8
Afar	8.8	95,000	2.8
Amhara	11.1	124,267	12.5
Oromia	12.8	120,663	15.2
Somalia (Ogaden)	16.3	97,833	3.1
Benishangul/Gumuz*	9.4	34.941	21.2
Southern Nations	8.3	114,512	15.2
Gambela*	18.4	19,500	20.9
Harari†	61.6	3,700	17.6
Addis Ababa†	100	12,808	16.9
Dire Dawa†	73.5	11,935	12.7
Ethiopia	15.8	59,971	13.8

* These are small states with a small population and have seen marked improvement in access to public health and education over the last two decades.

†These are urban areas and have greater access to public services.

Source: Ethiopia Statistical Abstract, 2004.

Uganda's ethnic- and region-based violent conflicts are mostly concentrated in the north. As Tables 2.5 and 2.6 show, historically the north has been the most impoverished area of the country. Although this can be traced to the colonial era, the cycle of violence has exacerbated the region's impoverishment (Uganda, APRM Report, 2009).

Kenya has experienced the fewest civil wars among the countries of the Horn of Africa, although it remains deeply divided along ethnic lines. Issues of access to land and political power have resulted in inter-ethnic strife, which has periodically erupted into violent conflicts. Nyaza, Western, and the North-East Provinces are the poorest (APRM, Kenya, 2006). These are also areas of

Table 2.5 Poverty by Region in Uganda

Rural/urban and by region	Poverty estimate 2005–6	2009–10	Gini coefficient for consumption 2005–6	2009–10
Rural	34.2	27.2	0.363	0.375
Urban	13.7	9.1	0.432	0.447
Central	16.4	10.7	0.417	0.451
Eastern	35.9	24.3	0.354	0.319
Northern	60.7	46.2	0.331	0.367
Western	20.5	21.8	0.342	0.375
Uganda	31.1	25.5	0.408	0.426

Source: Uganda Bureau of Statistics (2010). Uganda National Household Survey, 2009/10, Kampala, November.

Table 2.6 Inequalities in Uganda

Region	Average monthly income UGX	Mean monthly household consumption expenditure (2005–6 prices)	Literacy rate (per cent)	Access to telephone service (per cent)	Proportion of households that took one meal a day
Kampala	959,400	475,500	92.0	90	–
Central	389,600	291,250	83.0	80.4	7.2
Eastern	171,500	193,400	68.0	77.1	7.3
Northern	141,400	150,200	64.0	19.7	20.1
Western	303,200	210,450	71.0	84.7	5.7
National	303,700	232,700	73.0	70.8	9.3

Source: Uganda Bureau of Statistics (2010). Uganda National Household Survey, 2009/10, Kampala, November.

Table 2.7 Indicators of the Distribution of Poverty and Access to Public Services by Region in Kenya

Region	Income poverty, 2000	Households with access to electricity (per cent)	Gross primary school enrolments in 2000 (per cent)	Number of doctors
Nairobi	–	71.4	52	–
Central	35.3	19.2	106.0	190
Coast	69.9	19.3	71.0	147
East	65.9	6.9	96.9	147
North-East	73.1	3.2	17.8	9
Nyaza	70.9	5.1	94.0	165
Rift Valley	56.4	10.5	88.3	197
West	66.1	1.6	93.3	83

Source: African Peer Review Mechanism (APRM) (2006). Country Report of the Republic of Kenya, May; and Society for International Development, *Pulling Apart: Facts and Figures on Inequality in Kenya*.

conflict. The Akiwumi report, for example, attributes violence in the north-east and west of the country to the extreme marginalization of communities in the political, economic and social structures and processes (Kenya, APRM Report, p. 13). As Table 2.7 shows, poverty in the country is very high and extremely skewed, with the North-East Province as an outlier in all indicators.

A MODIFIED EXPLANATION

The data in the tables, although incomplete, suggest that the relative deprivation/grievance theory goes a long way in explaining the ethnic- and region-based conflicts in the Greater Horn. However, the theory needs to be placed within the context of the challenges of state- and nation-building in post-colonial Africa in order to provide a fuller explanation of the conflicts. Some of the conflicts, such as Eritrea's war of independence, the Ogaden wars, the conflicts in the North-East Province of Kenya as well as the Afar conflicts in Djibouti, Ethiopia and Eritrea, cannot be explained by relative deprivation alone, even though relative deprivation plays an important role in all these conflicts. In large part the conflicts in all these cases are over the incorporation of certain identities into states they do not want to be part of. The conflicts are thus primarily rebellions by ethnic identities who find themselves in the wrong state due to the creation of African states of mixed ethnic identities by the colonial powers or to annexation by a post-colonial state.

The Eritrean struggle for independence was essentially a response to the country's annexation by Ethiopia, although the political domination that followed annexation and the brutal repression perpetrated by successive Ethiopian governments during the conflict contributed in mobilizing the population to support the armed struggle. The origins of the conflicts in the Ogaden of Ethiopia and the North-East Province of Kenya were also largely because the Somali communities in those two areas found themselves in the wrong states backed by the republic of Somalia, which aspired to unite all Somalis under one state. No doubt, the marginalization of the Somali communities within their respective states added to their grievances. It is, however, unclear if absence of marginalization would have prevented the conflicts. Again the Afar conflicts in Djibouti, Ethiopia, and Eritrea are related to the fact that the Afar find themselves scattered across three states, where, as minorities, they are marginalized. At the root of Afar insurgencies in all three countries is Afar nationalism, although such nationalism may also have been propelled, at least in part, by the relative deprivation the Afar face.

CONCLUDING REMARKS

From the point of view of the relative deprivation/grievance theory, the states in the Horn of Africa could bring the conflicts under control by addressing the problems of deprivation. In other words, the states in the region need to target economic resources at the deprived areas to ensure that those areas receive adequate representation in the political process. The states also need to facilitate cultural empowerment of the culturally marginalized communities. There is little doubt that such measures are essential and the states of the region need to provide equitable citizenship rights to all identity groups. Northern Uganda's conflicts may, for example, be successfully resolved through such measures, as there is no strong separatist aspiration in the region.

From the perspective of the modified theoretical formulation, however, the states of the region need to do more than address the problem of deprivation. The problems of ethnic entities separated by national boundaries are likely to require flexible borders and close cooperation among the states of the region in order to address the burden of these ethnic groups. A new strategy of state-building with close regional cooperation that encompasses issues, such as open borders and dual citizenships, may be required.

NOTES

1. Inter-communal conflicts in Ethiopia and Kenya largely revolve around land and livestock theft (IDRC Report).
2. Casualty figures from Sudan's first North–South conflict (1955–72) are estimated at 500,000. The second (1983–2005) is said to have produced some two million dead, 420,000 refugees and over four million displaced. The casualty figures for the Darfur conflict are estimated at over 180, 000, with approximately two million displaced, although some human rights organizations estimate 300,000 deaths (Qugnivet 2006). The casualty figures for Ethiopia's various civil wars between 1962 and 1992 are estimated at about 1,400,000 (*Twentieth Century Atlas*).
3. Eritrea, Sudan and Ethiopia, in particular, have had periods of high security expenditures as a ratio of GDP. For the period 1998–2007, the ratio of military expenditures to total public expenditures was 34.88 per cent in Eritrea, 28 per cent in Sudan and 17 per cent in Ethiopia (UNICEF Information by Country 2010; www.unicef.org/infoby country).

4. Oil wealth may explain why the SPLM changed its long-held opposition to independence after the death of its leader John Garang de Mabior, but oil wealth was not a motivator for the conflict at least for the first 20 or so years before oil deposits were discovered.

REFERENCES

African Peer Review Mechanism (2006). *Country Report of the Republic of Kenya.* May.

African Peer Review Mechanism (2009). *Country Report of the Republic of Uganda.* January.

Auvinen, Juha and Nafziger, Wayne (1999). 'The Sources of Humanitarian Emergencies', *Journal of Conflict Resolution,* 43(3) (June), 267–90.

Ballentine, Karen and Nitzschke, Heiko (2003). *Beyond Greed and Grievance: Policy Lessons from Studies in the Political Economy of Armed Conflict,* International Peace Academy, Programme on Economic Agendas in Civil War (EACW), IPA Policy Report, October.

Ballentine, Karen and Nitzschke, Heiko (2005). *The Political Economy of Civil War and Conflict Transformation,* Berghof Research Centre for Constructive Conflict Management, April.

Cobham, Alex (2005). *Causes of Conflict in Sudan: Testing the Black Book,* QEH Working Paper No. 121, January.

Collier, Paul and Hoeffler, Anke (2000). *Greed and Grievance in Civil Wars,* Policy Research Paper No. 2355, Washington, DC: The World Bank.

Collier, Paul and Hoeffler, Anke (2004). *Greed and Grievance in Civil War.* Oxford, The World Bank, CEPR and CSAE.

Cramer, Christopher (2006). *Civil War is Not a Stupid Thing: Accounting for Violence in Developing Countries.* London: Hurst.

El-Tom, Abdullahi Osman (2006). 'Darfur People: Too Black for the Arab-Islamic Project', in Salah M. Hassan and Carina E. Ray (eds.), *Darfur and the Crisis of Governance in Sudan,* Ithaca, NY and London: Cornell University Press, pp. 84–102.

Gurr, Ted (1993). *Minorities at Risk: A Global View of Ethnopolitical Conflicts.* Washington, DC: United States Institute for Peace Press.

Hassan, Salah M. and Ray, Carina E. (eds.) (2006). *Darfur and the Crisis of Governance in Sudan,* Ithaca, NY and London: Cornell University Press.

Klugman, J. (2000). 'Kenya: Economic Decline and Ethnic Politics', in E. W. Nafszinger, F. Stewart and R. Vayrynen (eds.), *Weak States and Vulnerable Economies: Humanitarian Emergencies in the Third World.* Oxford: Oxford University Press.

Mwaura, Ciru, Baechler, Gunther and Kiplagat, Bethuel (2002). 'Background to Conflicts in the IGAD Region', in Ciru Mwaura and Susanne Schmeidl (eds.), in *Early Warning and Conflict Management in the Horn of Africa,* Lawrenceville, NJ and Asmara: Red Sea Press.

Nafziger, Wayne and Auvinen, Juha (2002). 'Economic Development, Inequality, War, and State Violence', *World Development* 30(2) (February), 153–63.

Qugnivet, Noelle (2006). 'The Report of the International Commission of Inquiry on Darfur: The Question of Genocide', *Human Rights Review,* vol. 7, no. 4, July: 38–68.

Ross, Michael (2003). 'Oil, Drugs, and Diamonds: the Varying Roles of Natural Resources in Civil War', in Karen Ballentine and Jake Sherman (eds.) *The Political Economy of Armed Conflict: Beyond Greed and Grievance*. Boulder, CO: Lynne Rienner, pp. 47–70.

Sambanis, Nicholas (2002). 'Defining and Measuring Civil War: Conceptual and Empirical Complexities', paper presented to the 43rd Annual Convention of the International Studies Association, New Orleans, LA, 2–27 March.

Society for International Development (2008). *Pulling Apart: Facts and Figures on Inequality in Kenya*, Washington, DC: SID.

Stewart, Frances (2000). 'Crisis Prevention: Tackling Horizontal Inequalities', *Oxford Development Studies*, vol. 28, no. 3: 245–62.

Wulf, Herbert and Debiel, Tobias (2009). *Conflict Early Warning Response Mechanisms: Tools for Enhancing the Effectiveness of Regional Organizations, A Comparative Study of the AU, ECOWAS, IGAD, ASEAN/ARF and PIF*. Working Paper no. 49, Regional and Global Axes of Conflict, Institut Für Entwicklung und Frieden (INEF) Duisburg.

3
Leadership in the Horn of Africa: The Emic/Etic Perspective

Hassan Mahadallah

It has almost become a universal dictum to say that leadership is contextual and culture-specific. Yet this dictum is consistently ignored when it comes to leadership in Africa. When Africanists discuss the subject, they talk about national leadership. But in Africa, leadership is ubiquitous. You encounter it in the church, in the market and in the village and hamlet. It pervades African life, yet it is layered and culture-specific. However, these layers and breaks, and how they affect leadership and governance, do not appear in the Africanist literature.[1]

The purpose of this chapter is to show that leadership is best understood in terms of the insider/outsider (emic/etic) perspective. We believe that the distorted view of the continent's leaders is caused by the universalization of the etic. Certain leadership qualities that are valued in the etic domain, such as craft, dominance, violence, may be viewed negatively in the emic. For instance, while non-Africans may embrace the idea of the 'naked leader',[2] Africans may find the idea unfathomable. Therefore, in this chapter we will examine the subject from both perspectives. Since these perspectives are informed by a life lived or empirically observed experiences (respectively) they offer the clearest understanding of the subject. The contrast reveals the nature of leadership in the continent.

In this chapter, we define leadership traditionally as the ability of one person to motivate and move others towards a desired goal without resort to coercion. It is important to us whether the goal is shared by both the leader and the led. Leadership, as we shall see, is culture-sensitive, though not always culture-contingent. Therefore, what is of interest is how leadership is understood and leaders evaluated by insiders and outsiders. In the first section, we briefly discuss how leadership is treated in the literature. In the second, we explain the emic and etic concepts and delineate their conceptual boundaries. In the third, we show the incongruence of the insider and the outsider views regarding leadership. We will locate these differences in the inter-ethnic or, in the case of Somalia, inter-clan discourses. These will show how certain country-specific factors affect leadership. Finally, we offer general remarks that may guide and inspire further research.

THE STATE OF THE CURRENT LITERATURE

Since the time of the Ancient Greeks, leadership has been widely investigated and debated. To the Greeks, leadership was, like any other human activity, a skill that could be learned. In the *Republic*, Plato depicted a philosopher-king, who was trained (or trained himself) in the affairs of the *polis*.[3] Later, with his colleagues, he established a school for leadership, the *Paideia*. Likewise, in the *Nicomachean Ethics* Aristotle discussed how legislators can learn leadership by habituation.[4] More importantly, both the Academy and the Lyceum were founded by the two philosophers respectively to educate Greeks for the attainment of life's calling, including leadership.

In the *Iliad* and the *Odyssey*, Homer identified four leadership qualities: legitimacy; judgement; cunning; and valour. Since these traits are distributed among the wider population, it is unlikely that a single person will possess them all. Therefore, Homer seems to advance a concept of group leadership that combines all four characteristics. As one author put it, 'The four leaders might reflect an early awareness that the best group of leaders includes those whose qualities balance and complement one another.'[5]

In Ancient Greece, leadership was essentially a community affair. Leaders were developed and ultimately evaluated by the political community. The character and performance of Greek leaders were judged according to local norms and standards. Etic understandings were alien to the early Greeks, who disdained foreign mores and cultures. Since the *polis* provided the necessary resources for their training, as well as the political space where leaders could exercise their functions, leadership was an emic experience.

The Bible and the Qur'an cite the exemplary accounts of great leaders, like Moses, Jesus and Mohammed. As law-givers, these men organized their disorganized followers into political communities and inspired them to seek higher ends.[6] In the Bible, leadership is service and the ideal leader of the Christian community is a servant. 'You know that the rulers of the nations lord it over them,' said

Jesus, 'and their great ones exercise authority over them. It shall not be so among you, but whoever desires to become great among you shall be your servant.'[7]

In terms of leadership the Qur'an is more explicit and forceful than the Bible. In Sura al-Nisa, the Qur'an commands: 'O ye who believe! Obey Allah, and obey the Messenger, and those charged authority among you.'[8] In one of his widely read utterances, Prophet Mohammed enjoined that every three Muslims should have a leader. In addition, Islam delineates the ideal attributes a Muslim leader should have. Overall, this individual is a virtuous person who rises above the masses by his personal qualities. 'Your need for a leader,' uttered the Caliph Uthman bin-Afan, 'whose acts are greater than your need for a leader who charts.'[9]

Modern studies of leadership date back to the sixteenth century, when Niccolò Machiavelli published his most famous book *The Prince*. In this book, Machiavelli depicted a virtuous prince who is both prudent and cunning. He had to be so, he posited, because the political environment is rife with treachery. Thus, in Machiavelli, the character and actions of the leader cannot be understood outside the existing socio-political landscape.[10]

The subject received its second most important contribution in the modern era in 1922, when Max Weber published *The Theory of Social and Economic Organization*, in which he propounded an enduring typology of leadership.[11] From 1922 until 1978, when James M. Burns published his seminal work, aptly titled *Leadership*, the subject received scant attention. Since then, a stream of publications from different disciplines has been produced. The *Encyclopedia of Leadership* alone contains 1.2 million words in 373 substantive entries and 300 sidebars of public records.[12]

Despite the volume of the existing literature, studies on leadership cluster round only two broad conceptual threads: one takes the leader as its primary referent, the other takes leadership as its focal point. Those that fall in the former cluster focus on the personality traits of leaders and equate leadership with what leaders do. Given the centrality of the leader in these studies, the context in which leadership is exercised is treated as marginal.[13] Typical among these studies is one by A. Lorri Manasse, titled 'Vision and Leadership: Paying Attention to Intention'. In this study, the leader is endowed with extraordinary capabilities, among them technical knowledge, foresight, hindsight, attentiveness, innovativeness, learning ability, creativity, self-awareness, even a sense of humour. The gist of the study is that such a person, regardless of the nature of the situation, would be a reliable leader.[14] A Harvard Business School publication, titled *Becoming an Effective Leader*, concurs. As a how-to book for result-driven managers, the work places the executive at the centre of the business universe. It offers pointers for successful business leaders. They alone, the study seems to suggest, can make or break corporations. Accordingly, successful CEOs, like Jack Welch of GE, are deified, as though he alone is responsible for the success of the company.[15]

Writing within the same leader-centric genre, Kotter offers a more nuanced view of leadership. To him, leadership is a 'core behaviour . . . that changes little over time, across different cultures, or in different industries'.[16] Although external factors may impinge on what leaders do, they may not frustrate their goals. This 'core behaviour', when brought to bear on any situation, he argues, will unfailingly produce desirable results.[17]

Conversely, those in the latter cluster investigate not only the leader, but also the context and the ideational formulations that confer meaning on the subject. Whereas the former portrays leadership as a personal quality, the latter considers it as a relational process involving human motivations, influences and expectations. Thus, the primary task of the political leader is to ascertain what these motivations and interests are and to foster collaborative relationships among them.[18]

> All leaders, even the most autocratic face limits on the scope of their power. Limits may include not only superior authority in a hierarchy, but also the existence of powerful competitors, the interest of key constituencies whose support is important if the leader is to retain power, the necessity for the leader to appeal to an electorate on some regular basis, or a board of trustees or directors that appoints, and may remove, the leader.[19]

These perspectives gave rise to various theories of leadership and leadership styles. The more noteworthy among these are charismatic/rational theory, transformational/transactional theory and servant leader theory. In addition, there are two main leadership styles known as the stewardship and constitutional styles. We have not employed any of these theories or styles in this chapter because our aim is not to show how leadership is practised in the Horn of Africa, but how it is understood by insiders and outsiders.

THE CONCEPTS OF EMIC AND ETIC

The terms emic and etic are derived from the Greek words *phonemic* and *phonetic*, which pertain to the basic sound of a word and the idea conveyed by it, respectively. While the former (the phoneme) refers to the sound system of a language, the latter (the phonetic) refers to the structure that gives meaning to it. Therefore, the emic is an unconscious reflection of the life-long experiences of a particular society. These experiences may be concrete, perceptive or symbolic. Therefore, an emic understanding of an object is invariably informed by what Karl Marx referred to in another context as 'sub-structure' – the ideas that motivate and give meaning to human action, such as beliefs and social codes. As Hans Zetterberg succinctly put it, 'Emic sentences are those that tell how the world is seen by a particular people who live in it.'[20]

The etic, on the other hand, is akin to the comprehension and interpretation of the experience of a society by an outside observer. The tales of Hermes in ancient Greece constitute a good example of etic communication.[21] Although, like the Hermes stories, etic communications contain inaccuracies and misrepresentations, they also offer insights and information previously hidden from their emic users. Today, etic productions are analogous to 'the language of science, scholarship and cultural criticism' which shed light on emic objects and experiences.[22]

To have any meaning, both the etic and emic units must occur where, when and how they are perceived or seen as appropriate. 'Appropriateness of an emic unit includes the feature of its relevant occurrence in relation to the total pattern of an individual or society.'[23] For instance, in the cultural documentary *The Gods Must Be Crazy*, a Coca-Cola bottle dropped from a plane flying over the Kalahari Desert has no meaning to the !Kung family who find it. Their initial marvel is indicative of its alienness (inappropriateness) to their material culture. Likewise, an etic unit that is valued in a classroom setting may be excluded from a museum of natural history as inappropriate.[24]

The accuracy of the emic and the etic depends on the distance one is removed from the object. In colonial Africa, there was a wide social gap between the European rulers and the indigenous population. A similar gulf existed between the populace and their African leaders.[25] As a result, each layer had a distorted view of what the other was actually doing. For example, when during an anti-colonial rally some Congolese who were trekking towards

Kisangani were asked where they were going, they replied, 'We are going to Stanleyville to hear Lumumba insult the Europeans.'[26] Of course, insulting Europeans was far from Lumumba's mind, but that was their emic understanding of the matter.

The emic and etic occur in multiple and overlapping contexts. Since most people participate in multiple settings and social relationships, 'what is emic or etic can shift from one context to the next'.[27] Depending on how far the audience is removed from the object, this author's understanding of leadership in Africa can be either an emic or etic unit. For instance, at the Nordic Institute of Africa Studies in Uppsala, this chapter was perceived as an emic communication.[28] On the other hand, since my presentation was research-based and objectively developed, it was also perceived as an etic unit. In short, depending on the distance a reader is removed from the situation, the information can be alternately perceived as an emic or etic communication.

COLONIALISM AND THE ETIC UNDERSTANDING OF LEADERSHIP

1884 is indelibly marked in the history of modern Africa. This is the year when 14 European and American diplomats met in Berlin and agreed to divide up the African continent among them.[29] Hegemonic and extensive in its effect – economically, socially, politically – European rule created a two-tier society in the colonies where the upper was occupied by European expatriates and the lower by the local population. Yet, despite the profound social rift it created, colonialism brought together large populations under one government, expanded the social and political spaces, and fostered a dynamic social discourse between and within these societies. It is these discourses that inform our understanding of political leadership in Africa.

Since it is conducted above the daily life of the village, the hamlet and the homestead, we appropriately call this discourse etic. According to Homi Bhabha, this discourse has distinct characteristics.

It is a form of colonial discourse that is uttered *inter dicta*: a discourse at the crossroads of what is known and permissible and that which though known must be kept concealed; a discourse uttered between the lines and as such both against the rules and within them.[30]

In this genre, both the colonial apologist and opponent situate Africa's modern political life in its colonial origins. Therefore, they are united in problematizing the 'colonial situation'. Since they share the same philosophical root, they form two sides of the same coin. Simply put, they 'mimic' one another, in Bhabha's word.[31]

In this grand discourse, the colonial man – his person, language, way of life – is banished from the scene. 'I remember that when I was a boy,' wrote Jawaharlal Nehru,

> the British-owned newspapers in India were full of official news and utterances; of service news, transfers, and promotions; of the doings of English society, of polo, races, dances, and amateur theatricals. There was hardly a word about the people of India, about their political, cultural, social, or economic life. Reading them, one would hardly suspect that they existed.[32]

Accordingly, in the European scheme of things, the colonial man appears in his crass attributes – docile or cantankerous, lethargic or anxious, agitator or nationalist, etc. He is almost present, but not quite, to paraphrase Bhabha. In this 'metonymy of presence', the native leader (administrator, teacher, preacher) can only mimic the real one, for he is 'both incomplete and virtual'.[33] Thus, 'Grant's colonial as partial imitator, Macaulay's translator, Naipaul's colonial politician as play-actor, Decoud as the scene setter of the *opéra bouffe* of the New World, these are the appropriate objects of a colonialist chain of command, authorized versions of otherness.'[34]

The colonial literature hardly mentions the discourse that goes on every day in the villages and hamlets, where most Africans live. Therefore, it is safe to say that the etic perspective captures only half the complete picture. Even the works of Christian missionaries and social anthropologists, who spend much of their active life in the field, often misrepresent native culture and way of life. According to Raymond Firth, the failure is primarily 'a function of the general structure of the situation in which the anthropologist works'. Since this colonial structure is founded on power, the mores of the powerful – the Europeans – provide the primary referent by which all things are judged. Therefore, Firth argues, the anthropologist, like the other expatriates, is a captive of his/her culture.[35]

The deficiency of the etic perspective does not end with the dissolution of the colonies. As Alexis de Tocqueville reminds us, no matter how fundamental a change a nation may undergo, old methods and mind-sets do not easily wither way.[36] In post-independence Africa, the retention of colonial structures and institutions guarantee the continuation of the etic distortions. This is why I. M. Lewis, founder of modern Somali studies, regretted his subjectivity: 'Reflecting on this, I now think that I have sometimes tended to be less critical and objective (too guilty of the professional anthropological "charity" Ernest Gellner [1962] rightly criticizes) about the policies and actions of successive independent Somali governments (including the present one).'[37]

The etic perspective has certainly expanded our understanding of social life outside 'our' own. However, leadership is culture-specific and does not easily lend itself to etic interpretations. Even the term 'leadership' has different meanings and connotations in different cultures. Calling an American a 'leader' may be taken as praise, but calling him a 'führer', which means the same thing in German, can be seen as offensive.[38] In Africa, not only the meaning of the word is different, but also how leadership is acquired and exercised. Unlike his European counterparts, the African leader may be a leader in one setting and a follower in another. This is why the idea of a sovereign was unknown in the Continent before colonialism. To elaborate the point, in the next section we will discuss African understanding of leadership.

THE EMIC UNDERSTANDING OF LEADERSHIP

In his book *Not Yet Uhuru*, Oginga Odinga incisively recounted African notions of leadership. Before colonialism, he said, the basic ingredients of African leadership were maturity, experience, steadfastness, wisdom and consensus-building. Power, which is a core ingredient of the etic understanding of leadership, did not enter the African calculation. Leaders were a collective product of the community and were perpetually joined to it by an umbilical cord. They may have been low on power, but they were certainly high in legitimacy. They led but did not reign. 'A chief', wrote Odinga, 'did not issue orders . . . His function was not to lay down the law, but to consult and arbitrate to learn the consensus of opinion, and to keep the unity of his people.'[39]

In the African tradition, leadership was distributed between the chief and the clan elders, who represented their respective lineages. The concept of a reigning sovereign was alien to the traditional African mind. The chief shared power with the village elders. Together, they constituted the government and decided on matters of war/peace, taxation/tribute and production/distribution of resources. The chief's unique task was 'to reconcile the sectional interests of the elders' and forge a working consensus.[40]

In terms of power and wealth, the African leader was marginally better off than the elders, who were his peers. 'The services and tributes which the chief received were to enable him to fulfil the obligations of his office, but not to enrich him.'[41] This imposed tight control on royal power and compelled a modest standard of living on royalty. Since most Africans lived in close proximity to the seat of government, relations between the rulers and ruled were intimate. Furthermore, the two shared a common culture, which informed their understanding of what good leadership entailed.[42]

The colonial encounter irreversibly overturned this stable traditional arrangement. The European system created new distant centres of power manned by a new crop of leaders, who honed their leadership skills, not in the villages, but in colonial schools and institutions. These leaders were taught universal rules (which they did not thoroughly digest), which they were expected to enforce in all cultural settings. More importantly, they had at their disposal the vast resources of the institutions of law and order. They were destined to rule badly and so they did.[43]

When outsiders refer to the leadership crisis in Africa they are usually talking about this crop of leaders, especially those at the national level. At this level, as Michael Crowder has observed, Africa's national leaders mimic the colonial governors they replaced. They prefer to rule by decree, live in large palaces, fly the national flag and lead an opulent lifestyle.[44] Like the Southern Bourbons who 'learned nothing and forgot nothing' they exchange favours and circulate power among themselves.[45] But leadership is more ubiquitous in Africa than the etic can account for. It occurs in churches, the marketplace and in the villages and hamlets, where most Africans live. It is contextual and culture-specific.

In his much cited work *No Shortcuts to Progress*, Goran Hyden correctly identifies the African state as a 'suspended' one, comparing it to a large balloon hovering over society.[46] Caught between two independent societies (national and international), the typical African leader governs 'in the context of a state that is suspended in mid-air above society'.[47] The solution lies, he states, in the development of new 'leadership codes' that are less affective and more task-oriented.[48] But Africa's leadership problem does not easily lend itself to technical resolution, as the Samatar brothers rightly pointed out. In Somalia, for instance, they demonstrate how the economy of affection continued to operate even after the institution of one-man rule. Said Barre, they contend, was as much attuned to the appeals of his clansmen as the civilian rulers he replaced.[49]

Africans have yet to make the psychological step necessary for the emergence of common leadership. If one does not respect the government of neighbouring tribesmen how can one esteem the leadership of a government located in a distant capital he rarely visits? This is why the village is still the locus of African leadership. The traditional chief, the local 'big man', and the priest are among the acknowledged leaders of the community. Their government is less contentious and less corrupt than the national one. Theirs is a moral regime.[50]

When it comes to African politics, I tend to agree with Patrick Chabal that our etic understanding is flawed. African politics cannot be easily understood by looking at what he calls 'high politics'. Rather, it is the 'low' politics, the politics of everyday life, as he put it, that carries the true meaning.[51] To an outsider, African politics is rife with corruption and ethnic strife. But the insider differentiates between politics at the state level and politics at the local level. At the former level, for instance, corruption is not only tolerated but may even be encouraged. At the latter, however, it is discouraged and rarely tolerated.[52] Ahmed Samatar agrees: 'No Somali feels guilty in the unlawful appropriation of public wealth and the people do not see it as a robbery. On the contrary, any person holding public office is encouraged to get rich and also to help his kin-relations at the same time.'[53]

Colonialism has created new states and new leaders without totally obliterating the pre-existing ones. Therefore, the modern African state has to compete for loyalty with more entrenched multiple centres of power. The primary task of today's leader is to negotiate the voluntary transfer of this loyalty to the centre. One way to achieve this is to offer incentives for this mental journey. Unless people are convinced that their lot will improve, they will not agree to change. More importantly, no one will agree to do so while the end-point is in a state of turmoil. This is why most Africans prefer the status quo to unfamiliar change.

In short, there is a conceptual incongruence – a tension, if you will – between the etic and the emic understandings of leadership. Whereas the former is concerned with the ideal leader – say, one with normative (preferably European) qualities – the latter is concerned with the practical leader whom people encounter on a daily basis. While the etic talks about presidents, prime ministers, ministers, deputies, directors, the emic talks about chiefs, elders, couriers, village councils. In the former context, leadership is based on power and authority, factors that transcend cultures. In the latter, leadership is founded on consensus and persuasion, factors that are culture-contingent. Therefore, to uncover what a leader is, one must take into account the ever-present tension between the emic and etic.

UNDERSTANDING LEADERSHIP IN THE HORN OF AFRICA

If Africa is 'a nation of singers and dancers', as Olaudah Equiano once described it, the Horn of Africa is a nation of great empires and leaders. Located in the eastern-most corner of the continent, the region abuts the Middle East, the cradle of civilization, and abuts Europe and Asia. Due to a long sustained interaction with its neighbours, the people of the area developed large towns and kingdoms before any other part of the continent. Despite their long experience with statehood, like other Africans they are still beset by poor national leadership.[54]

In December 2010, the *East Africa Magazine* assessed all of Africa's currently serving leaders. Although the rating was simplistic, it underscored the sorry state of the continent's leadership. Of the 52 rated presidents (two unrated), five of the six Horn of African leaders were rated ICU and mortuary cases. The only one who scored a pass, Mwai Kibaki of Kenya, was given a 'C'.[55] What is the cause of this leadership crisis in the region? It is our contention that this crisis is located at the national level and does not permeate the whole of social life in the region. Still the villages and small towns, where the majority of the population lives, are stable and, for the most part, well governed. In the next section we discuss leaders in specific countries.

LEADERSHIP IN ETHIOPIA

The kingdom (later empire) of Axum 'entered the wider light of history at the end of the first century A.D.'.[56] Unlike its neighbours, Ethiopia's state is home grown. However, like them it is a hybrid of nationalities and ethnic groups with different cultures. Since culture mediates the relationship between rulers and ruled, leadership in this multi-ethnic country is burdened by cultural differences and incompatible political organizations – those of the rulers and citizens.[57] For more than a century, the country's national leaders came from the core regions of Tigray and Amhara. Because of their alien origin and the manner in which they accede to power (usually by conquest), their legitimacy is locally contested throughout the country. This is why even when they possess incontestable national power Ethiopia's leaders lack 'hegemonic control'.[58]

Throughout Ethiopia's long history, leadership has always been a contested affair. Vanquishing one's rival, rather than an orderly succession, has been the normal path to the throne.[59] Despite its obvious brutality, the process is so culturally entrenched that some still look back to it with nostalgia. 'Often based on military prowess,' wrote one Ethiopian author, 'God's choice [victor] became formal the moment the Church anointed the elect.'[60] The current regime continues the tradition. Having come to power by force, Ethiopia's Prime Minister, Meles Zenawi, recently intimated to a visiting US Undersecretary of State for Democracy and Global Affairs, Maria Otero, that if Ethiopians wanted democracy, they should be 'willing to sacrifice and die for their cause', just as others before them had done.[61] As a cultural throwback without a common institution to 'anoint' him, the Prime Minister of Ethiopia rules without internal legitimacy.

That Ethiopia avoided colonialism is often stated. But what is not so readily mentioned is this African state was an old empire with its own colonial ambitions.[62] Vying for territorial aggrandizement, Emperor Menelik II pressed the European powers in the region for concessions: 'Ethiopia has been for fourteen centuries a Christian island in a sea of pagans. If powers at a distance come forward to partition Africa between them, I do not intend to be an indifferent spectator.'[63] By the late nineteenth century, when the empire established its current boundaries, it had been transformed into an internal colonial state with a two-tier society notorious for its oppression and economic exploitation.[64] Speaking to the true spirit of the era, one Ethiopian aristocrat reminisced:

> an edict would be made to prepare food for the journey and to clothe the servants and to fatten mules…on the road the men servants put up the tents and foraged for hay while maidservants washed our feet, baked bread, prepared coffee and served us dried meat and savouries . . . those who had hydromel drank that; those who had none took home-made beer . . . In addition the peasants had to bring us food and drink by way of tribute (*gibir*). We enjoyed hydromel and good meat on such journeys although the poorer soldiers slept in the bushes and ate dried

bread with only water to drink. What a marvellous way to spend thirty days travelling.[65]

Ethiopia's history is a history of conquest and the resistance of conquered peoples. For more than a century, the country's national leaders came from the core regions of Tigray and Amhara. Other ethnic groups, who are geographically and culturally further removed from the centre, continually contested the authority of the Christian highlanders. While the conquered peoples consider the dominant ethnie 'colonialists' and 'bandits', the latter consider the peripheral societies to be 'tribalists' and 'secessionists'. The controversy has spawned an inter-ethnic discourse reminiscent of a bygone era. The Oromos, wrote Professor Asafa Jalata, live under 'Ethiopian political slavery'.[66] 'The Oromo people,' he continued,

have no protection from political violence since there is no rule of law in the Ethiopian empire. They do not have personal and public safety in their homes and communities. Oromos live under Ethiopian settler colonialism that has taken away their sovereignty and exposed them to massive human rights violations and absolute poverty by denying them their fundamental needs and rights.[67]

The language of the conquered always privileges freedom, human rights and self-determination. On the other hand, the language of the conqueror emphasizes unity, stability and progress. In the Ethiopian milieu, the lines of the discourse are drawn accordingly. In a recent commentary, Shiferaw Abebe portrayed the Oromo Liberation Front (OLF), the champion of the Oromo cause, as a separatist organization engaged in political subterfuge. Despite its pretences, he argued, the OLF remains true to its original mission, which is the 'liberation of Oromia from the Colonial empire of Abyssinia',[68] In response, Dumessaa Diimmaa, a member of the OLF, after referring to his interlocutor's social position, *nefetegna*, recounted the painful history that placed his society in its subject position.[69] 'For the Abyssinians,' he wrote, 'these imperial marches of conquest and annexation may be viewed as nation building of glory and gallantry. For the polities in the south, it was rivers of blood and tears.'[70]

Even though national leadership in Ethiopia is highly contested, local leadership thrives because people trust traditional institutions. Based on 'cultural logic' they are familiar, accessible, timely and cost-effective. This is why, in order to 'nationalize' their leadership credentials, Ethiopia leaders have tried to link with and tap into the legitimacy of local institutions. Councils of elders, youth leadership, peasant associations and religious organizations – repositories of local legitimacy – were invariably targeted for penetration. So far, the effort has been without success.[71]

Not all multi-ethnic states have leadership problems. Ethiopia is however unique in three respects. First, the method of incorporating certain ethnic groups, especially the Oromos, was traumatic. During the state-building process, they were pillaged and massacred in large numbers. In the words of Martial de Salviac:

> The conduct of the Abyssinian armies invading a land is simply barbaric. They contrive a sudden irruption, more often at night. At daybreak, the fire begins; surprised men in the huts or in the fields are three quarters massacred and horribly mutilated; the women and the children and many men are reduced to captivity; the soldiers lead the frightened herds toward the camp, take away their grain and flour which they load on the shoulders of their prisoners spurred on by blows of whip, destroy the harvest, then, glutted with booty and intoxicated with blood, go to walk a bit further from the devastation. That is what they call 'civilizing a land'.[72]

Second, Ethiopia remains a two-tier society, a relic of its imperial past. Class, race and power inform social and political relations.[73] Finally, even though they are the largest ethnic group in the country, the Oromos do not have political power commensurate to their strength. 'The politics of numbers,' wrote Christopher Clapham, 'are foreign to Ethiopia's means of allocating power.'[74]

National leadership in Ethiopia thus lacks internal legitimacy. Recent attempts by Ethiopian leaders to link with local authorities are steps in the right direction. As a product of 'interactive dynamics' leadership partly inheres in such interactions.[75]

LEADERSHIP IN SOMALIA

Since Axum, other empires and principalities had emerged in the Horn of Africa. Noteworthy among these were the seven Muslim principalities of the Awdal empire in north-western Somalia. The trade and diplomatic relations they established with countries as distant as Morocco and Turkey, the wealth they amassed and the size of the armies they raised attest to the sophistication the Somali empire.[76] Despite their long experience with nationhood, Somalis did not develop a national consciousness, and, therefore, national leadership, until the colonial era. Battered and pulverized by the colonial onslaught, they congregated, for the first time since Awdal, around one leader, the Sayyid Mohamed Abdille Hassan, who took up their cause. According to Said S. Samatar, who studied the man and his movement, the Dervish regime was highly centralized, heralding 'a new order which was alien to the pastoral Somalis'.[77]

Until the rise of the first nationalist party in 1947, the Somali Youth League (SYL), the idea of 'Somaliness' existed as a plethora of ideas in the popular mind. The political agitation and the educational campaigns that the party leaders waged during the independence movement solidified the idea of nationhood. Thus, when independence came, the national credentials of the President, Aden Abdulle Osman, and his ministers were not questioned – at least not on cultural grounds. A share in the common heritage, territory, language, religion and belief in common descent with the general citizenry prevented the rise of that type of opposition.[78]

However, ethnic homogeneity did not confer special authority on Somali leaders any more than the escape from colonialism improved the legitimacy of Ethiopian rulers. Regionalism and clan subterfuge in the national politics repeatedly undermined the legitimacy of Somali leaders. In 1987, Laitin and Samatar correctly described the political situation in Somalia:

> The formation of political coalitions, the selection of presidents and prime ministers, the distribution of civil service (from minister down to the humblest office messenger), the allocation of national resources, the access to economic opportunities – these depend almost invariably on kinship patterns.[79]

In this competitive, clannish environment, power periodically shifts from one clan to another; and when it does, the legitimacy of the new leader is evaluated through the prism of Somali clan culture. Accordingly, it appreciates among his clansmen and declines among others. The vast post-independence inter-Somali discourse captures these sentiments. 'For us the years 1960–69 represented the neo-colonial era,' declared Mohamed Aden Sheikh, a relative of President Siad Barre and inner circle minister. 'The economy floundered,' he continued, 'the politics reflected confusion and tribalism . . . social relations were corrupted and our cultural heritage was allowed to disintegrate.'[80]

In his speech, Sheikh portrayed the military regime of General Siad Barre as a break with the past. His views were quickly disputed by others. In analysing the politics of the government, Abdi Sheikh Abdi highlighted the familial relationship of the President and three of his inner-circle ministers, including Sheikh himself.[81] Somali politics, Abdi argued, is 'a bewildering blend of radical rhetoric and clan politics'. Obviously, the military regime could not be any different. As a solution, he proposed a 'policy of national dialogue and reconciliation', which did not preclude Barre's removal.[82] 'Barre's regime, he said, 'has squandered whatever store of legitimacy it had left through the mismanagement of the Ogaden war'.[83]

Leadership thrives on legitimacy. In Somalia, the legitimacy of a ruler is viewed through the prism of clanism. Mindful of this, Siad Barre waged a long, though ineffective, anti-clan campaign. For a while, this won him some political credit. However, he squandered it in 1975 when he publicly executed ten prominent religious leaders.[84] The defeat of the national army in Ogaden in 1978 and the collapse of the economy further eroded his status as a national leader. Weak and unpopular, in the next ten years or so he maintained his power by force. His resort to crude force, manipulation and intimidation in the face of growing opposition finally dissolved whatever was left of his legitimacy.[85]

With the political demise of Siad Barre imminent, and violence looming, the people gravitated towards the strong men of their clans. So legitimized, and subsequently resourced by their kinsmen, the so-called 'warlords' quickly filled the leadership vacuum – many even adopting the title of president. During their long tenure, they carved up the country into many clan fiefdoms, which they jealously guarded. Based on ideology of clanism, and maintained by brute force, these fiefdoms enjoyed the sanction of local tradition.[86]

In some traditional societies, where the social unit – ethnic, tribe, clan – does not coincide with a given territory, there is usually some incongruence between the etic and emic understandings of leadership. However, in Somalia, where each clan is associated with a known district (and, if large enough, a region), there is less disagreement on where the locus of leadership is located. Simply stated, it is at the local level. This explains not only the proliferation but the resilience of local governance in post-state Somalia. By the same token, it explains why Somalis do not share the urgency of the international community in reconstituting the national state.[87]

Sheikh Sharif Sheikh Ahmed, the current President, came to prominence in 2006 through the Islamic Courts' Union (ICU), a coalition of clan courts in Mogadishu. The formation of the ICU was prompted by successive assassinations and kidnappings of prominent sheikhs carried out by a coalition of warlords who were hired by the CIA as a part of the war on terror. Under Sharif, the ICU defeated their opponents, pacified the city and instituted a semblance of national government.[88] Throughout this period, a youth faction, al Shabaab, was gestating in the ICU. Allied with international jihadists, they began to object to Sharif's leadership.[89]

Al Shabaab challenges the legitimacy of Sheikh Sharif on the basis of ideology. As believers in the caliphate system, they transcend the national state. To them, leadership entails universalist rather than nationalist principles. This is a reversal of the common thinking of the peoples of the Horn of Africa, who tend to look inwards for leadership. This ideological anomaly, though unpopular in Somalia, poses the strongest challenge to Sharif's leadership.[90]

LEADERSHIP IN KENYA

Unlike Somalia and Ethiopia, Kenya did not experience major internal or external wars. The country also avoided the military coups that swept across sub-Saharan Africa in the post-independence era. Unlike its neighbours, Kenya avoided the upheavals of the Cold War and the costly diversion of socialist ideology. Yet the country's leaders are, like their neighbours, underperforming in all facets of governance. Political patronage, corruption and judicial corruption are common in the highest echelons of power. What is the main reason for this leadership failure?

The answer lies in Kenya's social landscape. The country is multi-ethnic with more than 40 tribes. Since independence, political leaders were elected through their ethnic communities. Therefore, after election, they tend to enrich and empower their ethnic supporters. According to Africa Watch, Jomo Kenyatta, the first President of Kenya, started this practice and his successors continue it. 'By 1990, most senior positions in government, the military, security agencies, and state-owned corporations were held by Kalenjins.'[91] With all the levers of power in the hands of one ethnic group, others resented the President, Daniel Arab Moi. In one of his political discourses, Moi read them the Riot Act:

I call on all Ministers, Assistant Ministers and every other person to sing like parrots. During Mzee Kenyatta's period I persistently sang the Kenyatta tune until people said 'This fellow has nothing except to sing for Kenyatta.' I say: I didn't have any ideas of my own. Why was I to have my own ideas? I was in Kenyatta's shoes and therefore, I had to sing whatever Kenyatta wanted. If I had sung another song, do you think Kenyatta would have left me alone? Therefore, you ought to sing the song I sing. If I put a full stop, you should also put a full stop.[92]

The concept of *nyayo* is associated with the presidency of Moi, Kenyatta's successor.[93] According to the opposition group UMOJA, the President's rhetoric was at variance with his actions. They equated his economic, social and political programmes with neo-colonial practices aimed at undermining Kenya's hard-won independence. The practice, they predicted, will not only survive Moi but is bound to intensify after him. 'It will unleash even more violence on the people for it has absolutely no other base for its continued existence.'[94]

The group was prescient in its prediction of Kenya's political future. The presidential election of 2007 was contested by two political giants, Mwai Kibaki, a Kikuyu, and Raila Odinga, a Luo. After the election, each side claimed victory. Kibaki, the sitting president, declared himself winner and was sworn in. Odinga refused to concede. The political dispute rekindled old grievances between the Kikuyu and Luo over landownership and power-sharing. In less than two weeks, over 1,000 people were killed and 25,000 displaced.[95] Two years later, the ethnic tension was still simmering. In October 2009, BBC News reported Kenyans rearming in anticipation of violence in the 2012 presidential election.[96] As we have seen, under these conditions it is difficult to claim much legitimacy.

LEADERSHIP IN ERITREA AND DJIBOUTI

Eritrea and Djibouti are the smallest and newest countries in the Horn of Africa. They are also both colonial artefacts. Since its independence, Eritrea has had only one president, Issaias Afeworki, while Djibouti has had two, the current President, Ismael Omar Ghuelleh, and his predecessor, the late Hassan Gouled Aptidon.[97] Both countries are poor and sparsely populated.[98] Politically, they are both autocratic.[99] But this is where their similarities end.

The Republic of Djibouti has two main ethnic groups, the Afar and the Issa. Together, they constitute just over 55 per cent of the population. The rest of country's citizenry is divided into Isaaks, Gadaboursi, Europeans and Yemeni.[100] Ever since the country gained independence in 1977 the presidency has been held by an Issa. Control of the army, the security forces and until 1992 the country's only political party, gave Aptidon, the first president, immense power. Between 1977 and 1992 he ruled by executive decree as Djibouti did not have a formal constitution.[101]

Throughout the 1980s, the Afars contested this state of affairs by themselves. But having failed to effect political changes, they opened up negotiations with other opponents of the regime, including the Gudaboursi, Isaak, Yemenis and some disgruntled Issas, who were disaffected by Aptidon's autocracy. The opposition splintered in 1992 when the government met some of their demands, especially the unifying issue of single-party system. Thereafter, Aptidon was not seriously challenged and remained in power until spring 1999, when he voluntarily retired.[102] His successor, the current President Ghuelleh, retains Issa's hold on power. From 2005, when his party won all the seats in parliament, he emerged as the most dominant figure in Djiboutian politics.[103]

Unlike Djibouti, Eritrea's nine ethnic groups are not politicized. Perhaps, as Dan Connell says, it is because of the country's political culture which discourages people's involvement in politics.[104] Or, as Paul B. Henze argues, multi-ethnicity is not by itself sufficient to spark ethnic competition. The author rightly points out that some multi-ethnic nations, like the United States and Switzerland, have successfully managed their ethnic differences. Thus, he posits that multi-ethnicity poses a political problem only when it is coupled with authoritarianism, as in the former Soviet Union.[105] In Eritrea, although ethnic politicization did not occur, autocracy did. And herein lies the country's problems.

Since the Provisional Government of Eritrea was constituted in 1991, Eritrea has had only one president, Issaias Afeworki. According to Said Samatar, when many concerned Eritreans asked him to submit to the democratic process, he developed a bunker mentality.[106] In his recently published memoir, Bereket Habte Selassie, a former comrade-in-arms of the President, has painted a picture of paradise lost. During the liberation struggle, he wrote, the Eritrean People's Liberation Front (EPLF) told the nation that the country would be self-sufficient after independence. Unfortunately, though, since liberation Eritrea has become a beggar nation. He blames President Afeworki and his coterie in the EPLF for this failure.[107]

LEADERSHIP IN SUDAN

Sudan is geographically the largest country in Africa and the most ethnically diverse in the Horn. However, the country's more than 50 ethnic groups cannot be neatly divided according to race, religion, language or geography. Simply stated, the identities of the Sudanese people tend to overlap in all these categories. As a result, over the centuries they have developed interpenetrating social relationships. And had it not been for the long-sustained military dictatorship, and its uneven distribution of resources, Sudanese affairs would have taken a different trajectory.[108]

In his study of ethnic conflicts, Stefan Wolff lists political repression, economic deprivation and environmental disruption caused by governments as the main factors that politicize ethnic groups.[109] This seems to have been – and still is – the case in Sudan. With the exception of two brief periods in its history (1956–58 and 1986–89), Sudan has been governed by military leaders, who ruled by fiat, squandered the economy and poisoned the social relations. Colonel Ja'afar Muhammad Numeyri, who took power 25 May 1969, is the most notorious in this regard. During his tenure, Sudan's economy collapsed, the constitution was replaced with shari'a law and the North–South peace accord, signed in Addis Ababa in 1972, was abrogated. Thereafter, Sudan plunged into a civil war that would last for the next 20 years.[110]

Since he came to power in 1989, the current President, Omar Hassan al-Bashir, continues the trend. In the three years preceding his presidency, Sudan's economy plummeted and social relations further deteriorated. Using these as a pretext, on coming to power he banned unions, political parties and independent newspapers, and placed radio and television under government control. His political association with Sheikh Hassan al-Turabi, the leader of the Muslim Brotherhood in Sudan, had unsettling effects on secularists and Southerners. Their concerns were confirmed when al-Bashir's government imposed shari'a law even in the non-Muslim South, prorogued the Bar Association and enfeebled the judiciary.[111] In 2003, the Darfur eruption and the misfortune of criminal indictment at The Hague would be added to his repertoire.

When it comes to leadership in Sudan, the social discourse reveals part of the problem. It revolves around race and religion. Although the social reality is more complex than that, the Southerners tend to talk about 'Arab Muslims' while the Northerners speak of 'black Christians'. Their communication portrays domination and resistance.[112] Francis M. Deng, a Southerner and a former ambassador and Minister of State for Foreign Affairs, wrote:

> While Arabization was the first to take root, Islamization accentuated the process and became a determining factor in categorizing the races into slave masters and enslaved groups. The normative framework provided that a person who was a Muslim, Arabic-speaking, culturally Arabized, and could claim Arab descent was elevated to a position of respect and dignity, while in sharp contrast, a non-Muslim black African was deemed inferior, a heathen, and a legitimate target for enslavement.[113]

In Sudan, as elsewhere in the Horn of Africa, leadership is highly contested for two main reasons. The first is the inability of the leaders to enact policies that are socially equitable and economically progressive. Since independence, Sudan's leaders have done the opposite. This wrought the politicization of ethnic groups. The second is related to the cultural complexity of the nation. Depending on how one defines ethnicity, Sudan has between 50 and 115 different ethnic groups. Since leadership is culture-sensitive not culture-determined, it would be difficult for any leader to secure national legitimacy. This is even more so in traditional societies like southern Sudan, where the late John Garang, a local, was perceived as more legitimate than President al-Bashir.

CONCLUDING REMARKS

Leadership has been a subject of great interest since the dawn of civilization. Virtually every advanced society has had something to say about it. These discourses spawned a plethora of perspectives, theories and approaches. This chapter adds to the existing literature by approaching the subject from an insider/outsider (emic/etic) perspective. By using these useful tools, it offers a novel explanation of leadership without dwelling on what leaders do or the numerous exigencies that leadership entails. Equally important, this chapter brings out the incongruence that exists between the insider and outsider understanding of leadership. Finally, it strengthens the argument that leadership is contextual and culture sensitive.

We have used the state in the Horn of African as a backdrop for our investigation of the subject. Composed of unrelated tribes and ethnic groups, who espouse different notions of leadership, the states in the region are hard to govern. Since all ethnic groups are not equal in size and resources, one group tends to dominate the political arena for a long time. Unequal access to state power and resources inevitably leads to the politicization of ethnic groups, delegitimizing the national leader in some parts of the country.

For their part, the leaders are caught between an old tradition that binds them to their ethnic groups and the legitimate demands of citizens for democracy and the equitable distribution of economic resources. Therefore, despite the lofty rhetoric of national unity, the actions of the national leaders point to counter-projects of ethnic empowerment and self-aggrandizement. National leadership cannot be developed from sectarian foundations. Instead, it must be built on a shared national vision and interest. Before leaders can become national, the nation must be built. This is precisely what leaders in the Horn are currently lacking.

Colonialism added another layer of complexity by creating new distant centres of power and new leadership characters, who are neither tribal nor national in manner or outlook. The average person may never have the opportunity to talk to them or see them. This is why, after independence, virtually all African societies have experienced a leadership crisis. These crises have been most acute and enduring in the Horn of Africa, where tradition and modernity coexist in cross-currents.

Cultural differences can be overcome by strong institutions. Perhaps the greatest challenges that the states of the Horn of Africa face are related to institutionalism. As regularized human activities, institutions reduce uncertainty and create opportunities for 'the meetings of the minds'.[114] Undeveloped and inchoate, the Horn of Africa institutions create more uncertainties and suspicion than they solve. Therefore, logic tells us that the main aim of the states must be institution-building.

Creating a state that simultaneously controls its behaviour and that of its citizenry is not beyond the capacity of most of the leaders in the region. Rather, the issue is how to inspire the task. Unless he is convinced that, by doing so, his lot will improve, no leader will agree to an abrupt change of tack. This is why they prefer the status quo to unfamiliar change. By the same token, this is why, when it comes to leadership and governance, the states of the Horn of Africa demonstrate an utter lack of creativity and foresight.

A little courage and political creativity may suffice to alter the course of history in the region. Creating a political space where citizens can exercise their political rights is not a complicated undertaking. Civil society, though currently unimpressive, can be a good pilot in this direction. Issues of power-sharing, business contracts, protection of private property and free market supervision are not too complicated for civil society. Yet these are important prerequisites for the stability and prosperity of the region. The matter requires only foresight and political courage on the part of the leaders.

NOTES

1. See Robert H. Jackson and Carl G. Rosberg (1982). *Personal Rule in Black Africa* Berkeley, Los Angeles, CA and London: University of California Press.
2. The naked leader is one who is not restrained by the socio-political context.
3. In the *Republic*, Plato conceptualized an ideal state ruled by a philosopher-king. He thought that an ideal leader could be had by making a philosopher a king, or a king a philosopher. The word *polis* is synonymous with political community.
4. Aristotle, *Nicomachean Ethics*, II, 1.
5. Bernard Sarachek (1968). 'Greek Concepts of Leadership', *Academy of Management Journal*, vol. 11, no. 1 (March): 39-40.
6. The concept of the law-giver is associated with Machiavelli. It means 'hero-founder' of a political community. A good discussion can be found in J. G. A. Pocock (1975). *The Machiavellian Moment*, Princeton, NJ: Princeton University Press, 1975.
7. See Matthew 20:25-26. Robert K. Greenleaf further developed the concept of servant leader in his *The Servant as Leader* (1970).
8. See v. 59.
9. www.tribune.com.ng/index.php/eyes-of-islam/11227-leadership-auccession-in-islam.
10. For an expanded treatment of Machiavelli's Philosophy, see Pocock, *The Machiavellian Moment*. For succinct commentaries, see George H. Sabine and Thomas L. Thorson (1965). *A History of Political Theory*, New York: Holt, Rinehart and Winston; and J. S. McClelland (1996). *A History of Western Political Thought*, London: Routledge.
11. Weber identified three types of leader: traditional/feudal, charismatic and legal/rational. This typology is often cited in leadership studies. The English translation was published by Free Press (New York, 1947).
12. See Murray Hiebert and Bruce Klatt (eds.) (2004). *Encyclopedia of Leadership*, New York: McGraw-Hill, p. xxxiii.
13. The naked leader concept is derived from this perspective.
14. A. Lorri Manasse (1985). 'Vision and Leadership: Paying Attention to Intention', *Peabody Journal of Education*, vol. 63, no. 1 (Autumn), pp. 150-73.
15. Harvard Business School (2005). *Becoming an Effective Leader*, Boston, MA: Harvard Business School Press, pp. 21-32.

16. John P. Kotter (1999). 'What Leaders Really Do', *Harvard Business Review Books*, p. 2.
17. Ibid.
18. Jean Hartley and Clive Fletcher (2008). 'Leading with Political Awareness: Leadership across Diverse Interests Inside and Outside the Organization', in Kim T. James and James Collins (eds.), *Leadership Perspectives*, Basingstoke and New York: Palgrave Macmillan, p. 171.
19. Nannerl O. Keohane (2005). 'On Leadership', *Perspectives on Politics*, vol. 3, no. 4 (December): 708.
20. Hans L. Zetterberg (2006). 'The Grammar of Social Science', *Acta Sociologica*, vol. 49, no. 3 (September): 245.
21. Hermes was a messenger of the Greek gods one of whose task was to observe and report the way other cities worshipped their gods. Hence the derivative word 'hermeneutics', which is the study and theory of interpretation.
22. Zetterberg, 'The Grammar of Social Science,' p. 245.
23. Kenneth L. Pike (1990). 'On the Emic and Etics of Pike and Harris', in Thomas N. Headland, Kenneth L. Pike and Marvin Harris (eds.), *Emics and Etics: The Insider/Outsider Debate*, Newbury Park, CA: Sage, p. 29.
24. Joseph Gugler (2003). *African Film: Re-Imagining a Continent*, Bloomington, IN: Indiana University Press, pp. 71–3.
25. William H. Friedland (1964). 'For a Sociological Concept of Charisma', *Social Forces*, vol. 43, no. 1 (October): 21–2.
26. As quoted in Friedland, 'For a Sociological Concept of Charisma', p. 23. Stanleyville was renamed Kisangani after independence.
27. Francis Danquah and Stephen K. Miller (2007). 'Cocoa Farming in Ghana: Emic Experience, Etic Interpretation', *Southern Rural Sociology*, vol. 22, no. 1.
28. In fact, my invitation to the conference was meant to elicit my insider knowledge of the subject.
29. The Berlin conference was prompted by the so-called Fashoda incident. Fashoda is a small village in Sudan, where French and British colonial forces met and almost clashed during exploration. The conference was held to forestall war between the great powers over colonial outposts in Africa.
30. Homi Bhabha (1984). 'Of Mimicry and Man: The Ambivalence of Colonial Discourse,' *October*, vol. 28 (Spring): 130.
31. Ibid., p. 126.
32. 'The Discovery of India (1946)' (1966). In Immanuel Wallerstein (ed.), *Social Change: The Colonial Situation*, New York, London, and Sydney: John Wiles & Sons, p. 67.
33. Bhabha, 'Of Mimicry and Man, p. 127.
34. Ibid., p. 129.
35. 'Whose Frame of Reference? One Anthropologist's Experience', *Anthropological Forum*, vol. IV, no. 2 (1977): 11.
36. See Alexis de Tocqueville (1955), *The Old Regime and the French Revolution*, New York: Anchor Books.
37. I. M. Lewis (1977). 'Confessions of a "Government" Anthropologist', *Anthropological Forum*, vol. IV, no. 2: 101.
38. Deanne N. Den Hartog and Marcus W. Dickson (2004). 'Leadership and Culture', in John Antonakis, Anna T. Cianciolo, and Robert J. Stenberg (eds.),

The Nature of Leadership, Thousand Oaks, CA, London and New Delhi: Sage, p. 250.

39. Oginga Odinga (1977). *Not Yet Uhuru*, London, Ibadan, Nairobi and Lusaka: Heinemann, p. 612. Odinga was warmly called Jaramogi (chief) by his tribesmen.

40. See K. A. Busia (1951). *The Position of the Chief in the Modern Political System of the Ashanti*, London, New York and Toronto: Oxford University Press, pp. 14–15.

41. K. A. Busia (1951). *The Position of the Chief in the Modern Political System of Ashanti*, London, New York and Toronto: Oxford University Press, p. 51.

42. For a good discussion of culture and leadership, see Deanne N. Den Hartog et al. (1999). 'Culture Specific and Cross-Culturally Generalizable Implicit Leadership Theories: Are Attributes of Charismatic/Transformational Leadership Universally Endorsed?' *The Leadership Quarterly*, vol. 10, no. 2: 219–56.

43. Busia, *The Position of the Chief*, p. 105.

44. Michael Crowder (1987). 'Whose Dream Was It Anyway? Twenty-Five Years of African Independence', *African Affairs*, vol. 86, no. 343 (January): 15.

45. The Southern Bourbons were post-civil war leaders in the Southern United States. They retained their methods and leadership styles after the war.

46. Goran Hyden (1983). *No Shortcuts to Progress*, Berkeley and Los Angeles, CA: University of California Press, p. 19.

47. Ibid., p. 36.

48. Ibid., p. 26.

49. Abdi Samatar and A. I. Samatar (1987). 'The Material Roots of the Suspended African State: Arguments from Somalia', *Journal of Modern African Studies*, vol. 25, no. 4 (December): pp. 669–90, esp. 683–8.

50. This is what Ekeh calls a primordial public. See Peter P. Ekeh (1975). 'Colonialism and the Two Publics in Africa: A Theoretical Statement', *Comparative Studies in Society and History*, vol. 17, no. 1: 92. The author distinguishes it from what he calls the 'civic public', which is amoral society, where corruption and social strife are common.

51. Patrick Chabal (1996). 'The Africa Crisis: Context and Interpretation', in Richard Webner and Terence Ranger (eds.), *Postcolonial Identities in Africa*, London and Atlantic Highlands, NJ: Zed Books, p. 52. By high politics Chabal means politics at the national and international levels.

52. See Ekeh, 'Colonialism and the Two Publics in Africa', p. 110. The author describes the two publics as 'civic' and 'primordial'. The former is amoral, while the latter is moral. Accordingly, corruption in the former is admissible, but not the latter. See p. 92.

53. Samatar and Samatar (1987). 'The Material Roots of the Suspended African State'.

54. See 'The Heart of the Matter,' *The Economist* (13 May 2000): 22–4.

55. The ratings were A, B, C, D, F, ICU (intensive care unit) and mortuary. Meles Zenawi Asres of Ethiopia, ICU; Ismail Omar Guelleh of Jibuti, ICU; Asaias Afwerki of Eritrea, mortuary; Omar Hassan Al-Bashir of Sudan, mortuary; and Sheikh Sharif Sheikh Ahmed of Somalia, mortuary.

56. Harold G. Marcus (1994). *A History of Ethiopia*, Berkeley, Los Angeles, CA and London: University of California Press, p. 5.

57. For the effect of culture on leadership, see Stanley A. Renshon (2000). 'Political Leadership as a Social Capital: Governing in a Divided National Culture', *Political Psychology*, vol. 21, no. 1 (March): 207.
58. I use the phrase 'hegemonic control' in its Gramscian sense. Leadership is not only about power, but also about established ideas that are universally accepted.
59. R. A. Caulk (1972). 'Firearms and Princely Power in Ethiopia in the Nineteenth Century', *Journal of African History*, vol. 13, no. 4: 609–30.
60. www.ethiopianreview.com/content/10016.
61. www.wikileaks.ch/cable/2010/02/10ADDISABABA163.html#par4.
62. See Teshale Tibebu (1996). 'Ethiopia: The "Anomaly" and "Paradox" of Africa', *Journal of Black Studies*, vol. 26, no. 4 (March): 414–30, esp. 421–2.
63. www.unpo.org/images/Sam_Jana/compressed%20ogaden%20presentation. pdf.
64. P. T. W. Baxter (1978). 'Ethiopia's Unacknowledged Problem: The Oromo', *African Affairs*, vol. 77, no. 308 (July): 283–96, esp. 283–6.
65. Quoted in R. A. Caulk (1978). 'Armies as Predators: Soldiers and Peasants in Ethiopia c. 1850–1935', *International Journal of African Historical Studies*, vol. 11, no. 3: 457. The theory of internal colonialism conceptualizes a two-tier society whereby the dominant one oppresses and exploits the other. See Harold Wolpe (1975). 'The Theory of Internal Colonialism: the South African Case', in Ivar Oxaal, Tony Barnett and David Booth (eds.), *Beyond the Sociology of Development: Economy and Society in Latin America and Africa*, London and Boston, MA: Routledge & Kegan Paul, pp. 229–52, esp. 230–1.
66. Asafa Jalata (2007). 'Ethiopia on the Fire of Competing Nationalisms: The Oromo People's Movement, the State and the West', *The Horn of Africa Journal*, vol. 25: 91.
67. Ibid., p. 112.
68. www.ethiopianreview.com/content/28452.
69. *Nefetegna* is Amharic for feudal lord.
70. www.ethiopianreview.com/content/28700.
71. Philippa Bevan and Alula Pankhurst (2007). 'Power Structures and Agency in Rural Ethiopia: Development Lessons From Four Community Case Studies', paper prepared for the Endowment Team in the World Bank Poverty Reduction Group (31 July).
72. Quoted in www.jpanafrican.com/docs/vol3no6/3.5EthiopianState.pdf.
73. www.jpanafrican.com/docs/vol3no6/3.5EthiopianState.pdf.
74. Christopher Clapham (1975). 'Centralization and Local Response in Southern Ethiopia', *African Affairs*, vol. 74, no. 294: 72–3.
75. Complexity leadership theory views leadership as an evolving social process. See Benyamin B. Lichtenstein et al. (2006). 'Complexity Leadership Theory: An Interactive Perspective on Leading in Complex Adaptive System', *E: Co Issue*, vol. 8, no. 4: 2–12.
76. See Sihab ad-Din Ahmed bin Abd al-Qader bin Salem bin Utman (Arab Faqih) (2003). *The Conquest of Abyssinia*, Hollywood, CA: Tsehai Publishers; Mohamed Hussein Hadi (2007). *Muliyooy Saa See*, Ottawa: Somali Resource and Heritage Centre, esp. pp. 1–17.
77. See Said S. Samatar (1982). *Oral Poetry and Somali Nationalism: The Case of Sayyid Mohammad 'Abdille Hassan*, Cambridge, London, and New York:

Cambridge University Press, pp. 120–1. Samatar compares the regimentation of the Dervish army to those of the Ndebele in Zimbabwe in the same era. I think the comparison is weak for, unlike the Somali warriors, who were partially herdsmen, they cannot be compared to the imbies in, say, Lobengula's army, who were lifetime warriors and raiders.

78.   Saadia Touval (1963). *Somali Nationalism: International Politics and the Drive for Unity in the Horn of Africa*, Cambridge, MA: Harvard University Press, p. 24.

79.   David D. Laitin and Said S. Samatar (1987). *Somalia: Nation in Search of a State*, Boulder, CO: Westview Press, p. 155.

80.   Mohamed Aden Sheikh (1979). 'Political Participation: The Somali Experience', in Hussein M. Aden (ed.), *Somalia: Revolutionary Transformation*, Mogadishu: State Printing Agency, p. 36.

81.   Abdi Sheikh Abdi (1981). 'Ideology and Leadership in Somalia', *Journal of Modern African Studies*, vol. 19, no. 1: 168.

82.   Ibid., p. 171.

83.   Ibid.

84.   Andre Le Sage (2001). 'Prospects for Al-Itihad and Islamist Radicalism in Somalia,' *Review of African Political Economy*, vol. 28, no. 89: 473.

85.   For a detailed discussion of Barre's leadership, see Jama Mohamed Ghalib (1995), *The Cost of Dictatorship: The Somali Experience*, New York: Lilian Barber Press, chapter 11.

86.   For a good discussion, see I. M. Lewis (2004). 'Visible and Invisible Differences: The Somali Paradox', *Africa: Journal of the International African Institute*, vol. 74, no. 1: 489–515, esp. 503–8.

87.   For an opposite argument, see Anna Simons (1995). *Networks of Dissolution: Somalia Undone*, Boulder, CO: Westview Press, chapter 12.

88.   For a good discussion, see Hassan Mahadallah (2007). 'The Islamic Courts, Ethiopia's Intervention in Somalia, and its Implications for Regional Stability', *Horn of Africa*, vol. 25: 135–64, esp. 145–53.

89.   See Abdirahman Aynte (2009). 'The Anatomy of Somalia's Al-Shabab Jihadists', *Horn of Africa*, vol. 27: 1–35.

90.   Abdirahman Aynte (2009). 'The Anatomy of Somalia's Al-Shabab Jihadists', *Horn of Africa*, vol. 27: 1–35.

91.   Quoted in Africa Watch (1993). *Divide and Rule: State-Sponsored Ethnic Violence in Kenya*, New York: Human Rights Watch, p. 7.

92.   Ibid., p. 8.

93.   *Nyayo* means footprints in Swahili. During his tenure, Moi used to say that he was following in the footprints of Kenyatta who, according to Moi, stood for, peace, love and unity.

94.   UMOJA (1989). *Moi's Reign of Terror: A Decade of Nyayo Crimes against the People of Kenya*, London: UMOJA Publications, pp. 1–4.

95.   See 'Ethnic Bloodletting Spreads in Kenya,' *USA Today*, 28 January 2008.

96.   See 'Kenyans Rearming for 2012 Poll', BBC News, 7 October 2009.

97.   There are different spellings of these names. However, the spellings used here are the most commonly used.

98.   Eritrea is 124,320 km² with a population of 4.3 million; Djibouti is 23,000 km² with below one million inhabitants.

99.   In Freedom House's political rights index, Djibouti scored 5 and Eritrea 7.

100. The Issas, Gadaboursi and Isaak are ethnic Somalis. Together, they constitute more than 60 per cent of the population in Djibouti.
101. Peter J. Schraeder (1993). 'Ethnic Politics in Djibouti: From "Eye of the Hurricane" to "Boiling Cauldron"', *African Affairs*, vol. 92, no. 367 (April): 206–7.
102. Mohamed Kademy (1996). 'Djibouti: Between War and Peace' *Review of African Political Economy*, vol. 23, no. 70 (December): 511–21, esp. 511–18.
103. US Department of State (2008). 'Country Reports on Human Rights Practices', August.
104. Dan Connell (1995). 'Eritrea: Starting from Scratch', *Review of African Political Economy*, vol. 22, no. 66 (December): 591.
105. Paul B. Henze (1995). *Ethiopia and Eritrea in Transition: The Impact of Ethnicity on Politics and Development*, Santa Monica, CA: Rand, pp. 1–13.
106. Personal discussion, 20 May 2011.
107. Bereket Habte Selassie (2010). *Wounded Nation: How a Once Promising Eritrea Was Betrayed and its Future Compromised*, Trenton, NJ: The Red Sea Press, chapter 4.
108. For a good introduction, see Ann Mosely Lesch (2003). 'Sudan: Ethnic Conflict in the Sudan', in Joseph R. Rudolph (ed.), *Encyclopedia of Modern Ethnic Conflicts*, Westport, CT: Greenwood Press, pp. 235–42.
109. Stefan Wolff (2006). *Ethnic Conflict: A Global Perspective*, Oxford: Oxford University Press, chapter 3.
110. For a good discussion, see Robert O. Collins (2008). *A History of Modern Sudan*, New York: Cambridge University Press, chapter 4.
111. Ibid., chapter 7, esp. pp. 185–95.
112. John Garang (1987). *John Garang Speaks*, London and New York: KPI, Introduction.
113. Francis M. Deng (2006). 'Sudan: A Nation in Turbulent Search of Itself', *Annals of the American Academy of Political and Social Science*, vol. 603 (January): 155–6.
114. For the role of institutions, see Douglas C. North (1990). *Institutions, Institutional Change and Economic Performance*, Cambridge: Cambridge University Press.

Part II
Conflict Dynamics

Part II
Conflict Dynamics

4
Conflicts in the Horn of Africa and Implications for Regional Security

Kassahun Berhanu

INTRODUCTION

The conflicts that unfold in the Horn of Africa are closely interconnected and feed into each other by assuming sub-regional and regional dimensions. In both the past and the present almost all the countries of the Horn have experienced intra- and inter-state conflicts of varying degrees and intensity. These variations notwithstanding, there is no instance of any one member country that has managed to avert the taking shape and escalation of intra-state violent episodes and move towards fundamentally resolving the adverse consequences in a sustainable manner. Violent conflicts between disaffected groups and the state on the one hand, and between different non-state actors on the other, in the sub-region are mainly driven by economic factors. These often find concrete expression in the unfolding of divergent drives anchored in incompatible claims and counter-claims. In the absence of negotiated settlements mediated through mutually agreed principles and regulatory mechanisms, divergent and competing socio-economic and political drives and interests with regard to control over and access to political and economic resources have resulted in intra- and inter-state periods of conflict, which have assumed various forms in the past and continue into the present. These range from internal rebellions and protracted insurgencies to full-scale inter-state wars.

The failure of mainstream political establishments, the power elite and different aspirants in finding lasting solutions to the root causes of conflicts, which generally escalate beyond national frontiers, is driven by several closely intertwined socio-historical and structural factors. Most importantly, these relate to the inability and lack of the necessary political will on the part of mainstream establishments to foster a climate in which the causes of intra- and inter-state conflict can be addressed. It is largely recognized that conflicts and their consequences have become a defining feature of the sub-region. This chapter examines the implications of the conflicts in the countries of the Horn for entrenching sub-regional security architecture.

The central argument advanced here is that in the absence of a lasting peace and stability at both the intra- and inter-state levels, it is hardly possible to envisage prospects for facing the challenges posed by the socio-economic and political ills plaguing individual countries and the sub-region at large. To this end, an attempt is made to identify the major causes of conflict and shed light on the prospects for bringing about sub-regional cooperation and security. An attempt is made to provide the contextual settings within which past and present conflicts unfold in the purview of pertinent conceptual and theoretical underpinnings, which is followed by a description of the causes, processes and consequences of intra- and inter-state conflicts which have erupted in the sub-region.

THE PROBLEM IN CONTEXT

The composition of the entities of the sub-region known as the Horn of Africa is understood differently depending on the determinants used on the basis of historical, demographic, geographic, cultural and geopolitical considerations. According to Herui (2007: 77) the term 'Horn of Africa' was first used to denote Ethiopia, Eritrea, Somalia and Djibouti. Later this was extended to include the Sudan. In the conventional sense, these countries came to be known as the entities of the 'core Horn' as distinct from members of the 'Greater Horn' in the geopolitical sense. Mwagiru (2002: 7) views all member countries of IGAD as forming the Horn of Africa, and so includes Kenya and Uganda. In this connection, Ayoob (1996: 59) argues that attributes used to identify regional sub-systems tend to take into account 'geographic proximity, regularity and intensity of interaction between actors . . . internal and external recognition of a group of states as a distinctive area' consisting of two or more countries.

Over the last four decades, the Horn of Africa has been wracked by major conflicts in Somalia, Sudan, Ethiopia, Eritrea (IGAD 2008) and, to a lesser extent, Djibouti. Conflicts in individual countries are often compounded by inter-state conflicts of varying degree and intensity which take place at different times. Moreover, recurrent droughts resulting in famine, and other troubles, among them environmental degradation and economic hardship, are expressed in the impoverishment of broad sections of the populations, internal displacement and flows of refugees, which became the hallmark of the 1970s and 1980s and later. In addition to a broad range of indicators of underdevelopment tearing apart the lives of the people of the Horn, the effects of the vagaries of nature and human folly depict the sub-region as one of the most fragile and crisis-ridden in the world. The major manifestations of the crisis are expressed in devastating intra- and inter-state wars, state failure and breakdown, and the proliferation of the flow of small arms and human trafficking, among others. Hence it is rightly believed that there is no other zone of regional conflict that has produced a greater concentration of death and destruction since the Second World War than the Horn of Africa. It is estimated that the death toll is eight times the number of those who perished in the Balkan conflict (Prendergast 1999: 7). In a similar vein, the Inter-Governmental Authority on Development (IGAD 2007: 7) estimates that the sub-region hosts about 33 per cent of the world's internally displaced persons (IDPs). In 1982–92 alone, two million people lost their lives in the Horn due to war and famine, and more than 25 million faced serious food shortages in 1992 (Prendergast 1992). Moreover, the major countries of the sub-region – Ethiopia and Sudan – are experiencing massive deforestation, which continues unchecked every year. These and similar disasters by themselves are illustrative of the sorry state in the Horn, without taking into account the destruction that took place following the end of the Cold War and the ushering in of what came to be known as the democratization wave signified by the termination of authoritarian dispensations, which was expected to bring an end to the multi-layered conditions of conflict and lack of security.

In the light of all this, posing a number of questions and then addressing them is worthwhile. To this end, it is necessary to investigate the directions that future developments are bound to take if the current trends militating against peace and stability are allowed to persist unchecked. In line with this, this chapter seeks to examine and deal with a number of issues, including what Somalia's fate will be if radical Islamic movements like al-Shabaab are not defeated. What are the relations between Ethiopia and Eritrea bound to be and what are the implications of this for entrenching peace and stability in the sub-region? What does the future hold with regard to resolving the Darfur crisis and what will be the outcome of the accession of South Sudan to independent statehood in view of subsequent relations between different state actors in the Horn of Africa? All these indicate that an enormous task lies ahead for anyone engaged in the planning and execution of conflict mitigation and resolution in the sub-region.

CONCEPTUAL AND THEORETICAL UNDERPINNINGS

Heated debates have been raging recently over issues pertaining to what drives conflict in different parts of the world. Proponents of globalization argue that the world is becoming increasingly smaller and that 'the age of nation states is already passing' due to a host of new developments, as a result of which discrete events of the past have begun to transcend national identities, boundaries and nationalism (Hopper 2007: 87). Opponents of this view argue that the world remains diverse despite the homogenizing trend of globalization. The proponents of the latter view thus emphasize the desirability of turning the focus of attention from globalization to the escalating world-wide tensions caused by terrorism, ethnic distinctiveness and the quest for regional autonomy and political independence (Rowntree et al. 2005: 8). Hence, it is claimed, this is why most wars are currently fought within rather than between countries, albeit subsumed under the terms 'insurgency', 'ethnic unrest', 'nationalist movements' and 'tribalism' (Nisbet 1999: 5). One of the insidious legacies of the Cold War has been the resumption of old conflicts rooted in language, culture, race and religion (McWhinney 2007: 8). Consequently, multinational political entities, greater in number than those that are homogeneous states, are rocked by conflicts associated with group identity. This is propelled by the quest for self-determination within an existing nation state and in some cases secession. As a consequence, the potency of drives emphasizing self-determination as a cherished goal are on the rise in the Horn of Africa, rendering the sub-region vulnerable to serious security deficits (Medhane 2004: 1).

Conflicts occur when two or more parties perceive that their interests are incompatible. As a result they pursue their goals through actions that are detrimental to their adversaries. Divergences of interests may arise over access to resources, power, identity, value or status (Oquaye 2000: 72) and may assume peaceful or violent dimensions. Peaceful or non-violent conflict episodes can be regulated through established mechanisms and norms that allow for the interplay of competing interests without recourse to violence. Conflict resolution mechanisms may be traditional or modern, formal or informal. On the other hand, violent conflicts occur when protagonists seek to attain their objectives prompted by either systemic or proximate causes often triggered by acts and events associated with internal and/or external factors. Hence conflicts should not be understood as immutable or static phenomena but as historical processes (Suliman 1999: 26) mediated by a situation of constraint when groups and social actors feel that they are denied access to resources and amenities deemed crucial to their livelihood. Rupesinghe (1998: 33) identified four loose typologies of conflict: resource-based, governance issues, ideological and identity. Resource-based conflicts pertain to competition for economic power and access to renewable resources, whereas conflicts over governance issues are propelled by competition for political power and the quest for the meaningful participation of potential and actual stakeholders in mainstream socio-economic and political processes. The contest between rival world outlooks and value systems that culminate in ideological disagreements may lead to the unfolding of identity conflicts expressed in competition between rival ethnic, religious or other communal groups whose actions are often driven by the urge to secure privileged or better access to political and economic resources.

Among the several triggers of conflict, competition over scarce resources is the most potent. The dwindling of the resource base erodes established social fabrics prompting fierce competition. Jeong (2000: 71) argues that the struggle to satisfy basic needs is a key motivational factor driving human behaviour and social interaction. In the absence of an enabling social space and entrenched mechanisms that facilitate dialogue between diverse identities and value and belief systems, competition over resources is likely to culminate in violent struggles. Hence scarcity and the shrinking resource bases, combined with a rapidly growing population, engenders a volatile social situation that breeds group conflict (Homer-Dixon 1994). The imbalance between population growth and resources adversely impacts on the maintenance of an acceptable quality of life. Markakis (1998: 2) notes that sustainability requires that the rate of consumption of renewable resources should not exceed their rate of renewal and failure to maintain this equilibrium often culminates in serious challenges that militate against security and stability. It could thus be argued that during times of severe economic stress characterized by shortfalls in supplies, competition over scarce and renewable resources assumes a very serious and acute dimension. Primordial attributes like ethnicity, religion and value and belief systems are invoked to forge common identities and a sense of belonging aimed at bolstering collective bargaining positions.

Conflicts in the Horn of Africa in general are intractable and closely interconnected in the sense that the unfolding of conflict in one country can easily spill over into neighbouring areas (Närman 2002: 86). This is why it is better to conceptualize the entire sub-region as a 'conflict system'. Mwagiru (1997: 3) was among those who introduced the concept of an interlinked conflict system with regard to the Horn of Africa by emphasizing that conflicts in the region are not only interconnected but also form a region-wide conflict system. This forms the basis for claiming that 'what might at first appear as isolated conflicts in fact are parts of a wider pattern of conflict regionally' (ibid.). Hence the conflict in the Horn tends to counter the assertion that there is a dominant tendency signifying a considerable decline in the incidence of war at the global level since the end of the Cold War, which is partly attributed to the absence of viable sub-regional peace and security architecture (de Waal 2007: 1). By way of lending credence to Mwagiru's thesis, inter-state conflicts in the region lead to the formation of organic linkages with intra-state conflicts. Owing to a lack of internal legitimacy and political consensus and the problematic surrounding the mode and manner in which state formation processes took shape, political regimes in the Horn more often seek to externalize their domestic problems to the extent of internationalizing them. Moreover, the arbitrary nature of the drawing of boundaries during the colonial era resulted in fragmentation of ethno-cultural formations and other trans-border ethnic identities, thereby blurring the distinction between intra- and inter-state conflicts.

THE ANATOMY OF INTRA- AND INTER-STATE CONFLICTS IN THE HORN

In this section an overview of the profile and structural and proximate causes and consequences of conflicts in the countries of the Horn is provided by taking into account the socio-economic and political dimensions of the current situation with a view to determining the prospects for cooperation and integration in the sub-region. Almost all the countries of the Horn have suffered from the effects of violent conflicts. Given that these conflicts have both internal and external dimensions, it is necessary and appropriate to provide a complete picture of the underlying causes and their consequences in order to understand current conflict trends and determine their implications for economic cooperation and integration in the sub-region.

DJIBOUTI

Geopolitical factors have immensely influenced the history of Djibouti and its domestic and international affairs. The major structural cause of conflict in Djibouti is the perception of political and economic marginalization on the part of the minority population, the Afar. Political frustration on the part of the Afar was coupled with economic marginalization. Even before independence, as compared to the Issa the Afars were not visible in terms of engagement in business and other gainful employment. After independence, the Issa economic elite emerged as dominant players in the economy by purchasing land and business enterprises left by Europeans through loans obtained from the Djibouti branch of the Commercial Bank of Somalia (Aden and Rirash 2001: 6). Moreover, the political leverage enjoyed by the Issa power elite also immensely facilitated the furthering of their economic fortunes. In contrast, the Afars were under-represented in the political and security structures of the country (Schraeder 1993: 203).

Djibouti has been remarkably stable compared to its neighbours, particularly Ethiopia and Somalia, as a result of which it was dubbed the 'eye of the hurricane' (Schraeder 1993). This, however, changed after the Afars embarked on armed insurgency in the early 1990s. Rivalry and conflict between the Somali/Issa and the Afar, can be traced to the historical legacy of French colonial rule which favoured the former as a response to the opposition of the Afars' traditional chiefs on the issue of the French acquisition of Obock. According to Aden and Rirash (2001), the conflict landscape in Djibouti can be seen from two angles. First, there is conflict between pastoral communities and the state and second, tension between the two communities that has been experienced for decades since the country's independence in 1977 exploded into a major conflict at the beginning of the 1990s when the disgruntled Afar established the Front for the Restoration of Unity and Democracy (FRUD) and launched a guerrilla war against the Issa-dominated regime. FRUD rebels initially overwhelmed the government forces (Schraeder 1993: 211), albeit for a relatively short period, after which the armed insurgency was brought under control with the support of French troops stationed in the country and the neighbouring states of Ethiopia and Eritrea. The latter two were alarmed by the implication of FRUD's success for their own Afar populations. As the two major ethnic groups in Djibouti also live in the neighbouring countries – the Issa in Ethiopia and Somalia and the Afar in Ethiopia and

Eritrea – inter-ethnic relationships in Djibouti are often influenced by political developments in several countries of the Horn. Djibouti was also affected by the 1998–2000 Ethiopian-Eritrean conflict, which had mixed outcomes for the situation in the country. On the one hand, Djibouti benefited economically as Ethiopia became entirely dependent on it for port services; this revitalized Djibouti's economy. On the other hand, the Eritrean government, which sought to undermine Ethiopia's quest for a sea outlet, seems to have resorted to supporting the remnants of FRUD against the Djiboutian regime.

ERITREA

Eritrea's contemporary history is largely identified with the secessionist war against Ethiopian rule, which culminated in its independent statehood at the beginning of the 1990s. The 30-year war of liberation between different Eritrean liberation fronts and successive Ethiopian regimes continues to influence the politics, economics and international relations of that country. In 1991, the Eritrean People Liberation Front (EPLF), which led the successful armed insurgency against Ethiopia, seized power and changed its name to the People's Front for Democracy and Justice, (PFDJ) in 1994. Since its formal accession to independent statehood in 1993, Eritrea has been mired in intra- and inter-state conflicts. Internally, the PFDJ regime has become increasingly repressive and seems unwilling to tolerate any form of dissent. Externally, Eritrea has been engaged in conflicts with almost all of its neighbours – Yemen, Djibouti, Ethiopia and the Sudan. It is also widely believed that the Eritrean regime continues to provide assistance to anti-government movements in its neighbours, most notably Ethiopia.

While the long and bitter conflict that pitted different Eritrean liberation fronts against Ethiopia and each other can be partly explained by external factors alone, internal developments to a major degree account for the poor political and economic state in which independent Eritrea finds itself. The structural sources of the conflicts in Eritrea can be seen from different angles. First, the economy is not well developed and remains fragile despite the government's tight grip on the economic resources of the country, including the lucrative transfer of remittances from the estimated 150,000 Eritreans who live abroad. Second, there is an intense militarization of state and society in independent Eritrea. Eritrea and Ethiopia are still at a standoff after the end of their two-year border. war. The decision of the Ethiopia–Eritrea Boundary Commission (EBBC) regarding the contested territory – Badme – has not translated into practice due to Ethiopia's refusal to comply. In light of this, both Eritrea and Ethiopia are engaged in bringing down each other's government. Eritrea, for example, supports Ethiopian opposition forces like the Oromo Liberation Front (OLF) and the Ogaden National Liberation Front (ONLF), while Ethiopia sponsors several activities of the Eritrean opposition. The Eritrean government is also accused of providing strong support to the Somali Islamists who are currently locked in a bitter war with the African Union contingents drawn from Uganda and Burundi, including Ethiopia, Kenya and the highly beleaguered Somali Transitional Federal Government (TFG).

ETHIOPIA

The structural sources of conflicts in Ethiopia are also many and interconnected. The legacy of unequal ethnic relations continues to haunt the politics of the country. This particularly is rooted in the wars of expansion undertaken at the end of the nineteenth century by the traditional Christian kingdom. Moreover, the economic and political inequality that unfolded following the formation of the modern state served as a driver of the violent conflicts that have engulfed the country during the last five decades. In this connection, the chief slogans of leftist opposition forces, which have been challenging the legitimacy of imperial rule since the mid-1960s, emphasized the quest for equity, social justice and democratic freedoms, including ethnic rights, among others. The other major structural source of conflict in Ethiopia, in both the past and present, is the absence of an inclusive political system, which could have facilitated efforts towards fair and democratic contestation for power. So far, the country has not experienced a peaceful transition of power, exemplified by the forcible seizure of power by successive regimes. Rapid population growth and escalating ecological fragility have added to the problems of the diminishing resource base and have contributed to the persistence of violent conflicts in Ethiopia. Like almost all countries of the sub-region, the conflicts that take shape there often assume regional and international dimensions – for instance, the conflict in Somalia between the TFG and the Islamic insurgents has domestic, regional and international dimensions.

For Ethiopia, the conflict in Somalia has domestic, regional and international implications. At the domestic level, the conflict is inextricably connected with the intra-state conflict in Ethiopia's Somali region, the Ogaden. Regionally, the war in Somalia indirectly has a tendency to pit Ethiopia against Eritrea as the latter attempts to take advantage of this situation which is presumed to weaken the former. Internationally, the conflict in Somalia puts Ethiopia in the group of countries that support the US-led war on terror, signified by the fact that the latter not only provided intelligence support but also bombed sites which were suspected of harbouring Islamists whom it accuses of masterminding the 1998 bombings of its embassies in Nairobi and Dar es Salaam. Notwithstanding this, however, it should be noted that Ethiopia's intervention in Somalia appears to have been prompted by its urge to neutralize the Eritrean factor on the one hand, and contain the bellicose irredentist stance of the Union of Islamic Courts (UIC) on the other. The emergence of Ethiopia as a key ally of the United States in the Horn of Africa has advantages and disadvantages. On the one hand, the Ethiopians receive uncritical political support and economic assistance. The anti-terror alliance, on the other hand, could make the country a target of international terrorist groups and their sympathizers in the region.

SOMALIA

It is now over two decades since Somalia spiralled into chaos and endless conflicts. So far, dozens of reconciliation conferences have been held with the aim of restoring Somalia's statehood and ending the conflicts that continue to cause colossal humanitarian crises. The conflicts in Somalia have claimed hundreds of thousands of lives and displaced millions. The rise of the UIC in 2005 and its success in enforcing law and order in Mogadishu and parts of southern Somalia for the first time since the collapse of Mohammed Siad Barre's regime was a phenomenal event. It was hoped that anarchy in the country would finally come to an end. Nevertheless, the failure of the UIC and TFG to cooperate in a power-sharing arrangement on the one hand, and the bellicose stance of the former against the latter and neighbouring Ethiopia on the other, prompted Ethiopia's intervention in December 2006. Though Ethiopian forces managed swiftly to oust the ICU from its strongholds, Ethiopian troops and their TFG allies failed to translate their military victory into political success. Somalia has also attracted considerable international attention due to the pirates who threaten the international shipping route that connects Africa, Asia and Europe. In 2008 alone, pirates hijacked several ships and received millions of dollars in ransom monies. Even though several warships are now deployed to guard the Somali coast, piracy continues. Somaliland, which declared de facto independence in 1991, remains without international recognition despite the fact that developments in the south are bound to affect its fragile peace and stability.

The sources of the conflicts in Somalia are several and interrelated in many respects. For ease of presentation, however, they can be viewed from the point of view of the economic and socio-cultural perspectives and external factors that contributed to their escalation. In economic terms, Somalia is a poor country with a highly underdeveloped economic base. In the arid and semi-arid environment, Somali pastoralists endlessly compete for control of land resources and water sources. According to Markakis (1987: 16), 'clashes over pasture and water were the perennial bone of contention among lineage groups and clans. Force was the only effective means to serve such claims and it was a constant factor of nomadic life.' The weakening of traditional means of conflict management which arises from the ongoing crisis and ceaseless conflicts among Somali clans has rendered the containment of violence increasingly challenging. Socio-political factors also explain the structural causes of conflict in Somalia. In this regard, the clan system plays a central role as the most potent mode of socio-political organization. The majority of Somalis are nomadic pastoralists whose livelihood depends on transhumance. Although clan organizations are important in regulating conflicts, their fragmented nature has implications for domestic and international politics. In other words, the Somali clan system is both 'centripetal and centrifugal, at once drawing the Somalis into a powerful social fabric of kinship affinity and cultural solidarity while setting them against one another in . . . antagonistic clan interests' (Laitin and Samatar 1987: 30–1).

The other major socio-political problem that explains the conflict in Somalia is the difficulty in reconciling institutions of traditional governance with those of the modern state, which follow the Western model. Despite the call for Somali unity, Somali governments have been inherently unstable because of the political use of clan divisions in the distribution of resources and positional goods. This has given rise to immense difficulties in nation-building endeavours. When examining the external dimensions of conflict in Somalia, the legacy of Balkanization resulting in the separation of the Somali people across different countries of the Horn of Africa still impacts on the politics and security of the country. In fact, immediately after independence Somalia vigorously promoted the 'Greater Somalia' doctrine which was pursued as a guiding principle of successive regimes by way of advancing irredentist policies. This was viewed as detrimental to the territorial integrity of its neighbours, Ethiopia and Kenya, which have sizeable Somali populations. Somalia has twice engaged in a full-scale war with Ethiopia: first in 1964 and again in 1977–78. The second war in particular had grave consequences for both countries, precipitating the collapse of the Somali state in 1991 and rendering efforts aimed at finding solution to the problem in Somalia extremely challenging.

Entrenching peace and stability in the war-torn country became increasingly elusive in the face of the intervention of several external players whose objectives were contradictory. The United States and its Western allies are solely focused on the war against terror and seek to prevent forces espousing political Islam from using Somalia as their operational base. Ethiopia, for its part, was and still is preoccupied with installing a friendly regime, which will not resurrect the Greater Somalia doctrine as a principle of state ideology. With the aim of destabilizing its nemesis – Ethiopia – the Eritrean regime is accused of providing assistance even to Islamist groups, which it does not tolerate within its own territory. The combination of all these is a lethal brew that nourishes animosity between regional state actors and results in conflicts with devastating consequences. So far, the TFG has failed to bring about national reconciliation because of a number of internal and external factors. Internally, there is a wide gulf between two loose groups – the Mogadishu-based Somali Reconciliation Council and the Somali Reconciliation and Restoration Council (SRRC) – whose divergent positions on various issues are the expression of clan and regional differences. It is believed that Eritrean support for the insurgents and those who opposed the intervention of Ethiopia was instrumental in reviving the prestige of the Islamists. In this connection it is claimed that the leaders of the disbanded UIC and other Somali politicians who are allegedly given sanctuary by Eritrea formed what is known as the Alliance for the Re-Liberation of Somalia (ARS) in Asmara in 2007. In typical Somali fashion, the ARS, which brought Islamists of various persuasions, civil society organizations and other players under its wing, began to unravel due to differences between the so-called moderate and radical factions. The moderate wing led by Sheik Ahmed Shariff joined the UN-sponsored peace negotiations that led to the withdrawal of Ethiopian troops and in October

2008, they signed a peace agreement with the TFG in Djibouti. The militant wing of the ARS in response labelled the 'deal' a betrayal and urged its supporters to ignore the call for a ceasefire. Similarly, al-Shabaab, which is fighting on the ground, continued its attacks on Ethiopian and TFG forces. To what extent the moderate wing of the Islamists can control the fighters and how the peace agreement will translate into practice remains to be seen.

SUDAN

Sudan is one of the countries in the sub-region that has suffered from chronic and multidimensional conflicts. The country experienced relative peace between 1972 and 1983. But the independent history of the country is marred by several interrelated conflicts, which brought mayhem and destruction to millions. The structural sources of the conflicts in the Sudan are several and complex. The conflicts that erupted in the country are, however, usually expressed in terms of a dichotomy – Arab/Islam vs. African/Christian and Animist. When one approaches Sudanese conflicts from this narrow angle, ethnicity and religion take centre place. Abel Ghaffar Ahmed (cited in Zeleza 2008: 17) criticized this approach, arguing that even if religion and ethnicity did play a role in the ongoing tragedy in the Sudan, the conflict is characterized by multiple complexities. Hence any approach that examines the structural causes of conflicts there should consider the entrenched social, economic and political marginalization of groups in the periphery. The colonial legacy of under- and uneven development and, more importantly, the opportunistic Sudanese power elite which is engaged in fomenting ethnic, religious and other divisions so that it can stay in power and control the economic resources of the country, have immensely contributed to the predicament of the country.

For several decades, Sudan suffered from multidimensional conflicts. In particular, the conflict that raged between the Islamic and Afro-Arabic North and the Christian/Animist African South has caused the death and dislocation of millions of people. After the Comprehensive Peace Agreement (CPA) between the Government of Sudan (GoS) and the SPLM/A was signed in 2005, relative peace appears to have reigned. There are, however, several unresolved problems, such as boundary demarcation, the issue of Abyei and the pending resolution in other parts of the country could derail the peace process as manifested in some alarming incidents that have transpired since the signing of the CPA. It is to be recalled that the principle of a United Sudan advocated by the late SPLM/A leader John Garang is now defunct, as expressed by the division of the country following South Sudan's secession in 2011. In contrast, the Darfur conflict in western Sudan is still raging and has caused one of the worst humanitarian crises witnessed to date. Many international actors accuse the Sudanese government of perpetrating massive human rights abuses in the region. Hence, this conflict has received worldwide attention. In 2004, the African Union (AU) established a peacekeeping force, the African Union Mission in Sudan (AMIS), with the aim of providing security to civilians in Darfur. AMIS, which started its operation with a token force of 150 troops, had been expanded to a force of 7,000 by mid-2005. Following the AU's recognition that the task of providing security to Darfurians is beyond its means, the United Nations Security Council (UNSC) decided in favour of the formation of a joint AU–UN peacekeeping force, the United Nations Mission in Darfur (UNMID), in 2007. Neither the deployment of international troops nor the signing of the Darfur Peace Agreement (DPA) in May 2006 between the GoS and the Sudan Liberation Movement/Army (SLM/A) led to the restoration of relative calm in the region despite the fact that the problem persists in several respects.

In summary, conflicts in the Horn in general take shape and escalate due to divergences in policy drives and attendant practices that often fail to pay due attention to the need to promote mutually beneficial measures that could result in win–win outcomes. On justifiable grounds, it could be expected that addressing issues surrounding governance failure could considerably reduce intra-state conflicts despite the presence of spoilers whose detrimental role cannot be ruled out. Moreover, incompatibilities between the divergent interests, behaviours and actions of neighbouring countries could be tackled through perseverance and commitment to enhance dialogue and negotiation that emphasize the need for according primacy to the forging and consolidation of sub-regional cooperation and partnership aimed at the realization of goals presumed to effectively address common dangers and problems. In the absence of a radical shift from the state of affairs that bedevils state–society and inter-state relations, the Horn will undoubtedly remain the bastion of the multifaceted crisis in which it finds itself. It could even be claimed that the tribulations experienced to date in terms of shortfalls in security arrangements will significantly worsen if the factors that nourish them remain essentially unaltered.

CAUSES AND MANIFESTATIONS OF SECURITY DEFICITS IN THE HORN

In general terms, security refers to the absence of threats to cherished values (Evans and Newham 1998: 490), which are interpreted differently by those who uphold the need to preserve them as essential to their well-being. Hence, variations are observed with regard to according primacy to certain values at the expense of others. The traditional conception of security emphasized regime and/or state security without paying sufficient attention to other dimensions, such as human security, that are equally important. According to some (Dorn 2001), human security in essence means protecting people from both violent and non-violent threats by laying the ground for freedom from pervasive menace to rights, liberties and life. Hence human security relates to situations where vulnerability to risks of threat from want, lack of rights and legitimate liberties, physical violence and psychological anxieties are significantly reduced or totally eliminated. Hubert (1999) argues that human security is closely associated with the legal and socially sanctioned protection of the worth, dignity and safety of individuals and groups in the family, community and the polity.

The traditional concept of security espoused by most state actors in the countries of the Horn is grounded in the understanding that state security is far more important than other concerns. This line of thinking is flawed since human security is not the antithesis of state security but rather is complementary to it. In other words, state and human security can be mutually interdependent. In fact, promoting and preserving human security in a sustainable manner guarantees the security of the state against internal threats which are often caused by widespread disaffection. In the likelihood of external threats posed against the security of the state, human security at the domestic level serves as an instrument for forging cohesion and unity to withstand challenges originating from sources beyond the borders of a given country. With this as a starting point, the causes and manifestations of the security deficit in the Horn are examined.

IRREDENTISM AND BOUNDARY CONFLICTS

Most of the boundaries of the countries in the Horn, as elsewhere in the African continent, were imposed by colonial powers. These boundaries typically cut through ethno-cultural and geographic divides, as a result of which some ethnic communities in the region are partitioned among neighbouring countries. The corresponding political arrangements made during decolonization have thus led to fluidity and volatility in inter-state relations anchored in adherence to the core value of territorial integrity which is highly valued by post-colonial states in Africa. These for the most part pose as mainstays of unhealthy developments impeding efforts to forge integration and cooperation. While the majority of the countries of Africa appear to have accepted the colonial boundaries,[1] countries of the Horn like Somalia have pursued an aggressive irredentist foreign policy as expressed by the quest of different Somali regimes to bring all Somali-speaking populations within a single Pan-Somali nation. Hence relationships between Somalia and its neighbours, Ethiopia and Kenya, were adversely affected, as signified by the 1964 and 1977–78 inter-state wars. In addition, the contested borders between Ethiopia and the Sudan, the contention between Ethiopia and Eritrea over control of the Badme Triangle, border disputes between the autonomous entities of Puntland and Somaliland, and the unresolved boundary issues between North and South Sudan[2] can be seen as bearing the seeds of potential and actual conflict.

ACCESS TO AND CONTROL OVER TRANS-BOUNDARY RESOURCES

Trans-boundary resources, particularly rivers, can either contribute to efforts to forge regional cooperation and security or foster mistrust and antagonism. In the Horn of Africa there are no mutually agreed mechanisms for sharing trans-boundary water resources. As a result, there is mistrust and incompatible positions with regard to the use of common resources. For instance, despite the establishment of the Nile Basin Initiative (NBI) there are persistent differences regarding the use of the waters of the Nile between some countries of the core and Greater Horn. In this regard, the major bone of contention refers to two agreements – the 1929 Nile Water Agreement[3] and the 1959 Agreement between Egypt and the Sudan – on the utilization of the Nile waters. The upper riparian countries in general and Ethiopia and Uganda in particular resent the 1959 Treaty which apportioned the Nile waters between Egypt and the Sudan. For their part, Egypt and the Sudan are not willing to enter into a new agreement regarding the desire of others for equitable sharing.[4] Hence this issue continues to strain relations between state actors in the sub-region. It is widely believed in Ethiopia that Egypt in particular, supported by Sudan, is actively engaged in fanning the flames of instability within Ethiopia (Medhane 2004).

PROXY WARS AND MUTUAL INTERVENTIONS

Proxy war through reciprocal interventions using intra-state protagonists remains one of the major instruments of foreign policy among the countries of the Horn of Africa (Cliffe 1999; Abbink 2003). In the context of the Horn of Africa in particular, proxy warfare refers to the practice of states using rebel movements that originate from the territories of their adversaries (usually neighbouring countries). This strategy is aimed at weakening actual and presumed adversaries with the hope of bolstering their bargaining position in their dealings with each other. Through this practice, neighbouring countries like Ethiopia, Eritrea, Uganda and Sudan are often locked in a vicious circle of mutual interventions. The motto and practice of 'the enemy of my enemy is my friend', which underpins intervention by proxy, has been used by Ethiopia, the Sudan, Somalia and of late independent Eritrea. Sudan and Somalia supported rebel movements such as the Eritrean insurgent groups, the Tigray People's Liberation Front, the Ethiopian Democratic Union (EDU) and the Oromo Liberation Front, among others, which were operating against the Ethiopian imperial and military regimes at varying times. Ethiopia responded in like manner by supporting rebel movements originating from both countries. This policy and practice persists with regard to the current disposition of the regimes in Ethiopia and Eritrea as a feature of their hostile inter-state relations in general and their involvement in supporting rival belligerent Somali factions in particular.

POLITICAL ISLAM AND THE 'WAR ON TERROR'

After the Cold War it was envisaged that Africa in general and the Horn sub-region in particular would lose geo-political and strategic significance vis-à-vis the vital interests of the Western powers (Buzan, cited in Rugumamu 2001: 9). But this proved to be unfounded owing to the rise of radical Islam as the major threat to the West. As a result, the importance of the sub-region appears to have been revitalized. Following the tragic events of 9/11, the United States and its Western allies strengthened their military ties with some countries of the Horn which had a polarizing effect. On the one hand, Ethiopia, Eritrea, Kenya and Uganda appear to be hostile to radical Islam whereas this is not the case in Sudan, for example. In fact, hostility to Islamist ideology in official circles in both Ethiopia and Eritrea is intense partly out of fear that 'division along religious lines would present a [serious] threat not only to regime survival but also to the survival of the state itself' given the large size of the Ethiopian and Eritrean populations professing Islam (Clapham 2007: 72). It should be remembered that in the 1990s Ethiopia suffered a series of terrorist attacks in the eastern parts of the country, which were reportedly perpetrated by al Ittihad al-Islam which is believed to have links to al-Qaeda. Despite the Sudanese regime's desire to improve relations with its neighbours following the removal of Islamist hardliners from positions of influence in 2004, it seems to have persisted in its pursuit of militant Islamic ideology. Besides, the temporary leverage that the UIC enjoyed in Somalia by declaring its wish to entrench political Islam as a guiding ideology prompted Ethiopia's military intervention, with the justification provided by the public utterances of UIC leaders which threatened Ethiopia's territorial integrity and national security.

GOVERNANCE FAILURE AND STATE FRAGILITY

Governance failure and state fragility have helped the conflict system and security complex to gain ground in the Horn of Africa. The majority of the countries are fragile with multiple shortfalls characterized by stress and lack of strong institutions and capacity which render them vulnerable to insecurity (Cliffe 2007). It is also noted that fragile states 'pose the risk of negative spill-over regarding their neighbours and the wider global community through spread of conflict and organized crime, refugee flows, epidemic diseases and barriers to trade and development' (ibid.: xi). The problem is even worse in Somalia, which has been without a strong and legitimate central government for several years. Statelessness and insecurity pose multifaceted risks not only to member countries of the sub-region but also to international commerce, as expressed in the form of piracy in and around the Somali coast. It is also noteworthy that almost all the countries of the Horn experience varying degrees of state fragility, expressed in different levels of deficit with regard to regime legitimacy and acceptance. This in turn lends force to the unfolding of conflict situations that the power holders are unable or unwilling to address. Even Kenya, which was seen as relatively immune to the escalation of conflicts in the sub-region, was rocked by post-election unrest in 2007, the effects of which it is feared will last for years. In view of this, governance failure and state fragility are bound to pose major challenges to the prospects of experiencing durable security in the area. The adverse impacts of inter-state conflicts on regional cooperation are too obvious to require further elaboration. Hence in an environment where there is no common security and governance architecture and commonly agreed and recognized mechanisms and structures for conflict resolution, it would be naïve to expect any improvements in the socio-economic and political spheres at both the intra- and inter-state levels. For instance, Ethiopia and Eritrea have closed their common borders, thereby destroying any possibilities of official bilateral commerce and cross-border trade.

PROSPECTS FOR ENTRENCHING SECURITY AND INTER-STATE COOPERATION

In spite of the bleak state of affairs in the Horn of Africa, there are some positive initiatives that could ameliorate the security predicaments of some countries. This refers in particular to developments pertaining to the brokering of negotiated settlements of conflicts in some countries like Sudan and Somalia through the agency of IGAD. This culminated in the signing of the CPA and the establishment of a Government of National Unity and a Transitional Federal Government in Sudan and Somalia respectively. Although these moves have encountered formidable setbacks in fully implementing the terms of the accords, persevering with efforts instrumental in withstanding the negative outcomes would be worthwhile. Unfortunately, serious concerns which have not been addressed continue to rock the security of the area as expressed in low-intensity intra-state conflicts in Ethiopia and Eritrea, the uneasy truce characterizing current Ethiopian–Eritrean relations, the worsening insurgency in Somalia, the unresolved issues between Ethiopia and Sudan with regard to sharing the water resources of the Nile and the Darfur crisis, among others. Across the sub-region, there is a perception that the vested interests of ethno-nationalist and other mainstream political elites who control the central governments impose unfair policies and practices with the objective of maintaining self-serving privileges, in terms of the distribution of political and economic resources, at the expense of large sections of the population. There is also a widespread belief that any group that controls the state extends preferential treatment to its clients in the context of a deeply entrenched system of neo-patrimonial arrangement. Hence unresolved issues, unbridged gaps and incompatible dispositions between formal and official pledges on the one hand, and actual practice on the other, continue to sow discord and resentment and potentially serve as a hotbed of conflicts. The opportunity that the end of the Cold War presented for the development of a common security framework has not been grasped by state actors in the sub-region due to a number of negative developments that have developed since then. The vacuum left by the major powers was replaced by the unfolding of intense competition between actors within the Horn and beyond. The incompatible hegemonic interests and aspirations of Ethiopia, Eritrea, Egypt and Libya supported by their respective allies and sympathizers are detrimental to efforts attempting to lay the ground for the realization of a viable security arrangement and coordination in the Horn of Africa. Menkhaus and Prendergast (1999: 216) argue that these and others are involved in the provision of military training and material support to different Somali factions, thereby rendering efforts to bring about peace and security in the war-torn country increasingly futile. This is compounded by the ineptitude and shortcomings of IGAD and the AU, which, as sub-regional and continental organizations respectively, are charged with responsibility for securing peace and security in line with their mandate. Undoubtedly, efforts to this end will succeed only when the actors concerned manage to develop a common security framework based on mutually agreed principles and binding regulatory mechanisms that can address the underlying causes of conflict at the intra- and inter-state levels. The question then would be how to identify what is required to bring about durable security and sustainable peace. According to de Waal (2007: 1), extricating the sub-region from the present quagmire of crises requires 'credible democratization in the states of the region, a durable resolution of internal conflicts, a stable sub-regional inter-state order, autonomous and capable multilateral institutions'.

CONCLUDING REMARKS

It is frequently stated that almost all the countries of the Horn suffer from recurrent and prolonged conflicts impeding efforts to address the major causes and ushering in security in all its dimensions. Lack of peace and stability in individual countries and the perennial practice of lending primacy to regime survival and elite privilege to the detriment and neglect of human security preoccupy all state actors in the sub-region and hence continue to sap the energy, sense of purpose and resources of member countries. It could, therefore, be argued that there is no option for committed engagement in addressing the deficits that adversely affect the socio-economic and political life of societies and inter-state relations. Conflicts in the sub-region are increasingly interwoven, making the task of managing and resolving them increasingly intractable and complex. The time-tested practice of mutual and reciprocal interventions aimed at reaping political benefits from upheavals in neighbouring countries that are designated as adversaries continues to prompt negative action and entails counter-responses. At present, the preoccupation of the Eritrean and Ethiopian regimes, among others, with supporting one another's armed opposition movements for effecting regime change in the target country is illuminating. Moreover, the two countries are currently at each other's throats in Somalia through varying levels of involvement, thereby adding to the predicaments of the already failed state. The track record of the countries of the Horn in terms of a peaceful transition of power and democratic governance is also far from commendable.

Paucity of trustworthy systems for holding elections, which ensure fairness and a level ground for all contestants and competing legitimate interests continue to bedevil the prospects for peace. The other observation that emerges from the review of the current state of conflicts in the Horn of Africa relates to the lack of a comprehensive approach to conflict resolution. In the case of the Sudan, the politics of exclusion and poorly thought through measures underlie efforts aimed at bringing about a durable peace and stability based on the equitable sharing and justice. Hence it could be argued that the prerequisite for realizing durable security at the sub-regional level continues to be adversely affected. It should be emphasized that the realization of goals pertaining to lasting security is dependent on the commitment of all stakeholders to putting things right by abandoning flawed and narrow-minded policies and attendant practices that continue to plague all façades of life in the Horn.

NOTES

1. To this effect, the predecessor of the African Union, the Organization of African Unity (OAU), agreed in the Cairo Declaration (1964) to respect colonial boundaries.

2. The boundary issue remains the principal bone of contention even after South Sudan's accession to independent statehood following the 2011 referendum as stipulated by the January 2005 CPA.
3 Unilaterally prescribed by the British Colonial Administration.
4. As recently as June 2010 Egypt and Sudan stood against the position of the majority of the Nile Basin countries which sought change based on equitable sharing. Opportunistically, Eritrea has expressed sympathy with the position of Egypt and Sudan aimed at preserving the status quo in the hope that this could undermine Ethiopia's leading role in advocating a new arrangement.

REFERENCES

Abbink, J. (2003). 'Ethiopia–Eritrea: Proxy Wars and Prospects of Peace in the Horn of Africa', *Journal of Contemporary African Studies*, vol. 21, no. 3: 407–25.

Aden, O. Abrar and Rirash, Mohamed Abdullahi (2001). *Conflict Prevention, Management and Resolution: Capacity Assessment Study for the IGAD Sub-region, Phase 2: Implementation Reports by National Experts: Djibouti*. Conflict, Disasters and Development Group, Centre for Development Studies, University of Leeds, Leeds.

Ayoob, M. (1996). *The Third World Security Predicament: State Making, Regional Conflict, and the International System*, Boulder, CO: Lynne Rienner.

Clapham, C. (2007). 'Regional Implications of the Eritrea–Ethiopia Boundary Dispute', paper presented at the Conference on the Current Peace and Security Challenges in the Horn of Africa, 12-13 March, Centre for Policy Research and Dialogue and InterAfrica Group Addis Ababa.

Cliffe, L. (1999). 'Regional Dimensions of Conflict in the Horn of Africa', *Third World Quarterly*, vol. 20.

Cliffe, S. (2007). 'Preface', in J. Manor (ed.), *Aid That Works: Successful Development in Fragile States*, Washington, DC: The World Bank.

de Waal, A. (2007). 'In Search of a Peace and Security Framework for the Horn of Africa', paper presented at the Conference on the Current Peace and Security Challenges in the Horn of Africa, 12-13 March, Centre for Policy Research and Dialogue and InterAfrica Group, Addis Ababa.

Dorn, W. (2001). 'Of Guns and Goods: Small Arms, Development and Human Security', in M. V. Naidu (ed.), *Perspectives of Human Security: National Sovereignty and Humanitarian Intervention*, Brandon, Manitoba: Canadian Peace Research and Education Association.

Evans, G. and Newham, J. (1998). *The Penguin Dictionary of International Relations*, London: Penguin Books.

Herui Tedla Bairu (2007). 'The Eritrean–Ethiopian Conflict and Security in the Horn of Africa', paper presented at the Conference on the Current Peace and Security Challenges in the Horn of Africa, 12-13 March, Centre for Policy Research and Dialogue and InterAfrica Group, Addis Ababa.

Homer-Dixon, T. F. (1994). 'Environmental Scarcities and Violent Conflict', *International Security*, vol. 19, no. 1: 5–40.

Hubert, D. (1999). 'Human Security; Safety for People in a Changing World', paper presented at the Conference on the Management of African Security in the 21st Century, Nigerian Institute of International Affairs, Lagos (unpublished).

IGAD (2007). 'Strategy and Implementation Plan 2004–8: Midterm Review Final Report', Djibouti.

IGAD (2008). 'IGAD, Minimum Regional Integration Plan (MIP)', November.

Jeong, Ho-Won (2000). *Peace and Conflict Studies: An Introduction*, Aldershot: Ashgate.

Laitin, David D. and Samatar, Said S. (1987), *Somalia: Nation in Search of a State*. Boulder, CO and London: Westview Press and Gower.

Markakis, John (1987). *National and Class Conflict in the Horn of Africa*, Cambridge: Cambridge University Press.

Markakis, J. (1998). *Resource Conflict in the Horn of Africa*, London and New Delhi: Sage.

McWhinney, Edward (2007). *Self-Determination of Peoples and Plural Ethnic States in Contemporary International Law: Failed States, Nation Building and the Alternative, Federal Option*, Boston, MA: Martinus Nijhoff.

Medhane, Taddesse (2004). *Turning Conflicts to Cooperation: Towards an Energy-led Integration in the Horn of Africa*. Addis Ababa: Friedrich–Ebert-Stiftung, Ethiopia Office.

Menkhaus, Ken and Prendergast, John (1999). 'Conflict and Crisis in the Greater Horn of Africa', *Current History* (May).

Mwagiru, M. (1997). 'The Greater Horn of Africa Conflict System: Conflict Patterns, Strategies and Management Practices', paper prepared for the USAID project on Conflict and Conflict Management in the Greater Horn of Africa, n.p. (April).

Mwagiru, M. (2002). *The Legal Framework for the Conflict Early Warning and Response Mechanism (CEWARN)*, Djibouti: IGAD.

Närman, A. (2002). *The Greater Horn of Africa: Conflicts and the Civil Society in Somalia*, SIRC Report 3, Lund: International Rehabilitation Centre.

Nisbet, R. Jackson (1999). 'Secession and Non-Secession in Four States: US, USSR, Ethiopia, and Belgium' (unpublished).

Oquaye, M. (2000). 'Culture, Conflict and Traditional Authority: A Ghanaian Perspective', in L. A. Jinadu (ed.), *The Political Economy of Peace and Security in Africa: Ethnocultural and Economic Perspectives*, Harare: Print Source.

Prendergast, J. (1992). *Peace, Development, and People of the Horn of Africa*, Washington, DC: Center of Concern.

Prendergast, J. (1999), *Building for Peace in the Horn of Africa: Diplomacy and Beyond*, Special Report, Washington, DC: United States Institute of Peace.

Rowntree, L., Lewis, Martin, Price, Marie and Wyckoff, William (2005) *Globalization and Diversity: Geography of a Changing World*, London: Pearson/Prentice Hall.

Rugumamu, S. (2001). 'Conflict Management in Africa: Diagnosis and Prescriptions', in A. Taye, S. M. Rugumamu, and A. G. M. Ahmed (eds.), *Globalization, Democracy and Development in Africa: Challenges and Prospects*, Addis Ababa: OSSREA.

Rupesinghe, K. (1998). *Civil Wars, Civil Peace: An Introduction to Conflict Resolution*, London: Pluto Press.

Schraeder, Peter J. (1993). 'Ethnic Politics in Djibouti: From "Eye of the Hurricane" to "Boiling Cauldron"', African *Affairs*, 90.

Suliman, M. (1999). 'The Rationality and Irrationality of Violence in Sub-Saharan Africa', in M. Suliman (ed.), *Ecology, Politics and Violent Conflict*, London and New York: Zed Books.

Zeleza, Paul Tiyambe (2008). 'Introduction: The Causes and Costs of War in Africa: From Liberation Struggles to the "War on Terror"', in A. Nhema and P. T. Zeleza (eds.), *The Roots of African Conflicts: The Causes and Costs*, Oxford, Athens, OH and Pretoria: James Currey, Ohio State University Press and UNISA Press in association with OSSREA.

5
Border Changes: North Sudan–South Sudan Regional Dynamics

Abdalbasit Saeed

INTRODUCTION: PRIMARY ASSUMPTION, KEY ISSUES AND THE STRUCTURE OF THE CHAPTER

The primary fact of the post-separation situation in Sudan is that, in the referendum held in January 2011, the people of South Sudan chose to create their own country, independent from the mother country, the Republic of the Sudan (TRS), in which they had lived in aversive association for almost two centuries, since 1821. The referendum that led to the creation of the independent state of the Republic of South Sudan (RSS) was premised on the 1 January 1956 border, which is yet to be demarcated with an outcome agreeable to the two states. Hence, separation and independence pose the greatest of emerging challenges for both countries as they grapple with 'post-mortem' issues. Unless urgently addressed, such risks and challenges may haunt the two countries throughout the decade.

This chapter contributes to drawing out a future redirection or perspective towards good neighbourliness, mindful of the inter-dependences between them for cooperation and collaboration to replace past confrontation. The role of countries in the sub-region and international actors during the post-separation decade is to help them manage their differences thoughtfully through deliberation and dialogue. The redirection after separation is seen in terms of the short term (two years) and medium term (five years). For the short term, reference landmarks that could be detailed further through dialogue have been provided under the loose title 'post-referendum arrangements', just before separation occurred. This chapter synthesizes internal causal dynamics as a diagnostic assessment of possible options for relations of cooperation between TRS and RSS, instead of the confrontation that preceded the CPA of 2005. It presents the main arguments why certain factors for the malfunctioning of vertical legitimacy of the state form are linked to a possible surge of conflict in certain locations in the Borderline Belt (BLB) between North and South where the Technical Border Committee had been encountering problems on delineation and demarcation.

Six key issues are outstanding, well after separation took place, from the slow CPA implementation. They can be stated as follows:

1. How the referendum on self-determination for South Sudan was conducted.
2. The conduct of a plebiscite for the Abyei area and resolution of issues associated with the incomplete enactment of Permanent Court of Arbitration (PCA) Award of 22 July 2009 which defined the boundaries for Abyei territory that are yet to be drawn, mainly due to objection or rejection of the PCA Award by the Misiriyae, allies of the ruling National Congress Party (NCP), who share the Abyei area with the Ngok-Dinka, allies of SPLM/A. The result has been the incomplete implementation, and hence shelving of the Abyei Protocol which envisaged a Special Administrative Status for Ngok-Dinka.
3. The organization of elections for the State Legislative Assembly in South Kordofan State (SKS), deferred in April 2010 as a result of a dispute between the SPLM and NCP over the 2008 population census results for SKS.
4. Border demarcation.
5. The imperative to conduct a Popular Consultation; the object of the Two Areas Protocol (TAP) in SKS has been compromised as war broke out in June following the defeat of SPLM/A when the deferred election was held in May 2011.
6. Unresolved security-related issues, including redeployment of forces away from the perceived border on either side, as on 1 January 1956.

There are also some issues not specifically stated in the CPA text, but which are seen to warrant resolution as post-separation issues, including easy transport of RSS oil using TRS infrastructure. Major among such issues is border delineation and demarcation, as well as oil wealth and related issues. Delay on these issues could impair relations between the two countries. They also include nationality, citizenship that could 'tailgate' on the future status of political, economic and social rights of citizens of one country in the territory of the other. Harnessing such issues requires TRS and RSS to settle their differences immediately and expeditiously so that relevant institutional and legal frameworks are agreed and put in place.

IMPLICATIONS AND RAMIFICATIONS OF SOUTH SUDAN'S SEPARATION FOR THE SUB-REGION

Sudan's neighbours have been reduced in number from nine to seven: Ethiopia, Eritrea, Egypt, Libya, Chad, the Central African Republic and the RSS. Kenya, Uganda and the DRC are no longer immediate neighbours. Sudan's outreach to Africa will, to this extent, be impaired. Most important are issues related to the waters of the Nile. The RSS is now the third richest country in natural precipitation in sub-Saharan African, after Ethiopia and the Congo. The abundance of seasonal streams will turn the RSS into a water giant as regards future strategies for the Nile waters. The 'old' Sudan will become a water-deficit country, in spite of the fact that the Nile traverses it from South to North. It will, furthermore, forfeit to the RSS eight billion cubic metres of water, equal to 40 per cent of its pre-separation share in the Nile Waters Agreement. It will result in the inability of its major agricultural sector to feed its people. Since the 1980s Sudan has been prey to one drought every three years, making it reliant on humanitarian food aid in the range of US$100 million every year. The country is now floundering to secure its own subsistence, already jeopardized due to the loss of 70 per cent of oil produced before separation. This grim picture is made worse by the fact that 75 per cent of the land mass of the North, (1,882,000 km^2) after separation is desert lying between the 13th and 21st parallels. The desert is unsuitable for agriculture except along the River Nile. Irrigation is too expensive in both the short and medium term. North Sudan's closed window on the Arab world might be less of an attraction. The long-standing, ill-fated developmentalist ideology of an 'Arab bread-basket' might collapse in view of the expected loss of foreign investment. Almost all investment in oil exploration and production in the BLB comes from China. In addition to the country's current foreign debt of US$38 billion, it will cost North Sudan much more expensive foreign financing to reach present oil production levels, estimated at 500,000 barrels per day. In addition, environmental and surface resource issues, oil and mineral resource issues, as well as the drawing of an internationally agreed boundary, which the two CPA partners failed to put in place during the six-year interim period, are primary issues that have immediate relevance to oil wealth for which the borderline states are the main producers, yet the most marginalized in benefiting from the 'oil wealth dividend' or fending off the deleterious environmental impact of 'produced water' as a result of oil exploration and production. An important note here is that oil for RSS will no longer be a matter of 'wealth-sharing' as it was under the CPA. Rather, it will be an issue of *division* and *ownership* of resources' by a country-in-the-making, including ownership of land, water, minerals and forest resources that must be bestowed upon present and future generations of the people of South Sudan.

General Country Context and External Dimensions

Sudan gained independence in 1956. The infamous North–South conflict and war generated, throughout 50 years of protracted hostilities, major challenges to stability and threats to peace and security in Africa and the wider world, as reflected in resolutions of the UN Security Council. In terms of international politics, during the years of conflict and war, the consequences of the conflict compromised Sudan's relations with its African neighbours. Relations with international finance institutions have been adversely affected. Economic sanctions and an embargo, though unnecessary, were intensified to add to the country's isolation. Most importantly, the conditions made it imperative on the world community to seek concerted efforts not only to stop the war, resolve the conflict and incorporate development strategies through power-sharing and wealth-sharing, but also to imagine the future state of the country at the end of the interim period. There are also emerging challenges with multiple implications for Sudan as regards the African region and 'Sudan-in-the-Middle-East'. Of particular relevance to South Sudan are Egypt and Uganda (for water), Ethiopia (for water and gold in the Kurmuk area on the border with Blue Nile State (BNS)), the Central African Republic (CAR), and Kenya as major trading partner. Some of Sudan's neighbours are also members of multilateral organizations in which Sudan cooperates: the African Union (AU), Arab League (AL), Organization of Islamic Conference (OIC) and United Nations (UN) – particularly, the Group of 77. They are also members of intergovernmental institutions, including IGAD, which sponsored the 2005 CPA which brought an end to the war in Sudan.

Now that the RSS has seceded, foreign countries already imposing sanctions on TRS on account of the war in Darfur and the non-implementation of the verdict of the International Criminal Court are expected to pursue those fugitives hitherto considered 'hiding in the open'. Sudan's severing of diplomatic relations with Kenya on 28 November 2011 on account of a Kenyan court order to 'catch' Sudan's President if he steps on Kenyan soil is a clear indication of Sudan's future strategy. Tied to the US ideology of the war on terror, the AL and oil-rich states of the Arab Gulf, currently paying only lip-service to Sudan, might side-track all issues. Two of Sudan's neighbours will continue to share international borders with both Sudan and South Sudan: Ethiopia (water and gold in Kurmuk area in BNS), and CAR (gold, copper and uranium). The eastern and western tips of the BLB are also affected by spill-over from the war in Blue Nile and Darfur, respectively, and have a direct bearing on relations with Chad and the Central African Republic. Furthermore, South Sudan shares a 2,000 km, indefensible border with North Sudan. It must be a safe and soft border. It must not be allowed to become porous. The litmus test could be vibrant border trade and strong cross-border infrastructure. Otherwise, the border could prove to be the soft underbelly for North Sudan as it might be used to smuggle arms to the post-separation insurgents in BNS, SKS and southern Darfur who have recently declared a tripartite coalition which will use arms to topple the NCP-led regime in Khartoum.

The African Union and Sudan's Neighbours

As part of the overall efforts to support the implementation of the CPA, the political process to achieve a solution to the Sudanese crisis in Darfur and in order to facilitate the democratic transformation of the Sudan, the AU Commission convened a high-level strategic review meeting under its chairmanship. The meeting reviewed and assessed the political situation in Sudan in anticipation of the final year of the CPA implementation, which includes holding referendums in South Sudan and Abyei. In this respect, the meeting acknowledged new realities arising from the elections and responsibilities imposed on the President of Sudan and the President of Government of Southern Sudan to promote inclusiveness and build on the progress achieved in furtherance of democracy, peace and security. The meeting recognized the magnitude and complexity of the challenges facing the Sudan, the tight timeframe within which they are operating and the multiplicity of international actors engaged in Sudan. In light of this, the meeting agreed on the need for greater support from the international community and close coordination among international actors, in support of the Sudanese actors who have demonstrated a determination and capacity to address these challenges. More generally, the meeting recognized that developments in Sudan are of critical importance to the region and to the African continent, and emphasized the importance of the AU–UN partnership in this regard, which needs to be supported by international partners.

Regarding the implementation of outstanding provisions of the CPA and the negotiation of post-separation arrangements, the meeting agreed on the following: (1) the need to do everything possible to assist the Sudanese partners to fulfil their CPA commitments; (2) creating the conditions, including at the technical level, to hold successful referendums in Southern Sudan and Abyei; (3) support for capacity building and conflict mitigation in South Sudan; (4) continued and strengthened coordination between international partners. Taking into account other recommendations, the meeting agreed on the need for all the international actors to work closely together and to coordinate their efforts for peace and security, social and economic issues, justice and reconciliation.

THE BORDERLINE BELT BETWEEN NORTH SUDAN AND SOUTH SUDAN: *NO AGREED BORDER*

The Borderline Belt Descriptively Defined

The Borderline Belt (BLB) between TRS and RSS lies between latitudes 9:30N and 12:00N and is where over 60 per cent of the Sudanese population make their livelihoods. It covers ten Borderline States (BLS) which extend from Sudan's international border at the Ethiopian plateau to the Zairian highlands. Using a metaphor to denote the prospect for stability, the BLB is a social and political 'dragon space' for the North Sudan because, looked at from east to west, the states that form the BLB take the form of a Chinese dragon. The BLB context also bears the term coined here 'North Sudan Dragon Belt' (NSDB). It denotes continued trouble between North and South Sudan since independence in 1956, with no indication of how to bring to an end the causes leading to it. The dragon's head faces the Ethiopian plateau and its tail touches the CAR. The BLB is plagued by disputes and conflict. Most importantly, in terms of the provisions of the Comprehensive Peace Agreement (CPA) which regulates national institutional and political processes, the BLB includes not only the Three Transitional Areas (TTAs) – Blue Nile, South Kordofan and Abyei – covering 66 per cent of borderline, which are governed by a separate CPA Protocol, and the disputed Abyei Area with a protocol specific to it, but also five states in South Sudan which are subject to the other major CPA Protocols governing power-sharing, resource-sharing and security. The BLB is approximately 1,936 km long in the form of a rectangle and covers three latitudes (9:30–12:30). Some 1,355 km (70 per cent) of this border lies in Southern Darfur State and Southern Kordofan State. This sector comprises the west-central hinterland of the White Nile. The eastern hinterland of the White Nile, along the BLB, comprises the White Nile State, Sinnar State and Blue Nile State. The BLB has an estimated land area of 436,000 km², equivalent to 20 per cent of the total area of Sudan. The borderline states are home to 12 million people, 31 per cent of the total population of Sudan. The average population density is 28 persons per km², almost double the national average of 15 persons per km², according to the 2008 census. It encompasses ten states on both sides of the border separating North Sudan and South Sudan.

According to the 2008 census, the five states to the north of the borderline are home to some eight million – equivalent to the total population of South Sudan. Their number is double the population of the five states that face them across the border in the South. The five borderline states of South Sudan contain an estimated 50 per cent of the total population of South Sudan. The implication for a future successor state in the South, with half of its population living north of the Sudds and mangroves, poses a strategic security concern. Of particular importance is the 'head and neck' of the Upper Nile State, protruding to reach latitude 12:20N and 'rubbing shoulders' with four states in North Sudan, two of which are not only in a state of conflict but also well armed.

In terms of resources, the BLB encompasses 13 million people, all active oil production in Sudan, the greater part (80 per cent) of the land area covered by semi-mechanized farming and over 60 per cent of the national livestock during the dry season as well as the majority of wildlife and game reserves. Mineral resources include gold in Kurmuk (BNS), oil, natural gas, iron ore and bauxite in south-west Kordofan (inhabited by Misiriyae and Ngok-Dinka agro-pastoralists), as well as uranium, gold and copper in Hufrat-en-Nahas (SDS), claimed to be part of South Sudan according to the 1 January 1956 boundary line. Overall, some 80 per cent of Sudan's population is said to be dependent on the direct use of natural resources, mostly through the production, processing and marketing of crops and livestock products, and other environmental products from trees. The BLB, therefore, is the main source of food production and food security, with the Nile as its primary endowment. A substantial strategic threat and risk arose when the southern 25 per cent of the country was lost on referendum day 2011.

In terms of development potential, the BLB has an annual average seasonal (June–October) rainfall of 400–800 mm. In terms of surface resources the BLB has savannah grasslands of varying quality and forest cover. The ten borderline states house more than 80 per cent of the national livestock herd, particularly during the long dry season. The BLB is home to the majority of wildlife and game reserves of Sudan. It is suitable habitat for wildlife, forests for lumber, trees for harvesting, fertile land for agriculture and pasture for livestock migrating to the South across BLB in dry season. The BLB enjoys varied soil types, including alluvium soils suitable for many crops, including cereals (sorghum and millet) and oil seeds (sesame, groundnuts, as well as watermelon seeds and sunflower) as cash crops. Inland water bodies are also encompassed by the BLB, including Lake Abyad and Lake Kailak in Southern Kordofan, as well as Lake Kundi and Lake Kalaka Natural Depression in Southern Darfur, which are used for fish farming.

The Borderline Belt and the Ten Borderline States

The CPA 2005 called for a precise demarcation of the North–South border as it existed on 1 January 1956. An ad hoc Technical Border Committee (TBC), established by Presidential Decree 29 in September 2005, has been appointed to the task, charged to and supported by national and international experts. The CPA 'pre-interim period' (January–July 2005) was the envisaged timeframe to determine the border. The task of the TBC is yet to be completed, with five sectors causing delay, three of which involve SKS, WNS and UNS. Establishing the exact borderline has been considered important not only for the conditionality of successor state sovereignty to finalize the respective territories of the North and South, but also for implementing other aspects of CPA, such as population censuses, voter registration for referendums and redeploying the Sudan Armed Forces (SAF) and Sudan People Liberation Army (SPLA). However, the TBC not only suffered an initial delay of two months, but also started functioning in mid-2006, one year later than envisaged in the CPA. The fundamental challenge for the TBC has been that no map exists that accurately depicts the North–South boundary at independence. In addition, its work has met multiple hurdles, including procedural disputes and accusations of political meddling. The founding decree stipulated that: the TBC demarcates the borderline between South and North Sudan, as of

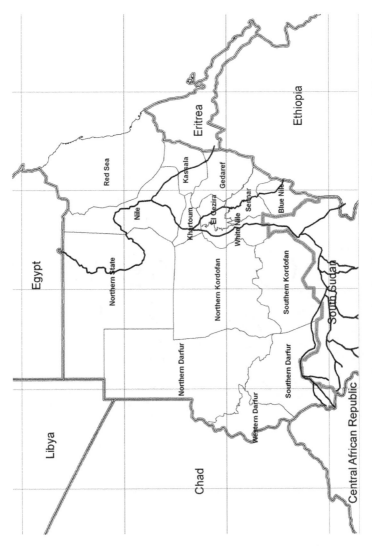

Map 5.1 Borderline States of Sudan after the Separation of South Sudan: South Darfur, East Darfur, South Kordofan, White Nile, Sinnar (Sennar) and Blue Nile.

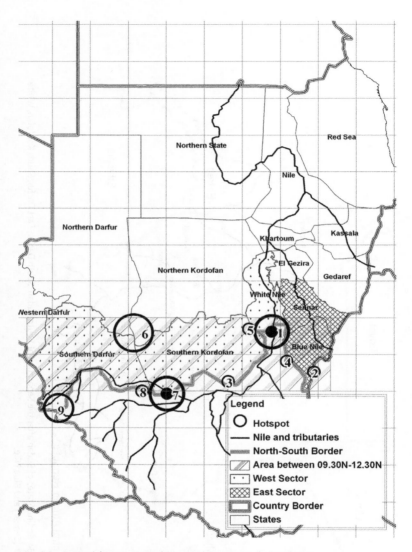

Map 5.2   Potential Hotspots and Disputed Sectors on the Borderline.

1 January 1956; and without contradicting the generality of the text in the preceding item, the TBC has functions and powers to consult all maps, drawings and documents, visit all border areas between North and South Sudan and overlapping areas, consult tribal leaders and civil administrators in overlapping areas, and

listen to their statements and review any documents provided by them, and solicit internal and foreign expertise, if necessary. There is disagreement in the work of the TBC over several sectors on the border. Five have been identified as problematic in the TBC report (2010) to the presidency. Map 2 identifies nine hotspots, all within the BLB. They are the Jabalain-Joada sector at the point of convergence of White Nile State (WNS) and UNS; the Jabal Migeinis sector where the boundaries of three states (WNS, UNS and SKS) meet; Kaka town sector between Upper Nile State (UNS) and SKS; Abyei area where the SKS boundary meets Unity State, Warrap State and North Bahr-al-Ghazal; and Hufrat-en-Nahas (also known as Kafia-Kingi) where South Darfur and West Bahr-al-Ghazal meet. Starting with highlights on the implications of the indeterminate boundaries of Kordofan for the disputed sectors and border delineation, the White Nile (Jabalain-Joda) Sugar Bowl and Abyei Area will be addressed in detail.

Set in east-to-west geo-spatial sequence, there are five states on the northern side of the borderline. They fall into two sectors: east of the White Nile River sector and west of the White Nile River sector. On the east bank of the White Nile are the BNS, Sinnar State (SINS) and WNS. The WNS to the north of the borderline and UNS to the south of the borderline are dissected by the White Nile River from south to north. On the west bank of the White Nile are South Kordofan State (SKS), which encompasses Abyei (ABY) and South Darfur State (SDS).

The BLB lies within the realms of three medieval kingdoms: Funj Sultanate (1504–1820), headquartered at Sinnar and controlling the east bank of the White Nile and expanding to Kordofan and Darfur in the middle of the eighteenth century; Musabba'at Sultanate in North Kordofan and the Kingdom of Tegali, corresponding to the Southern Kordofan segment of the border; as well as Darfur Sultanate (1664–1916) with strong command-outreach in the Bahr-al-Arab border segment. The land covered by the ten borderline states was, historically, the meeting ground for inequitable and unequal groups of peoples from North and South Sudan. It was the fringe landscape for the medieval civilizations of the three tributary states/ kingdoms of the Funj kingdom in SINS and BNS; the kingdom of Tegali and Musabba'at Sultanate in Kordofan; as well as the Darfur Sultanate. The three segments (BNS, SKS, SDS) and marginal borderlands further south were used as corridors through which Turkish expeditions were mounted to supply the slave trade.

THE STRATEGIC IMPORTANCE OF THE BORDERLINE BELT FOR THE TWO STATES

The importance of the BLB arises from several considerations, occurring in the form of potential hotspots. They relate to internal geo-economics and geo-politics of the country. Four states from North Sudan touch the UNS at the intersection of latitude 12:00N/longitude 32:30E. A circle is formed where the borders meet. It encompasses portions of sugar cane plantations on both banks of the White Nile, controlled by Kinana Sugar Company and Sabina Sugar Company. South Sudan will be concerned over security issues regarding the 'neck and head cap' of the UNS, extending from latitude 11:30N to 12:00N. This is where border-related disputes, oil-related disputes and land disputes related to agricultural land use all converge or overlap and find expression not only in tribalism and ethnicity for the local people but also in claims and counter-claims, by NCP and SPLM, to historical evidence from British colonial archival sources.

This section undertakes to describe the implications of major potential hotspots.

The BLB touches two focal neighbours of Sudan: Ethiopia in the east and the Central African Republic in the west. Since independence South Sudan has become water-rich, the second richest country in Africa, after the Congo. Of course, Nile water is of strategic concern to Sudan's neighbours, Egypt, Ethiopia and Uganda. The signing of a controversial agreement on River Nile Waters, in Uganda on 15 May 2010, and the establishment of a lame commission to the detriment of Sudan and Egypt, sends a negative signal to South Sudan in the Great Lakes Region. The BLB is the meeting ground for the majority of tributaries of the White Nile River (WNR), except Bahr-al-Jabel, which arises from Lake Victoria. The WNR carries an estimated 51 per cent of the annual discharge of the River Nile. Most of this (60 per cent) is generated by natural precipitation within the borders of the Sudan, and where the waters meet determines their flow. The tributaries of WNR prevail over South Sudan as major sources of surface water bodies. It also resupplies water-borne sedimentary basins. By contrast, the Blue Nile River (BNR) does not flow through South Sudan. It arises from the Ethiopian Plateau and is fed by three rivers: the Atbara, Dinder and Rahad. Together they contribute an estimated 48 per cent of the annual discharge of the River Nile. Internally, petroleum is of strategic concern to the North, South and within Border Line States. It also poses environmental risks and threats, of multiple dimensions. However, official data on oil exploration are not readily available.

POTENTIAL HOTSPOTS AND FUTURE CROSS-BORDER RELATIONS: THE WHITE NILE/UPPER NILE

Nine potential hotspots and flashpoints have been identified where resource-driven disputes are either current or could arise, internally or with neighbouring states, including Ethiopia, CAR and RSS. Four of these hotspots involve the border of South Kordofan, with borderline states in the South and others in North Sudan. One significant potential hotspot, where tribal/ethnic disputes are common, involves five states, four in the North and one in the South: NBS, SINS, WNS and SKS touch UNS. It is described here as the White Nile Sugar Bowl (WNSB), situated at the head of Upper Nile State. It is a descriptive phrase for the predicament not only for pastoralists entering the Upper Nile State but also for the security concerns of North Sudan as such. It comprises locations/ enclaves of the border where the four states in North Sudan touch UNS. From a security angle, the WNSB approaches everything that North Sudan wants to keep for itself. At the same time, it forms the soft underbelly for South Sudan, as its 'head cap and neck' is circumscribed by four well-armed states (BNS, SINS, WNS and SKS). The UNS is, therefore, a security concern to both states.

Irrigated sugar cane plantation agriculture in southern WNS, mechanized, rain-fed agriculture, migratory livestock herds and oil exploration companies – on both sides of the White Nile River in the five states – converge at WNSB, contributing to potential conflict. The disputes formerly designated as 'tribal' could be transformed, post-separation, into security concerns of strategic implications for the two states. The WNSB sits at the head cap of the UNS. The WNSB encompasses Jabalain Locality and al-Salam Locality. They are currently burdened with resource-based disputes and conflicts driven by competition over pasture and the inability of pastoralists to access the banks of the White Nile in order to water their livestock. This is because access is blocked by 'river-bank pasture-grabbers'. In addition, the sugar cane plantations manned by Kinana and Sabina companies complicate the situation as Kinana has relocated pastoralists southwards from Jabalain since the 1970s, and the currently implemented Sabina sugar cane farm (97,000 ha) is planning to relocate pastoralists in al-Salam Locality to the western pastures in South Kordofan, which will make it difficult for them to access the White Nile to water their livestock, as it will be some 40 km away.

Kaka Town: South Kordofan Dispute with Upper Nile

The Technical Border Committee has been divided over the border between Upper Nile and South Kordofan with regard to the 'Kaka town sector'. Kaka town is a small river port on the west bank of the White Nile, near the border between Upper Nile and South Kordofan states. In 1922 British colonial administrators of Sudan instituted the Closed Districts Ordinance (CDO). This was a policy which in effect divided North Sudan from South Sudan. The CDO policy severely restricted movement and trade from North to South, as the White Nile was the only access route. As a result, communities in Southeast Kordofan – presently the eastern parts of South Kordofan – could not obtain goods and services from North Sudan. Instead they looked to the South and the WNR.

To address the problem, a 1923 Sudan Government Gazette transferred administration of Kaka town – and in effect management of its port – from Upper Nile Province to Kordofan Province (now South Kordofan State), thereby granting Nuba settled communities a supply route and Silaim tribe pastoralists easy access to water sources for their livestock. Since then, communities from South Kordofan have sustained use through seasonal harvesting of gum arabic in the area. Large-scale mechanized farming was developed through the granting of leasehold permits by the government. After 90 years the North Sudan members of TBC claim that the administrative order of the condominium authority amounts to a permanent change of boundary. However, TBC members from South Sudan argue that these changes do not constitute a border change. The dispute has continued in the post-separation phase.

Migeinis Mountain: A Three-State Disputed Sector

Jebel Migeinis is a mountain located at the north-west point of Upper Nile State where it joins White Nile State to the north and Southern Kordofan to the west. The current boundary where Manyo County, inhabited by Shilluk people in Upper Nile State, converges with al-Salam Locality in WNS is where the Silaim agro-pastoralist cattle herders are found. Here, they collect gum arabic and other seasonal harvests. The cause of this dispute is that the Silaim agro-pastoralists claim this area as part of their traditional *dar*. In addition, the Migeinis sector has considerable agricultural potential as well as oil exploration in block 7. Oil potential was the prime mover behind TBC's technical claims and counter-claims during the CPA. However, as the TBC mandate was grounded in administrative boundary delineation and demarcation, it appeared there was little chance for traditional *dar* claims to prevail over official documents. In the course of TBC discussions, South Sudan members of the TBC argued that if North Sudan members (NCP) preferred that the committee expand its mandate to include 'historical tribal boundaries' in TBC deliberations, they would agree. They thought that South Sudan would undoubtedly benefit in several disputed locations, including the oil-rich Hejleej fields which South Sudan claims as Nuer land.

Sluggish Boundaries of Kordofan, Disputed Sectors and Border Delineation

South Kordofan borders eight states, four in North Sudan and four in South Sudan. With the exception of BNS and SINS in the east sector of the BLB and West Bahr-al-Ghazal state in the west sector of BLB, all states share borders with South Kordofan. Therefore, the issue of 'sluggish administrative boundaries' testifies to the fact that South Kordofan is not only directly involved as a central state sharing all the agonies of a country falling apart, but also constitutes the soft underbelly where oil-related disputes and pasture-related conflicts coincide with borderline delineation disputes on the left bank of the White Nile (the BLB's west sector) which the TBC has been trying to sort out for six years. However, sectors where the TBC differences are acute seem to coincide with those where oil-related exploration finds petroleum reserves in commercial quantities. The main locations where borderline disputes need to be resolved include: the meeting point of Upper Nile State with the White Nile State; Jebel Migeinis sector where White Nile State and South Kordofan in North Sudan meet/dispute with Upper Nile State in South Sudan; Kaka town sector where South Kordofan in North Sudan is in dispute with Upper Nile State in South Sudan; and Abyei Area as disputed domain where a micro-conflict with multiple ramifications is aggravated by local disagreement between Misiriyae – Ngok-Dinka, national (NCP-SPLM), and international (non-implementation of Abyei protocol, and non-implementation of the PCA Award).

Anatomy of the Abyei Territory Puzzle: A Dispute that May Cause Another North–South War

Abyei is a disputed enclave in South Kordofan, situated in west-central Sudan and inhabited by Ngok-Dinka and Misiriyae since the middle of the eighteenth century. According to the Abyei Protocol, the Ngok-Dinka have the right to decide whether they should remain in the North or merge with the South. In the meantime, its boundary was decided upon by a special Abyei Boundaries Commission (ABC). Its 'final and binding decision' was rejected by the NCP on presentation to the presidency on 14 July 2005. This situation generated the Abyei Territory Puzzle (ATP). Thus, with the future of Abyei uncertain, tensions began in 2008 and led to the unseating and expelling ofthe SPLA by the SAF in May 2011. The two communities who share resources are traditionally north–south long-distance transhumance agro-pastoralists (Misiriyae) and west–east short-distance transhumance agro-pastoralists (Ngok-Dinka). Since the peak of violence in 1965, they have tended towards partly settled livelihoods, mainly due to conditions that made pastoralism increasingly difficult for both communities, namely, desertification and land degradation in the North and persistent conflict and war in the South. The separation of South Sudan relegates north–south long-distance transhumance increasingly redundant as a way of life. This is borne out by the decline in the number of pastoralists as shown in five national censuses: 13 per cent in 1956, and 10 per cent in the 1973, 1983 and 1993, and 8 per cent in 2008.

The Main Actors Who Make up the Abyei Territory Puzzle

Despite the CPA peace agreement between North and South, the Abyei dispute kept fault lines alive within the shaky coalition government, shared by NCP and SPLM. Bloody clashes erupted in May 2008 over the control of Abyei oil-rich land. An unknown number of people were forced to flee during heavy fighting between the SAF and the SPLA. One further complication following this confrontation is that local ethnic feuds erupted and escalated between Misiriyae and Ngok-Dinka pastoralists who, respectively, continue to serve as proxy forces for SAF and SPLA, including during the 20 years of conflict and war (1985–2005) that preceded the CPA. The three main contenders are the NCP and the SPLM; the SAF and the SPLA; and the Misiriyae and Ngok-Dinka pastoralists, as local clients for NCP and SPLM. While Sudanese political parties wrangle over the question of oil-sharing, they are not united on a national programme in the face of the NCP. Lurking in the wings are the oil exploration and production companies. Some 40 Sudanese service companies work under them and ally with their interests. The oil exploration companies have their interests aligned with the governing partners (NCP and SPLM) and their respective armies, who protect the oil interests. Furthermore, there are five categories of international (external) actors operating in Abyei Territory: UN agencies, international humanitarian organizations, UN international monitors commissioned under chapter 6 of the UN Charter (now chapter 7 of the Charter), and joint integrated units (JIUs) foreseen in the CPA (now replaced by an AU-backed force of 4,200).

The Positions Taken by the Major Actors

It is the oil wealth of Abyei Territory that really matters to both the NCP and SPLM. It is surface land resources that matter to the local pastoralist clients, Ngok-Dinka/Misiriyae, particularly water, pasture and forest resources for livestock herding. However, as a disputed territory, Abyei may hold the key to Sudan's future stability. Northern Sudan, NCP and SAF fear that if they concede Abyei Territory, they will not only lose vast (50,000 bpd) oil reserves but also other contested resource-rich areas across the controversial 1956 North–South borderline, including other oil blocs, as well as gold and copper in Hufrat-al-Nahhas. In Khartoum, the NCP will do everything in its power to keep the area from becoming the first domino to fall. If this does happen, they will be held responsible for allowing the country to be dismembered. Southern Sudan, SPLM and SPLA, while publicly disavowing a return to war, nevertheless maintain their unity by provoking confrontation with the North and are also desperate to hang on to Abyei oil resources. In October 2010, as the CPA timelines were approaching the referendum on self-determination for South Sudan, NCP and SPLM realized that slow implementation during the first six years would be the undoing of at least the Abyei referendum, posited to be concurrent with that for the South. The NCP and SPLM also realized that the Abyei referendum could not be held. Therefore, the Abyei Protocol had by default become impossible to implement. At this late stage they tried to bring on board representatives of the Misiriyae and Ngok-Dinka to attend supplementary negotiations in Ethiopia which must look seriously into acceptable/amicable solutions and arrangements that could uphold the substance of the CPA and at the same time reach a settlement that would avoid resort to violence. The attempt failed. The Abyei Territory puzzle remains unresolved. In the first week of January 2011, just two days before the referendum of South Sudan, heavy fighting broke out in Abyei in which some 33 persons were killed (14 Ngok-Dinka and 19 Misiriyae) and more than 30 persons reportedly injured. The reason given was that the

Misiriyae wanted to take their livestock to water in the Regeba-ez-Zerga, the only water resource at that time of the year. Access was denied because the Misiriyae were accompanying their herds 'arms-in-hand', which is construed as 'fingers-on-the-trigger' by the Ngok-Dinka. This is evidence of the mistrust between the two communities, a cognitive issue, which is at the heart of animosity. No further details are available.

CONCLUDING REMARKS

The outstanding issues foreseen in the CPA have now been overtaken. The question of wealth-sharing has been transformed into one of *resource division with, and ownership by* the South. The issues of citizenship and nationality in the post-separation decade must now be addressed as matters of the sovereign domain of each state. The challenges of boundary delineation and demarcation are now matters for the constitutional identity of the state. The outstanding issues in Abyei Area (under chapter 7 of the UN Charter), SKS, BNS and Darfur have become so complex that international mediation has become imperative. They must demand that the TRS and the RSS distance themselves from piecemeal attempts and converge in a more holistic manner to re-engage the CPA guarantors, the IGAD and the Troika countries (the United States, Britain and Norway). Further, there is an urgent need for the international community to work towards the creation of sustainable post-separation arrangements and to pursue democratization and a sustainable peace. The African Union, United Nations and individual contributors to UNAMID and the UN force in Abyei need to work hard in order to enhance the capacity of their missions for civilian protection in both countries.

This chapter, based on desk work, has addressed three main challenges: macro-level challenges for the two states in respect of their neighbours; problems and risks of the Borderline States; and local stakeholders within them, who face enormous political, security and development challenges since separation. The first challenge is to identify activities that best serve the stated objectives in each unique context. The second is for the two states to agree on strategies that can replace long-standing confrontational attitudes with post-separation strategies for cooperation and collaboration through the creation of effective leadership, coordination and accountability. The third challenge, which arises from the second, is to commission quick assessment and planning commissions for the establishment of a coherent strategy in a fast-moving post-separation environment. Such tasks require support and cooperation from a diverse range of national and international actors. There are, however, no quick fixes for holding and sustaining peace in a volatile context. However, the litmus test is the need to realize that innocent men, women and children all too often bear the costs of war. They cannot, as Kofi Annan says, 'be asked to pay the price of peace as well'.

With the wounds of the past reopened in Abyei area, it could be apposite to conclude this account with an unconventional closing, and leave the chapter open for a revisiting of the Abyei Territory Puzzle. It could be stated that in spite of fielding the largest peace-keeping mission in the world to the region (30,000 UN and AU troops in North Sudan and 7,000 in South Sudan), the international community, including the UN Security Council, appears unable, unwilling and/or powerless to keep armed violence at bay, particularly in Abyei, SKS, BNS and South Darfur. If the issues, questions and contentions in these areas are to be satisfactorily addressed and resolved, at a minimum NCP and SPLM senior politicians and military personnel must urgently be made to adhere to signed agreements and seek new ones to sign. They should persuade or coerce their local clients, including both the Misiriyae and the Ngok-Dinka, to realize that the PCA Award must be honoured. The SAF and SPLA must also realize that their local clients, as primary stakeholders and counterparts in other areas, feel increasingly excluded and restless. So, senior politicians and military personnel must not only bring their respective local partners into line, but also cease exploiting emotional susceptibilities and local tensions. The educated and tribal elites, as local leaders of ethnic groups in disputed locations and flashpoints, should remember that the local communities have coexisted, and will continue to do so, as long as they can equitably share local resources and obtain a just peace dividend.

REFERENCES AND FURTHER READING

Abdalbasit, Saeed (1982). 'The State and Socioeconomic Transformation in the Sudan: The Case of Social Conflict in Southwest Kurdufan', PhD dissertation, University of Connecticut (unpublished).

Abdalbasit, Saeed (2009). 'Environment, Constrained Livelihoods and Human Settlement: The Case for the Future of Pastoralists in Southwest Kurdufan', paper presented at the 4th Horn of Africa Network Conference, Khartoum.

Abdalbasit, Saeed (2010). 'Strained Livelihoods: Conditions of Pastoralist and Farming Communities in Southern Kurdufan, Sudan: Persistent Contentions and Emerging Challenges for a Better Future', discussion item presented to the Cairo Papers Symposium on Agrarian Transformation in the Arab World.

Deng, Francis M. (1995). *War of Visions: Conflict of Identities in the Sudan*, Washington, DC, Brookings Institution.

Galal el-Din el-Tayeb (ed.) (2006). *Land Issues and Peace in Sudan*, Khartoum: Publications of the Sudanese Environment Conservation Society.

Obeid Hag Ali (2005). *Anglo-American Studies of Tribal Law: Concepts and Methods*, Sudan: Gezira Printing and Publishing Company.

6
Political Violence in the Horn of Africa: A Framework for Analysis

Seifudein Adem

INTRODUCTION

Two decades ago two events with potentially far-reaching implications took place in the Horn of Africa. In 1991 Eritrea successfully seceded from Ethiopia – the first such case in post-colonial Africa. Also in 1991 the Somali Republic, which was created in 1960, split into Somaliland (a former British colony) and Somalia (a former Italian colony). International institutions played varying roles in the birth of these states and in the aftermath, reflecting wider changes in the world as well as in the domestic structures of these societies. What is also intriguing is that Somaliland seceded from a greater Somalia to which it had originally consented, but Eritrea seceded from a union with Ethiopia which had been imposed on it. In the case of the Somali Republic, the union of the former British and former Italian Somaliland was an attempt to reject European colonial boundaries. In the case of Eritrea, its annexation to Ethiopia had been an attempt to substitute European colonial boundaries with indigenous imperial expansionism. Despite lack of external sovereignty Somaliland has survived for more than a decade. Challenging the Westphalian notion, the experience of Somaliland so far suggests a state can indeed survive without external recognition. On the other hand, the state of Eritrea – a relatively more culturally pluralistic society than Somalia – won recognition from the international community from its birth, including from Ethiopia, of which it was a part. Ethnic tensions continue to simmer in the post-EPRDF Ethiopia. This chapter reviews theories of state formation and state disintegration and examines their relevance to the Horn of Africa, with a special focus on Ethiopia.

There is a broad consensus that the proliferation of communal movements[1] that challenged state authority in recent years can be explained in terms of the reawakening or rekindling of ethnic and national sentiments which had hitherto been smothered by Cold War politics. At various levels of generalizations, different explanations have been advanced to make sense of the circumstances that foster or inhibit these movements. One theory maintains that the process of economic modernization leads to a division of labour which has the potential to replace organically integrated society with mechanically integrated society.[2] Ethnic identification, having been rendered dysfunctional, will therefore disappear. For the proponents of the opposing view, modernization, rather than resulting in a new form of integration, increases ethnic group interaction which may heighten conflict because as ascriptive ties lose their political relevance, unintegrated citizens, looking for an anchor in a sea of change, will cling to an increasingly anachronistic ethnic identity, which bursts onto the scene and then withdraws as the process of structural differentiation moves towards a reintegrated society.[3]

The experience of the Horn of Africa does not vindicate the universality of either of these arguments. Underlying both theories is the assumption that ethnic or cultural heterogeneity or dualism is a *sine qua non* of ethnic conflict.[4] It is argued here that cultural homogeneity does not guarantee social peace. This view, while less popular, has a long pedigree.[5] This does not mean that 'modernization' arguments are irrelevant to the analyses of state disintegration. What it does mean is that the plausibility of the arguments varies with the individual cases and that a more useful theory should be able, or at least aspire, to account for the phenomena more widely.

At a lower level of abstraction, some analysts have focused on what triggers violent communal conflicts and singled out different sets of factors that purportedly account for the eruption of intra-state violence. Richard Shultz identified four major characteristics of groups involved in ethnic conflicts: the groups are part of a severely divided society; they see their differences from other ethnic groups as irreconcilable; ethnicity is a principal form of identification; and, in the extreme form, such groups are subject to the manipulation of the elite.[6] de Samarasinghe also pointed out that, in general, the dynamics of ethnic conflicts suggest that given the appropriate conditions, such as a culturally homogeneous group, a 'homeland', a common set of grievances, political leadership and political mobilization, a movement with modest aims that do not extend beyond devolution of power within the existing state can easily evolve into a full-blown secessionist movement.[7] Druckman similarly observed that extreme attachment to ethnic, religious, national or clan identities leads to brutal acts against those perceived to be the enemy.[8]

This chapter seeks, among other things, to formulate a broad explanation of state disintegration which is based on both positivist – though not in the more meta-theoretically rigid and unimaginative sense – and postmodernist epistemological foundations.[9] However, the aim is not to advance a causal explanation of state formation and state disintegration but to take the first step towards that end by identifying what appear to be the components of this phenomenon and teasing out the underlying patterns that link them. Once such a framework is in place, I hope that a causal relationship among the variables can be sought and the dynamics of state disintegration elaborated more easily. This should ultimately pave the way for ascertaining empirically the correspondence between the derivatives of the theory and the realities on the ground.

ELEMENTS OF STATE DISINTEGRATION

What is state disintegration? The term is used here in the most basic sense interchangeably with the term state failure to denote a situation in which a central government's power to discharge its 'crucial' functions is progressively eroded or curtailed as a result of revolutionary wars, ethnic wars, genocides or politicides and/or adverse or disruptive regime changes.[10] These crucial functions include:

> Sovereign control of a territory; sovereign supervision (though not necessarily ownership) of the nation's resources; effective and rational revenue extraction from people, goods and services; the capacity to build and maintain an adequate national infrastructure (roads, postal services, telephone systems, railways and the like); the capacity to render such basic services as sanitation, education, housing, and health care; and the capacity for governance and the maintenance of law and order.[11]

The ultimate source of communal conflicts, which in many cases lead to state disintegration and emerge under a variety of circumstances and take various forms,[12] can perhaps be reduced *to the crises of citizenship and legitimacy*.[13] When these crises reach an acute level they lead to the total collapse of the institution of state. Demonstrating the processes and stages through which the transformation of the crises takes place is the objective of this chapter. But first it is appropriate to clarify the building blocks of our hypothesis – its key concepts.

A citizen is defined here as a member of a political community, entitled to whatever prerogatives and encumbered with whatever responsibilities are attached to membership.[14] As citizenship is such an expression of membership in a community, its real meaning has varied widely depending on the community and the historical period.[15] One of the basic questions which arises, therefore, is whether we can refer in the same way and across societies to citizenship as the bonds that bind individuals into a political community. The answer is a qualified yes. Although it had not been in vogue at the time, J. P. Nettl argued decades ago that for analytic reasons statehood should be viewed as a quantitative variable according to which one can speak of a political entity as having more or fewer qualities of statehood.[16] In this sense, it may be truer to refer to both the principle and the real meaning of citizenship as similarly more or less developed. That is to say, the condition of citizenship ought to be judged by the degree to which its constituent parts are present.[17] But it would be incorrect to regard the notion of citizenship as totally irrelevant to or absent from the minds of the 'peripheral' people. Citizenship implies full status in a political community and it is developed to the extent that all sections of the population subject to a shared authority have political rights in common, including the right to participate in political life.[18]

Another key concept to which our leading argument in this chapter anchors itself is legitimacy.[19] In the Weberian tradition, power relations are legitimate when those involved in them, the subordinate as well as the dominant, believe them to be so.[20] David Beetham provides an alternative definition: 'for power to be legitimate, three conditions are required: its conformity to established rules; the justifiability of the rules by reference to shared beliefs; the express consent of the subordinate, or the most significant among them, to the particular relations of power.'[21] The Weberian definition is used here despite the criticism levelled at it by some,[22] rather than Beetham's, since the former is as adequate as and yet more parsimonious than the latter and is therefore more useful for approaching the issue of legitimacy across historical societies.

Less abstractly, there are two interrelated ways by which legitimacy of a government can be better evaluated and understood.[23] One is by considering how a government came into being or the mechanism through which the political leaders assumed power. In this sense, governments which assume power through constitutional, legal means are legitimate and those which do so otherwise are illegitimate. Legitimacy can also be judged on the basis of the policy outputs of those who govern. As Scharr notes, the regime or the leaders provide the stimuli, first in the form of policies improving citizens' welfare and then in the form of symbolic materials which function as secondary reinforcements, and the followers respond by assuming either a favourable or unfavourable attitude towards the simulators.[24] In short, the central issues involved in political outputs pertain to the questions of what values will be allocated, who will benefit from them and who will be burdened by the particular configuration of value allocations.[25]

Judging the legitimacy of a ruling group by its policy output assumes greater significance especially in 'post-colonial states' where government administration is generally less concerned with public goods and where in both theory and practice the state is 'a source of power, prestige, and enrichment for those clever or fortunate enough to control and staff it'.[26] There is also growing evidence that a trend is emerging in which people increasingly judge the legitimacy of their leaders on the basis of policy outputs instead of solely on the mechanism by which political leaders assume power.[27]

This chapter postulates that there is an essential link between the crises of citizenship and legitimacy on the one hand, and on the other the onset of state disintegration which, in some cases, could lead to state failure and eventual collapse. What are the alternative mechanisms by which the mutation of peaceful communal movements into state disintegration can be forestalled and, if conflicts nevertheless erupt, regulated? The tentative answers to these questions will be given towards the end of the chapter, but first it is helpful to lay down the framework for analysing the distinct stages and the intricate processes that link the twin crises of citizenship and legitimacy on the one hand, and the phenomenon of state disintegration on the other.

PROCESS ANALYSIS OF STATE DISINTEGRATION

The origin of communal conflicts can be traced as far back as the time of the Assyrians, around 610 BC, when a coalition of Babylonians, Medes and Chaldeans rose in rebellion against Sardanapalus to end Assyrian rule.[28] For analytical and practical purposes, however, the dialectical process of state disintegration can be taken to begin when a state comes into being in national or imperial form. Generally, a state comes into being through institution or acquisition. Nettl characterized the two processes as implosion and explosion, respectively representing a particularization or narrowing of sovereignty into ethnically homogeneous or, at least, ethnically defined areas, and an extension of central authority across ethnic boundaries and particularly hitherto sovereign communities.[29]

More than how states are created, however, it is how they are ruled, or more precisely how their rule is perceived by those who are ruled, which conditions the emergence of communal movements. Almost invariably, states that came into being as a result of imposition from above or outside are multi-communal or have political boundaries that do not coincide with their cultural boundaries. This implies two things. First, free institutions are almost impossible to mould under these circumstances.[30] This difficulty also hampers the emergence and consolidation of legal and peaceful ways of airing dissenting views. Second, the authority of the state is likely to be perceived, or misperceived, as exclusive, alien, arbitrary or a combination of some or all of these.[31] In spite of this, or because of it, political leaders attempt to promote nationalism[32] with the declared goal of forging a nation coterminous with the state. It should be mentioned in passing that the meanings attached to nationalism in much scholarship and most political discourse reveal more about the users of the term than about the phenomenon.[33] This definitional problem is compounded by the paucity of the theory of nationalism.[34]

In any case, civic nationalism is an early variety based on a set of abstract principles of civic responsibility; and ethnic nationalism is a form of nationalism based on ethnic, and occasionally religious, identity. The first form is more inclusive, that is citizenship is theoretically open to anyone who can meet the requirements of civic duty. In states that promote the second variant of nationalism, citizenship cannot be acquired without the appropriate ethnic or religious stamp.[35] With few exceptions, civic nationalism is the officially preferred nationalism promoted by the ruling elite.

It is thus fair to assume that at least at the level of rhetoric virtually all states promote civic nationalism. That is probably why most communal groups seem to judge the legitimacy of the authority of their governments not against what they say but against what they do or are perceived to do. Once ethnic rather than civic nationalism is believed to be dominant in the face of an imagined or real threat emanating from ethnic or religious self-centredness of certain groups, political discontent will emerge. When that discontent becomes politicized, the beneficiaries of the governmental policy outputs begin to resent the reaction of the marginalized groups.

Correspondingly, the marginalized feel relegated to second-class citizen status, while at the same time being maligned as less than patriotic by the former. At this stage, a sense of relative deprivation begins to develop. The political scientist Ted Robert Gurr formulated the notion of relative deprivation and defined it as 'actors' perception of discrepancy between their own *value expectations* and their environment's apparent *value capability*'.[36] Hah and Martin's less abstract definition of the level of relative deprivation is also based on this conception: it represents the balance between the goods and conditions of life to which people believe they are rightfully entitled and the goods and conditions they think they are capable of acquiring or keeping, given the means available to them.[37]

However, for the sense of relative deprivation to emerge the situation need not necessarily and objectively be bad in relative or absolute terms. Many advocates of regional autonomy, observed Susan Olzak, indulge in the rhetoric of economic and/or political subjugation, even in regions that are enjoying an economic boom.[38] Neither the presence nor the absence of objective inequality leads to the corresponding appearance or disappearance of a sense of relative deprivation and political discontent. What is more crucial at this stage is how the situation is widely perceived. As Hah and Martin underscore, inequality engenders dysfunctional inputs to the political system only to the extent that they cause value expectations to outpace value capabilities. In this case, the elite can play a crucial role in the construction of images and their portrayal to the followers as empirical realities.[39] Once political discontent and a widespread sense of relative deprivation are in place, together with mutual distrust and wariness among different groups of 'citizens', we can speak of a state being confronted by the *crises of legitimacy and citizenship*.[40]

After these crises are initiated, the next stage comes to the fore when the marginalized communal groups begin to load the political system with something resembling what Gabriel Almond has, in a different context, called *dysfunctional inputs* that cause changes in the capabilities of a political system, in the conversion patterns and structures, and in the socialization and recruitment functions.[41] The demands of communal movements (hereafter referred to as dysfunctional inputs, or more simply inputs) may vary with respect to the direction in which they flow, as well as their quantity, substance or content, intensity, source and number of kinds affecting the system at any given point. Also relevant to our analysis is the nature of the groups who advance these inputs. Gurr identified the following broad categories of groups involved in significant conflicts with the state: nations without a state; communal contenders for state power; militant sects; peoples of the frontiers; and ethno-classes. The orientation of these groups towards the state would be one, or a combination, of the following: a demand for recognition of the cultural distinctiveness of the group; reform of some aspects of the political system; fair representation at the centre; and attainment of independent statehood. These orientations are categorized again under the more generic terms control, access, accommodation and exit.[42] It is true, however, that a group's orientation towards the state and the nature of its demands may, and in most cases will, change over time. It is thus important to elaborate the nature and sources of these processes.

The environment within which they are situated and operate profoundly affects the behaviour of states and communal movements. These contextual factors can be placed under the general rubric of the structural attributes of the international system. They include internationally and regionally recognized rules and norms, such as those relating to the formation and recognition of states, non-intervention in the internal affairs of other states and the inviolability of their national borders. The principle of self-determination also falls within this category.

The principle of non-intervention in the internal affairs of a sovereign state, which is laid down in the United Nations Charter, is reflected in the legal documents of other regional organizations. Clearly, this principle works against communal movements seeking to secede from an existing state. It should also be noted that although in theory this principle applies equally to both sides engaged in an internal conflict, the government is only marginally affected, if at all, in its relations with other sovereign states.

Other structural factors or attributes of the international system which have had significant bearings on the origin, development and outcome of communal movements include colonialism, Cold War politics, the end of the Cold War and what has come to be known as the global war on terror.[43] Colonialism played a significant role in setting the stage for the crises of legitimacy and citizenship in many 'post-colonial' states[44] through the arbitrary process by which it created these states.

It is clear that the disjuncture between state boundaries and those of ethnic groups laid the foundations for the crises of legitimacy and citizenship that engulfed many post-colonial African states. It is also the case that these structural problems made it difficult to introduce genuinely representative institutions. Generations ago John Stuart Mill noted that it is in general a necessary condition for free institutions that the boundaries of governments should coincide in the main with those of nationalities.[45] The fact that state-making processes brought together peoples who have nothing in common except, perhaps, the fact that they had been enemies in the past provided fertile soil for a sense of relative deprivation to emerge and flourish.[46] Yet despite the widespread awareness of the arbitrariness of colonial borders, contemporary leaders of these states did almost nothing to change the territorial status quo. Instead, they institutionalized it by creating norms that upheld the principle of the inviolability of the existing borders.

In general, the consequences of the prevailing structural attributes can be systematically analysed by employing George Modelski's classificatory schema of the structure of a political system, which is divided into two in the case of internal war, as those of authority, solidarity, culture and resources.[47] An authority structure includes the institutions and peoples engaged in authoritative decision-making, their skills as well as the nature of the decisions made. This structure is important in that for a sense of relative deprivation to emerge there should exist among a collectivity a belief that its members are unjustifiably disadvantaged. The elite in this regard play a crucial role in articulating this 'disadvantage' or, if it does not exist, in inventing it. A sense of being disadvantaged is paramount, at least in the initial stage of a communal movement. It is perhaps no coincidence that most communal movements make more of the fact that they are or were the victims of inequality and discrimination than they do of any claim that their group represents an embryonic nation.[48]

The structure of solidarity, on the other hand, does not coincide with political boundaries. As a rule, it is either larger or smaller than the latter and is very fluid in that the extent of its boundaries depends on the strength of the pressures from the other structures. As Alexis Heraclides elaborates:

> The primary targets of the secessionist [and also of the central government's] activities for assistance include those that are considered to be within the 'solidarity universe' because of ethnic or national identity, religion, ideology, language, culture, race or history. Then there are those who are seen as likely supporters because they are well known historical enemies of the opponent group.[49]

The structures of culture and communication encompass the language and religion, as well as the self-image of the actors. This structure is also instrumental in rallying support and its scope is influenced by, and sometimes parallel to, the structure of solidarity. Last but not least, a political system has a resource structure that also extends beyond its political boundaries. This includes domestic resources, international alliances, access to military and economic aid, and foreign bases of operations. These structures reinforce one another and are thus interdependent. For instance, the availability of a foreign base (element of resource structure) may depend on empathy based on religion and ideology (elements of structure of culture). Similarly, the scope of the structure of solidarity will significantly depend on the skill and styles of the decision-makers (aspects of authority structure).

Structural factors influence not only the effects of communal movements on the political system and their outcomes but also their defining features. What ultimate form such movements take – whether a group's orientation towards the state will be exit, control, access or accommodation – depends on a host of variables, including whether or not economic, political and ideological means are available (part of resource structure) and on whether or not the communal group has compatriots on the other side of the border and can get moral and material support from outside (aspects of solidarity structure).

The structural attributes of the international system play a crucial role, as indicated above, in determining and/or regulating involvement by external actors in state disintegration. The motive of outsiders in intervening in a domestic conflict can be divided into an instrumental and an affective type:

> Instrumental motives include international political (including general strategic) considerations, short-term and long-term economic motives, and domestic political reasons including fear of demonstration effects and short-term military gain. Affective involvement may be for reasons of justice humanitarian considerations, ethnic, religious, racial or ideological affinity or personal friendships between top protagonists.[50]

In a nutshell, the normative structure of the international system influences outcomes of the confrontations between communal movements and the state in one of the following ways: diffusion and encouragement, isolation and suppression, or reconciliation.[51]

States must enjoy a measure of legitimacy in order to survive.[52] In dealing with challenges to their legitimacy, the governing elite must and will, therefore, react in a variety of ways. Gabriel Almond gives three possible modes of reaction: adaptive, rejective and substitutive.[53] What he classifies as 'adaptive' and 'rejective' patterns of elite behaviour respectively correspond to Heraclides' policies of 'acceptance' and policies of 'denial':

> Denial includes strategies such as removal or elimination (extermination, population transfer, expulsion), coercion (subjugation, state terrorism), domination within a framework of institutionalized cultural divisions, assimilation as well as individualization of the problem by way of non-discrimination and human rights. Acceptance includes the following strategies: integration in the sense of equal and joint contribution by both groups involved to a new superordinate nation and culture; minority protection and safeguards, consociational democracy in a unitary system; federalism or extended autonomy, very loose federation akin to confederation, redrawing of boundaries with a neighboring country (in case of irredentism); and territorial partition.[54]

It is generally not difficult to identify the reactive pattern the elite is following. In less clear-cut cases, one might consider looking at whether what Stephen van Evera has called the three principal varieties of chauvinist myth-making are present. They are self-glorifying, self-whitewashing and other-maligning.[55] In most cases, these types of myth-making exhibit features of a rejective pattern of elite reaction to inputs considered dysfunctional. In other cases, they constitute the rejective pattern itself. Theodor Hanf, on the other hand, distinguishes five possible forms of reactive pattern: partition, domination, assimilation, consociation and political syncretism.[56]

There is a good deal of overlap between the different sets of reactive patterns listed above, but Almond's parsimonious classification appears to be preferable for the purpose of analysing the phenomena of state disintegration. In general, therefore, patterns of reaction of the elites to inputs considered dysfunctional can be identified by answering the following questions: Does the elite yield or adapt to the dysfunctional demands and adjust its policies accordingly? Does it ignore or reject the demands and adopt a policy of indifference? Or does it substitute, that is to say does it respond positively but not necessarily in a way communal movements had sought? As indicated above, the way in which the elite chooses to react to an input considered dysfunctional is also mediated by the structural attributes of the system, as well by as the nature of the inputs itself.

There seems to be no magic formula according to which one can identify a particular reactive pattern as being the most 'rational', for the effects of any form of reaction depend in large part on the depth of the crises of legitimacy or citizenship, as well as the nature of grievances they are intended to address. It needs to be stressed, however, that it is the interplay between the changing nature of the communal demands, the structural attributes of the system or sub-system and the reactive patterns of the elite that will ultimately determine whether the fate of the state will be consolidation or disintegration, or whether order or anarchy will prevail. If the latter is the case, it is possible that the political unit will fall into a Hobbesian state of nature, after which it may well be re-invented. The alternative scenario is a consolidated state. In either case, at this stage the dialectical process of state formation and state disintegration will have come full circle. And yet these phenomena should not be thought of as a process predestined to reach a final, predetermined goal, but instead as an ongoing, continuous and extremely uneven process of formation, consolidation and failure and, in some cases, a total disintegration of state.

CONCLUSION

Over the years a plethora of measures has been suggested as a possible cure for the problem of state failure and state disintegration. At the risk of oversimplification,[57] it is worth noting that realist, liberal, functionalist and legalist schools respectively approximate to the broader paradigmatic orientations of the putative panaceas.[58] For dealing with the phenomenon of state disintegration, one school of realism suggests 'strategies that would involve significant changes in international legal and diplomatic practices'.[59] This school considers unquestioned support for the principle of the inviolability of existing borders to be the major cause of the problem: 'if secession was a viable threat, as it had been during the pre-colonial period, politicians would have a profound incentive to reach accommodation with disaffected populations, especially those that were spatially defined, lest they threaten to leave the nation-state.'[60] For realism the ultimate criteria for recognizing a given communal group as a state ought to be based on who is actually providing order.

Liberals also make a case for supporting secessionist causes, but for a different reason: '[i]n particular cases, liberal values may be served by those who seek to break up multinational states rather than by those who seek to preserve them.'[61] Neo-functionalists and legalists side with realists and liberals in identifying the discrepancy between the juridical and the empirical attributes of statehood as constituting the core of the crises; and they uphold the view that most of today's weak states, those created by the colonialists and inaugurated on the day of independence, have proved incapable of coping with the economic, political and security demands of the modern era, and that the way to overcome this problem is to integrate them into regional (i.e. continental) or sub-regional entities.[62] Where the two schools diverge from realism is in the constitutional or peaceful means they propose: 'it is desirable for a group of these states to band together into an economic community that will also be a security community and, eventually, a political community with sovereign rights.'[63]

Which of these suggestions makes more sense in theory and in practice? It seems likely that solutions based on force or on the realist criterion of who is actually controlling the larger territory and providing order entail deeper moral and practical problems. Morally, the solution is unacceptable to many simply because it is based on the iniquitous idea of 'might makes right'. Let us also remind ourselves that it is not always easy to determine who is effectively providing order, when and where.[64] Realist solutions also make the states more vulnerable to what is called the domino theory of secession *in extremis* in which 'if a society had a right to proclaim its will and secede from the major unit, every district, every town, every village, every farmstead could declare itself independent'.[65]

It has been pointed out above that realism offers a solution that essentially boils down to a proposal for the granting of international recognition to whoever is providing political order over a territory with a significant size and population. Such a prescription is logically sound and persuasive. In practice, however, it raises more problems than it solves and fails to address the problem of legitimacy and citizenship discussed above. The alleged solution can be conceived as the outcome of a zero-sum game. In effect, order may not provide an answer to all the issues central to the emergence of communal movements which challenge the state. As the French philosopher Jean-Jacques Rousseau aptly asked very long ago, 'Life is tranquil in jail cells, too. Is that reason enough to like them?' This same question seems to underlie the beliefs of millions of people who take up arms to challenge the central authority.

The idea that political boundaries should be revised so that, sub-regionally, communities will replace the current arrangement based on nation states is excellent and attractive. This functionalist prescription, which is based on the theoretical supposition that behaviours can be explained in terms of their effects, appears to have identified one of the sources of the chronic crises that have afflicted many states as being the arbitrary, and sometimes forceful, incorporation of territories and peoples with nothing in common. But when it comes to the mechanisms of implementing such a proposal, several problems are likely to arise, again owing to the processes by which these states were created and are maintained. In other words, for the legalist-functionalist solution to work, in addition to a strong political will towards this end, the political economy of the states ought to be such that it is able to sustain regional integration. But today that does not seem to hold true in many cases.

It has also been argued that the structural attributes of the international system play a crucial role in influencing the outcome of the crises of legitimacy and citizenship which take the form of a challenge to a state. The normative framework of the international system does not, however, play a primary role in the inception of the crises. Therefore, while recognizing the fact that normative attributes of the international system do affect the transformation of communal movements over time, it is neither productive nor prudent to direct the main focus on the external environment in dealing with the issue.

Moreover, even if the evidence suggests that external factors play a more crucial role than domestic factors in regard to a given problem, curative measures should be more inward-looking since it is easier to influence domestic political systems than the former, which include international legal and diplomatic practices. Again, even if international rules and norms could be '(re)constructed', given the political will of a large number of states (or at least the most powerful among them), the task would prove to be complex and time-consuming. Outward-looking measures are also not worthwhile since, as indicated above, the problem can be tackled more effectively and directly if the cure is sought from within the political system in the same way as an effective vaccine to a disease is developed from the vector.

NOTES

1. A communal movement is a collectivity of people who define themselves on the basis of ethnicity, religion, region or other social attributes and are engaged in some form of political activity.
2. The terms 'mechanical society' and 'organic society' are used here in the same sense as Kenneth Waltz (2008: 39) used them in a different context. According to Waltz, a mechanical society rests on the similarity of the units that compose it; an organic society is based on their differences. In other words, mechanical societies are loosely linked through the resemblance of their members; organic societies become closely integrated through the differences of their members.
3. In this regard, one analyst observed: 'the differences in the two articulations at least partly arise out of the differing focus on the unit of analysis. If the modernists focus on the individual and conceive collectivity as an aggregation, the primordialists concentrate on collectivities and take an organic view of society' (Oommen 1997: 10). For a broadly similar view, see Tilly (1997: 499). A detailed discussion can be found in Hah and Martin (1975) and Neuman (1991). For a more comprehensive classification, see Heraclides (1991).
4. An example of a work that saw ethnic homogeneity and political stability as two sides of the same coin, see Laitin and Samatar (1987). For a *post facto* argument that ethnic homogeneity may be a necessary condition but not a sufficient one, see McFerson (1995). Perhaps it should be pointed out with the exception of Iceland, Metropolitan Portugal, Norway and one or two other countries, the other 170 more or less sovereign countries in the world are ethnically heterogeneous (Ra'anan 1991: 4).
5. More than two centuries ago, the philosopher John Stuart Mill observed: 'Switzerland has a strong sentiment of nationality, though the Cantons are of different races, different languages and different religions. Sicily has, throughout history, felt itself quite distinct in nationality from Naples, notwithstanding identity of religion, almost identity of language, and a considerable amount of common historical antecedent.' For Mill, a portion of mankind may be said to constitute a nationality if they are united by common sympathies which do not exist between them and any other, which make them cooperate with each other more willingly than with other people, desire to live under the same government and desire that it should be government by themselves, exclusively (Dahbour and Ishay 1995: 98).
6. Shultz (1995: 77–8).
7. Samarasinghe (1990: 2).
8. Druckman (1994: 44).
9. Positivism focuses on quantification and empirical relationships between phenomena whereas postmodernism underscores the role of rhetoric in constructing both power relations and bodies of language. For a concise elaboration of postmodernism in relation to other schools in international relations, see Porter (1994: 105–27). On positivism, Popper (1968: 34) had this to say: 'The older positivists wished to admit, as scientific or legitimate, only those concepts (or notions or ideas which were, as they put it, "derived from experience"; those concepts, i.e., which they believed to be logically reducible to elements of sense experience.'
10. This definition is my adaptation of categories of control cases for analysing state failures given in Ted Gurr et al. (1999: 50); and Mazrui (1994: 28).

11. Mazrui (1994: 28).
12. For a summary of the different forms ethnic and other movements can take, see Jalali and Lipset (1992: 586).
13. This hypothesis is arrived at through a combination of deductive and inductive reasoning. For a clear discussion of the distinctions between the two, see Popper (1968).
14. See Walzer (1995: 10); and Warner (1995: 45–7).
15. In the Aristotelian understanding of citizenship, the notion signifies a person who both rules and is ruled. It excludes slaves and women. In a sense, the Aristotelian understanding was thus political. Five centuries later, the Roman understanding of the concept evolved in which the legal aspect was emphasized: 'the status of a citizen came to denote membership in a community of shared or common law, which may or may not be identical with a territorial community' (Pocock 1995: 29–52). There are crucial differences in the meanings attached to citizenship even in liberal democracies. For a well-documented and concisely comparative analysis of the different conceptions of citizenship in four liberal democracies, see Safran (1997: 313–15).
16. Nettl (1968: 561). For this reason, the notion of the state is unfitting and its use needs reconsideration. For such reconsiderations, Sorensen's (1998: 256–64) recent typology of contemporary states into post-colonial, Westphalian and postmodern is an excellent starting point.
17. Warner (1995: 45–7) separates these elements into three: civil, political and legal. 'The civil element of citizenship is a positive form which, on the basis of equality, people can make certain claims against each other and/or against the government. The political element is that which allows an individual to participate in the decision of the government or to be a member of that government. Both the political and civil elements are part of what could be called the 'objective' elements of citizenship. In terms of political theory, it could be argued that the objective political and civil elements are part of the vertical contract between citizens and a government. The social element of citizenship is the horizontal contract in society, the subjective elements in citizenship.' In Europe, as elsewhere, the three elements of citizenship did not emerge simultaneously. According to Marshall (quoted in Warner 1995: 49), civil rights belong to the formative period of the eighteenth century, political rights to the nineteenth century and social rights to the twentieth century.
18. Kornhauser (1964: 151).
19. State legitimacy in the eyes of its citizens should be distinguished from international legitimacy and in this chapter by legitimacy the former is meant, which denotes 'the capacity of the system to engender and maintain the belief that the existing political institutions are the most appropriate ones for society' (Scharr 1984). The latter is referred to as international recognition, or simply recognition. For a discussion of the distinction between the two, see Jackson and Roseberg (1982: 7).
20. Quoted in Beetham (1991: 6). Janos's (1964: 132) definition roughly resembles Weber's. For Janos legitimacy is the ability to ensure compliance short of coercion. It is a psychological relationship between masses and elites, involving acceptance by the masses of a claim by an elite to act in the name of the community.
21. Beetham (1991: 19).

22. At one point, Beetham (ibid.: 23–5) refers to Weber's theory of legitimacy as 'one of the blindest of blind alleys in the history of social science'.
23. For a discussion of the different dimensions of legitimacy and the problems associated with them, see Beetham (ibid.: 3–41).
24. Scharr (1984: 109). The notion of popular reaction to stimulators is consistent with James Rosenau's idea of 'skill revolution' as a result of which individuals tend to judge the legitimacy of their rulers on the basis of the policy outputs rather than through the mere criterion of the mechanism by which leaders assume office. 'Historically,' declared Rosenau and Durfee (1995: 76), 'the authority structures have been founded on traditional criteria of legitimacy derived from constitutional and legal sources . . . the sources have [now] shifted from traditional to performance criteria of legitimacy.'
25. Danziger (1991: 374).
26. Sorensen (1997: 260).
27. Rothchild and Groth (1995: 78). For some thoughts about how legitimacy is judged in the Horn of Africa, see Bricker and Letherbee (1994: 1).
28. See, Flexner and Flexner (2000: 6).
29. Nettl (1968: 590–1). For a concise discussion of the case of the Horn of Africa in this respect, see Markakis (1990).
30. This representation is from Mill. See Dahbour and Ishay (1995: 590–1).
31. Exclusive authority is authority that is believed to be inaccessible to much of the population, alien authority is authority that is believed to be foreign rather than indigenous, especially authority imposed from without and displaying symbols of an alien culture; arbitrary authority is authority that is believed to be capricious and irresponsible. For discussions, see Kornhauser (1964: 134).
32. A cautionary note is in order regarding the thorny concept of 'nationalism'. Hah and Martin (1975: 360) define nationalism as 'consisting of organizationally heightened and articulated group demands, directed toward securing control of the distributive system in a society'. The usefulness of this definition is its amenability to operationalization. But a stricter application will lead one to believe that a trade union movement or an army revolt could be considered as constituting a nationalist movement. In fact, this is not necessarily the case. Such a definition diminishes the utility of the concept for our purpose. Furthermore, we avoid use of the term nationalism as much as possible because when the existence of a fully developed state itself is questionable, it does not make sense to talk about nationalism. As Gellner (1994: 4) notes, '[t]he existence of politically centralized units, and of a moral-political climate in which such centralized units are taken for granted and are treated as normative, is a necessary though by no means a sufficient condition for nationalism.'
33. See Motyl (1991: 3). For a brief review of the different views on the origin, essence and manifestations of nationalism, see Kellas (1991: 34–50).
34. According to Stokes (1978: 150), one reason for the thinness of a theory of nationalism, despite the volume of literature on the subject, is the fact that until recently most of its analysts have been historians, who tend to be more interested in description than explanation.
35. See Shultz (1995: 79). Kupchan's (1995: 1) typology of nationalism into civic and ethnic follows similar lines. For him, ethnic nationalism defines nationhood in terms of lineage. Civic nationalism defines nationhood in terms of citizenship and political participation and favours social cohesion and political equality in ethnically heterogeneous political communities. Similarly, Rothchild and Groth

(1995: 69–82) identify the following as the two principles of what they called ethnonationalism: 'the exclusiveness of the national group's definition based upon particular criteria; and the maintenance of internal cohesion and loyalty to the group on the basis of perceived threats from outside its confines.'

36. Gurr (1968: 245–8).
37. Hah and Martin (1975: 380).
38. Olzak (1998: 1).
39. Hah and Martin (1975: 380). For a good review and analysis of this subject, see Fearon and Laitin (2000: 845–77).
40. For the specific applicability of this general hypothesis to the situation in the Horn of Africa and relevant discussion see, for instance, John Markakis (1990) and the review of Markakis's book *Resource Conflict in the Horn of Africa* (1998) in *African Affairs* vol. 97, no. 389, October 1998.
41. Almond (1986: 41–72).
42. Gurr (1980: 191–209). For a different classification, see Olzak (1998: 192–7). For discussions on this issue directly relevant to the Horn of Africa, see Laitin and Samatar (1987); Bariagaber (1998); Adam (1995); Gebre Kidan (1995); Cliffe (1989: 143), Trevaskis (1960: 11); *Eritrea and Tigray*, Minority Rights Group Report (1983: 18).
43. For the experience in the Horn of Africa in this respect, see Schraeder (1992), Ottoway (1982), Keller (1985) Krause (1984), Makinda (1987), Habte Selassie (1980) and Woodward (2006) among others.
44. As Samatar (1997: 695) relates this explanation to the situation in Somalia, 'unlike the old pre-colonial order in which the elders did not control either a coercive machine or economic power over the community, the imposition of colonialism on Somalia removed the major social means of restraining those in positions of power.'
45. Mill (1861), in Dahbour and Ishay (1991: 101).
46. As Rothchild and Groth (1995) note: 'the problem of psychological displacement of deprivation, frustration and uncertainty is likely to be most acute among the so called divided nationalities. For those groups classified as majoritarian within a particular area, the minority entities are easily identifiable, visible, and tangible targets for this displacement. The psychologically "helpful" enemy does not have to be invented. He is there for all to see.'
47. Modelski (1961: 124).
48. Heraclides (1991: 71).
49. Ibid.: 39.
50. Ibid.: 152.
51. Modelski (1961: 19).
52. After studying the nature of the early African states, Donald Kurtz (1981: 177) concluded that the legitimacy of the authority structures of early states was essential for their survival and their legitimation is an exorable and integral part of the process of early state development; states have to attain legitimacy if they are to rule by means other than naked force and long survive the tests of history.
53. Almond (1986: 68–9).
54. Hericlides (1991:11).
55. Evera (1995: 150–1).
56. Hanf (1991: 40–3).

57. For a different classification of IR theories with regard to their positions on the issue of self-determination, see Freeman (1999: 335–70).

58. It should be clear that the classification of each idea into one or another school in International Relations is made solely on the basis of the judgement of this writer and may be at variance with others' classification. For example, Freeman's (1999: 365) description of what a realist theory of self-determination is, is significantly different from mine. For Freeman, such theories have two properties: (1) they endorse only those conceptions of the right to national self-determination that could be accepted by the power-holders (particularly, states) in the contemporary world; and (2) they accord priority to the stability of the existing state system. For a detailed discussion of the taxonomy, see Freeman (1999: 355–70); for a cogent analysis of this theme from a world systems perspective, see Olzak (1998: 187–217).

59. Herbst (1997: 120).

60. Ibid.

61. Lind (1994: 87–112).

62. Mukisa (1997: 24). Riggs (1998) elaborates another reason why secession does not provide an answer to the problem of divided societies: 'ethnic nationalism prevails among marginalized communities in modern states whose members reject citizenship and demand sovereignty. They normally have a territorial base or "homeland" which, in fact or fantasy can anchor the state they wish to establish by liberation or secession. However, population mobility has led to a wide-spread mingling of peoples, not only in cities but also in rural areas, seriously hampering efforts to carve independent states out of the enclaves which ethnonational movements claim for themselves.'

63. Mukisa (1997: 24).

64. In addition to geographical fluidity of the territorial space, in temporal terms too the issue is not as clear-cut as it appears at first glance. In the case of Algeria, for example, there are claims 'that certain suburbs of Algerian cities are under the control of the authorities during the day and the control of Islamic militants at night' (Mazrui 1994: 28).

65. Osterud (1997: 70); L. C. Buchheit (in Freeman 1998: 360) refers to this notion as the problem of 'indefinite divisibility'.

REFERENCES

Adam, H. M. (1995). 'Islam and Politics in Somalia', *Journal of Islamic Studies*, vol. 6, no. 2: 189–211.

Almond, G. (1986). 'A Developmental Approach to Political Systems', in I. Kabashima and W. Lynn (eds.), *Political System and Change*, Princeton, NJ: Princeton University Press.

Anderson, B. (1991). *Imagined Communities: Reflections on the Origin and Spread of Nationalism*, London and New York: Verso.

Arfi, B. (1998). 'State Collapse in a New Theoretical Framework: The Case of Yugoslavia', *International Journal of Sociology*, vol. 28, no. 3: 15–42.

Bariagaber, A. (1998). 'The Politics of Cultural Pluralism in Ethiopia and Eritrea: Trajectories of Ethnicity and Constitutional Experiments', *Ethnic and Racial Studies*, vol. 21, no. 6: 1056–73.

Beetham, D. (1991). *The Legitimation of Power*, Atlantic Heights, NJ: Humanities Press International.

Bricker, D. and Letherbee, L. (1994). 'Consensus and Dissent in the Horn of Africa', *The Fund for Peace*, New York: The Horn of Africa Program.

Cliffe, L. (1989). 'Forging a Nation: The Eritrean Experience', *Third World Quarterly*, vol. 11, no. 4: 131–41.

Dahbour, O. and Ishay, M. (1995). *The Nationalism Reader*, Atlantic Heights, NJ: Humanities Press.

Danziger, J. N. (1991). *Understanding the Political World: An Introduction to Political Science*, London and New York: Longman.

Druckman, D. (1994). 'Nationalism, Patriotism, and Group Loyalty: A Social Psychological Perspective', *Mershon International Studies Review*, vol. 38, no. 1: 43–68.

Evera, S. (1995). 'Hypotheses on Nationalism and the Causes of War', in C. Kupchan (ed.), *Nationalism and Nationalities in New Europe*, Ithaca, NY and London. Cornell University Press.

Freeman, M. (1999). 'The Right to Self-Determination in International Politics: Six Theories in Search of a Policy', *Review of International Studies*, vol. 25, no. 3: 355–70.

Friedman, J. (1998). 'Transnationalization, Socio-political Disorder and Ethnification as Expressions of Declining Global Economy', *International Political Science Review*, vol. 9, no. 3: 233–50.

Gashman, G. (1993). *What Causes War: An Introduction to International Conflict*, New York: Lexington Books.

Gebre Kidan, F. (1995). 'In Defense of Ethiopia: A Comparative Assessment of Caribbean and African-American Anti-Fascist Protests, 1935–41', *Northeast African Studies*, vol. 2, no. 1: 55–69.

Gellner, E. (1994). *Nations and Nationalism*, Oxford: Blackwell.

Gurr, T. (1968). 'Psychological Factors in Civil Violence', *World Politics*, vol. 20, no. 2: 245–78.

Gurr, T. (1980). *Handbook of Political Conflict. Theory and Research*, New York: Free Press.

Gurr, T. (2000). 'Ethnic Warfare on the Wane', *Foreign Affairs*, May/June: 52–64.

Gurr, T. et al. (1999). 'State Failure Task Force: Phase II Findings', *Environmental Change and Security Project Report*, 5: 49–72.

Habte Selassie, B. (1980). *Conflict and Intervention in the Horn of Africa*, New York: Monthly Review Press.

Haggard, S. and Simmons, B. (1987), 'Theories of International Regimes', *International Organization*, vol. 41, no. 3: 491–517.

Hah, C. and Martin, J. (1975). 'Toward a Synthesis of Conflict and Integration Theories of Nationalism', *World Politics*, vol. 27, no. 2: 361–86.

Hanf, T. (1991). 'Reducing Conflict through Cultural Autonomy: Karl Renner's Contribution', in U. Ra'anan et al. (eds.), *State and Nation in Multiethnic Societies: The Breakup of Multinational States*, Manchester and New York: Manchester University Press.

Helman, G. and Ratnner, S. (1993). 'Saving Failed States', *Foreign Policy*, no. 89: 3–20.

Heraclides, A. (1991). *The Self-Determination of Minorities in International Politics*, London: Frank Cass.

Herbst, J. (1989). 'The Creation and Maintenance of National Boundaries in Africa', *International Organization* vol. 43, no. 4: 673–92.

Herbst, J. (1990). 'War and State in Africa', *International Security*, vol. 14, no. 4: 117–39.

Herbst, J. (1997). 'Responding to State Failure in Africa', *International Security*, vol. 21, no. 30: 117–39.

Jackson, R. and Roseberg, C. (1982). 'Why Africa's Weak States Persist: The Empirical and the Juridical in Statehood', *World Politics*, vol. 35, no. 1: 1–24.

Jalali, R. and Lipset, M. (1992). 'Racial and Ethnic Conflicts: A Global Perspective', *Political Science Quarterly*, vol. 107, no. 4: 585–606.

Janos, A. (1964). 'Authority and Violence: The Political Framework of Internal War', in H. Eckstein (ed.), *Internal War: Problems and Approaches*, New York: Free Press.

Kellas, J. (1991). *The Politics of Nationalism and Identity*, London: Macmillan.

Keller, E. (1985). 'United States Foreign Policy in the Horn of Africa', in G. Bender et al. (eds.), *African Crisis Areas and US Foreign Policy*, Berkeley, CA: University of California Press, pp. 178–93.

Keohane, R. (1986). 'Reciprocity in International Relations', *International Organization*, vol. 40, no. 1: 1–27.

Kornhauser, W. (1964). 'Rebellion and Political Development', in H. Eckstein (ed.), *Internal War: Problems and Approaches*, New York: Free Press.

Krause J. (1984). 'Soviet Arms Transfer to Sub-Saharan Africa', in R. K. Nation and M. K. Kauppi (eds.), *The Soviet Impact in Africa*. Lexington, MA: D.C. Heath.

Kupchan, C. (1995). 'Introduction: Nationalism Resurgent', in C. Kupchan (ed.), *Nationalism and Nationalities in New Europe*, Ithaca, NY and London: Cornell University Press.

Kurtz, D. (1981). 'The Legitimation of Early Inchoate States', in H. Classen and P. Salnik (eds.), *The Study of the State*, The Hague: Mouton.

Laitin, D. D. and Samatar, S. S. (1987). *Somalia: A Nation in Search of a State*, Boulder, CO: Westview Press.

Lind, M. (1994). 'In Defence of Liberal Nationalism', *Foreign Affairs*, vol. 73, no. 3: 87–112.

Lipson, C. (1984). 'International Cooperation in Economic and Security Affairs', *World Politics*, vol. 37, no. 1: 1–23.

Makinda, S. (1987). *Superpower Diplomacy in the Horn of Africa*, London: Croom Helm.

Markakis, J. (1990). 'Nationalities and the State in Ethiopia', *Third World Quarterly*, vol. 11, no. 4: 118–30.

Mazrui, A. (1994). 'The Blood of Experience: The Failed State and Political Collapse in Africa', *World Policy Journal*, vol. 12, no. 1: 28–34.

McFerson, H. (1996). 'Rethinking Ethnic Conflict (Somalia and Fiji)', *American Behavioral Scientist*, vol. 40, no. 1: 1–32.

Minority Rights Group (1983). *Eritrea and Tigray*, no. 5, London: MRG.

Modelski, G. (1961), *The International Relations of Internal War*, Princeton, NJ: Princeton University Press.

Motyl, A. (1991). 'The Modernity of Nationalism: Nations, States and Nation-States in the Contemporary World', *Journal of International Affairs*, vol. 45, no. 2: 307–23.

Mueller, J. (2000). 'The Banality of "Ethnic War"', *International Security*, vol. 25, no. 1: 42–70.

Mukisa, R. (1997). 'Toward a Peaceful Resolution of Africa's Colonial Boundaries', *Africa Today*, vol. 44, no. 1: 7–32.

Nettl, J. (1968). 'The State as a Conceptual Variable', *World Politics*, vol.20, no. 4: 559–92.

Neuman, S. (1991). 'Does Modernization Breed Ethnic Political Conflict?' *World Politics*, vol. 43, no. 3: 451–78.

Olzak, S. (1998). 'Ethnic Protest in Core and Periphery States', *Ethnic and Racial Studies*, vol. 21, no. 2: 187–217.

Oommen, T. (1997). *Citizenship, Nationality and Ethnicity*, Cambridge: Polity Press.

Osterud, O. (1997). 'The Narrow Gate: Entry into the Club of Sovereign States', *Review of International Studies*, vol. 23, no. 2: 167–84.

Ottoway, M. (1982). *Soviet and American Influence in the Horn of Africa*, New York: Praeger.

Pocock, J. (1995). 'The Idea of Citizenship since Classical Times', in R. Beinen (ed.), *Theorizing Citizenship*, Albany, NY: SUNY Press.

Popper, K. (1968). *The Logic of Scientific Discovery*, New York: Harper & Row.

Porter, T. (1994). 'Postmodern Political Realism and International Relations Theory's Third Debate', in C. Sjolander and W. Cox (eds.), *Beyond Positivism: Critical Reflections on International Relations*, , Boulder, CO and London: Lynne Rienner.

Ra'anan, U. (1991). 'Nation and State: Order out of Chaos', in U. Ra'anan et al. (eds.), *State and Nation in Multi-ethnic Societies: The Breakup of Multi-national States*, Manchester and New York: Manchester University Press.

Riggs, F. (1998). 'The Modernity of Ethnic Identity and Conflict', *International Political Science Review*, vol. 19, no. 3, pp. 269–88.

Rosenau, J. (1990). *Turbulence in World Politics: A Theory of Change and Continuity*, Princeton, NJ: Princeton University Press.

Rosenau, J. (1995). 'Security in a Turbulent World', *Current History, Journal of Contemporary World Affairs*, vol. 94, no. 592: 193–200.

Rosenau, J. and Durfee, M. (1995). *Thinking Theory Thoroughly. Coherent Approaches to an Incoherent World*. Boulder, CO: Westview Press.

Rothchild, D. and Groth, A. (1995). 'Pathological Dimensions of Domestic and International Ethnicity', *Political Science Quarterly*, vol. 110, no. 1: 69–82.

Safran, W. (1997). 'Citizenship and Nationality in Democratic Systems: Approaches to Defining and Acquiring Membership in the Political Community', *International Political Science Review*, vol. 8, no. 3: 313–35.

Saideman, S. (1997). 'Explaining the International Relations of Secessionist Conflicts: Vulnerability versus Ethnic Ties', *International Organization*, vol. 51, no. 4: 721–53.

Samarasinghe, S. (1990). 'Introduction', in S. Samarasinghe et al. (eds.), *Secessionist Movements in Comparative Perspective*, London: Frances Pinter.

Samatar, A. (1997). 'Leadership and Ethnicity in the Making of African State Models: Botswana and Somalia', *Third World Quarterly*, vol. 18, no. 4: 687–707.

Scharr, J. (1984). 'Legitimacy in the Modern State', in W. Connolly (ed.), *Legitimacy and the State*, Oxford: Blackwell.

Schraeder, P. J. (1992). 'The Horn of Africa: US Foreign Policy in an Altered Cold War Environment', *The Middle East Journal*, vol. 46, no. 4: 571–93.

Shultz, R. (1995). 'State Disintegration and Ethnic Conflict: A Framework for Analysis', *The Annals of the American Academy of Political and Social Sciences*, no. 541: 75–88.

Smith, Z. (2000). 'The Impact of Political Liberalization and Democratization on Ethnic Conflict in Africa: An Empirical Test of Common Assumptions', *The Journal of Modern African Studies*, vol. 38, no. 1: 21–39.

Sorensen, G. (1997). 'Analysis of Contemporary Statehood: Consequences for Conflict and Cooperation', *Review of International Studies*, vol. 23: 253–69.

Stokes, G. (1978). 'The Undeveloped Theory of Nationalism', *World Politics*, vol. 31, no. 1: 150–60.

Tilley, V. (1997). 'The Terms of the Debate: Untangling Language about Ethnicity and Ethnic Movements', *Ethnic and Racial Studies*, vol. 20, no. 3: 497–522.

Trevaskis, G. K. N. (1960) *Eritrea: A Colony in Transition*, Westport, CT: Greenwood Press.

Walzer, M. (1995). 'Citizenship', in T. Ball et al. (eds.), *Political Innovation and Conceptual Change*, New York: Cambridge University Press.

Waltz, Kenneth (2008). *Realism and International Politics*. New York and London: Routledge.

Warner, D. (1995). 'Citizenship and Identity: A Double Reading of the Identity Crisis', in A. Liebich et al. (eds.), *Citizenship: East and West*, London and New York: Kegan Paul International.

Weber, M. (1958). *The Protestant Ethic and the Spirit of Capitalism*, trans. T. Parsons, New York: Charles Scribner's Sons.

Wendt, A. (1998). 'On Constitution and Causation in International Relations', *Review of International Studies*, special issue, vol. 24: 101–17.

Woodward, Peter (2006). *US Foreign Policy and the Horn of Africa*, Aldershot: Ashhgate.

Part III
Regional and International Interventions

7
The IGAD and Regional Relations in the Horn of Africa

Peter Woodward

'The most dangerous corner of Africa is its North-Eastern Horn where instability reigns and terrorism thrives on the antagonism of its governments.'

Africa Confidential, 9 September 2009

Regionalism has become one of the most discussed themes of international relations since the end of the Cold War, including the significance within those relations of specific regional organizations.[1] In the Horn that process was first centred on the emergence of the Inter-Governmental Authority on Drought and Development (IGADD). Its initial formation in 1986 owed much to the international community and especially the response to the famine that swept across the region in the earlier years of that decade.[2] At the time the region's international relations were largely divided by the Cold War, with Ethiopia firmly in the grip of a Marxist-Leninist regime closely supported by the USSR, while neighbouring Sudan and Somalia were backed by the United States.[3] (This was an exact reversal of a period in the previous decade.) The Cold War division meant that any attempt at a regional organization should be as 'non-political' as possible and, in theory, IGADD's founding approach, based on environmental and other measures to address drought and its consequences, appeared to adhere to that. Thus it was that in spite of different alignments with competing superpowers Ethiopia was able to join the new organization along with the then clear Western allies Sudan, Somalia, Djibouti, Uganda and Kenya, brought together in part at least by the allure of foreign development aid. However, in practice little was achieved, for although IGADD came up with a number of project proposals, the international donors generally found them less than convincing and IGADD appeared in danger of withering on the vine in its remote 'neutral' headquarters in Djibouti.

DOMESTIC CONFLICTS

The end of the Cold War appeared to lift the limitation of IGADD to unconvincing project proposals and it focused instead on conflicts on the understandable grounds that development would be limited unless and until the region proved itself capable of peace. IGADD thus had an opportunity to re-invent itself and was encouraged to do so by its international supporters. To this end it made its first major step by involving itself in 1994 in an attempt at peace-making in southern Sudan. Down the years there had been numerous failed peace talks, but the end of the Cold War, and the resolution of the conflicts in Eritrea and Ethiopia that swiftly followed, seemed to offer the opportunity for a new chapter of attempts.[4] With the international community somewhat reluctant to start the ball rolling, it was former US President Jimmy Carter who made an early but unsuccessful effort, as was a further attempt by Herman Cohen, US Assistant Secretary of State for Africa.[5] That was followed by efforts by the Nigerian government, backed by the Organization of African Unity (OAU), which led to a further failure, known as Abuja I and Abuja II. It was after that that Ethiopia, Eritrea (independent in 1993 and a new member of IGADD), Uganda and Kenya – all IGADD members directly affected by Sudan's wars in the South – decided to make a fresh attempt under the auspices of IGADD and with some encouragement from the OAU and the West.

The attempts in successive talks in 1994 in Nairobi failed, but during and after the talks the IGADD leaders, and especially Ethiopia's Prime Minister, Meles Zinawi, formulated what became known as the Declaration of Principles (DoP). The DoP recognized that, in theory at least, a major factor in the failure of successive talks had been the government's determination to preserve the Islamic state it had established after the 1989 coup, while the SPLA had sought a secular state for Sudan such as there had been before Nimeiri's introduction of shari'a law in 1983. The way out proposed by the DoP was that if the government side would not accept peace based on a secular state, then the South would have the right to hold a referendum to determine its future, including separation. It was probably a solution that could only have come from the Horn, for ever since the foundation of the OAU in 1963 African states had rejected separation and wars had been fought to prevent it, as in Nigeria, Congo, Kinshasa and Ethiopia itself. But after the fall of President Mengistu of Ethiopia in 1991 the idea of a referendum determining separation had been practised in the case of Eritrea, with the agreement of the new government in Ethiopia from which it was expecting to secede. The same principle was now being put forward by IGADD and accepted by its members with the exception of Sudan, where the government still hoped for outright victory in the South. IGADD had taken its first step into the conflict in southern Sudan. Partly in recognition of its changing role, in 1996 it dropped 'Drought' from its official title, becoming simply IGAD.

Although the Sudanese government had rejected the DoP proposed by IGAD, it was to find itself prepared to adopt the same position in a different context. In an attempt to escape from dealing with either the SPLA or IGAD the government was pushing for what it liked to call 'peace from within' with a breakaway movement from the SPLA led by Riek Machar. In the course of arriving at a settlement in 1997 (known as the Khartoum Peace Agreement) there was a statement that the southerners would be able to 'determine their political aspirations' through a referendum: it was the least that Machar would agree to if he was to retain any credibility, rather than a real acceptance by the government at that stage of the possibility of separation for the south. In the event Machar was later to abandon his rapprochement with the government and return to the SPLA, but it did leave the government on record as prepared to countenance a referendum along the lines that IGAD had proposed.

In the immediately following years IGAD sought to reopen Sudan's talks but without success. However, following 9/11 the government was more fearful of the United States and possible action against it as part of the 'war on terror' and responded positively when the new US administration, led by George W. Bush who had personal sympathy for the war-torn South, appointed former Senator John Danforth as his special representative to Sudan.[6] This wider internationalization of the IGAD efforts, with the United States joined by Britain and Norway in what became known as the Troika, was to be a vital additional dimension to the search for peace. At the same time Kenya, a close US ally in the region and keen to develop a role as a 'neutral' peace-maker, announced that it was setting up a permanent office to facilitate mediation on behalf of IGAD to be led by Lieutenant General Lazarus Sumbeiywo. Other IGAD members, as well as the wider international community, were strongly supportive of the move and continued to be so throughout the process. It was to start with the Machakos Protocol of 2002, which agreed the DoP formula by which the maintenance of shari'a law in the North would trigger the right of the South to hold a referendum on separation. Sumbeiywo was to continue presiding over a series of protocols, which led eventually to the Comprehensive Peace Agreement (CPA) three years later.

It seemed like a considerable achievement, however subsequently the Sudanese government, nominally a Government of National Unity (GNU) but in practice largely dominated by the ruling National Congress Party (NCP), proved resistant to attempts by IGAD to be significantly involved in the implementation of the CPA. Nevertheless IGAD showed persistence in its wish to be active in at least monitoring the implementation of the CPA, and in March 2010 it called a special meeting in Nairobi to discuss the forthcoming elections and the various problems that were occurring. It was encouraged in this by the Government of South Sudan (GoSS) which has put considerable store by IGAD in view of its own establishment by the IGAD-brokered CPA (in contrast to the African Union in which only Sudan's national government is recognized).[7] The elections went ahead in the following month in controversial circumstances. However, the express intention of the parties to the CPA that the manner of its implementation would make unity attractive to the southerners appeared not to be borne out in the intervening five years and IGAD members were left to address the implications of the overwhelming decision by the South in January 2011 to secede in the following July. However, as mentioned, the SPLM in particular wants IGAD to remain involved in post-referendum developments because of its role in the CPA, and in June 2010 it was announced that IGAD and the African Union's High Implementation Panel for Sudan, led by former South African President Thabo Mbeki, would play a continuing role.[8]

At the same time as IGAD was convening the negotiations that resulted in the CPA, the organization was also playing host to another round of talks in Kenya, this time focused on Somalia. It was the 15th time that there had been efforts to negotiate a solution to the collapse of the internationally recognized Somali state since Siad Barre's downfall in 1991. These new talks were supported by the European Union (EU) but proved much less focused than the Sudan talks. Over 1,000 Somalis descended on the venue claiming to be representatives of this or that, and talks seemed set to drag on more or less indefinitely until October 2004 when Uganda's President Museveni, then chair of IGAD, intervened to call time. A Transitional Federal Government (TFG) was then cobbled together but was unable to claim its capital in Mogadishu and instead was forced to idle in Kenya before unsuccessfully seeking to assume its place in Somalia.

Having committed itself to the TFG, IGAD responded positively when the TFG's choice of President, Abdulahi Yusuf, called for peacekeepers to assist him in the establishment of his authority in Somalia. It agreed to an IGAD Peace Support Mission in January 2005, but it was followed by a period of uncertainty, including concern among the TFG's Somali supporters of the likely source of forces for such a mission, especially as it was feared that they would in practice come largely from their traditional foe: Ethiopia. With Ethiopia backing the TFG there were reports in 2005 of its now bitter enemy Eritrea, with which it still had an unresolved border dispute, assisting Somali opponents of the TFG. By early 2006 Ethiopian forces, backed by US air support, invaded Mogadishu, driving out the nascent Islamic Courts' Union (ICU) authorities and contributing to a new wave of violence across the southern half of Somalia. The contrast between at least the short-term impact of IGAD's involvement in peace-making in Somalia and Sudan could hardly have been starker.[9]

BORDER CONFLICTS

IGAD's involvement in conflict was also to be reflected with regard to international borders within the region. It is notable that, in addition to the prevalence of domestic conflict, the region has been the scene of the two largest international wars in Africa since the Second World War, both involving Ethiopia. The carve-up of the Somali peoples during the imperial era was, as is widely known, reflected in the five stars on the Somali flag at independence in 1960, three of which represented areas outside the new state, in Djibouti, Kenya and Ethiopia, all, like Somalia, later to become members of IGAD. After a decade of guerrilla warfare and a few quieter years, eventually in 1977 Siad Barre launched Somalia's forces against Ethiopia and they were only eventually repelled with the help of a massive Soviet arms lift to Ethiopia and the deployment of thousands of Cuban troops. Somali hostility towards Ethiopia was longstanding and widely known, but the establishment of a new international border, a unique event in post-independence Africa, between Ethiopia and Eritrea suggested that borders might not after all be sacrosanct.[10]

Having seen the creation of the new state of Eritrea in 1993 as an amicable arrangement between two connected former guerrilla movements there was shock internationally when war broke out in 1998, ostensibly over a comparatively small and poor slither of borderland between the two countries. After further rounds of fighting an international inquiry ruled on the border, but its decision has not been implemented and the tension has persisted, with both sides maintaining substantial forces along it. While the wars between Ethiopia and two of its neighbours have been the most violent cases of disputed borders there are other border issues within the IGAD region as well as others connected to IGAD members' borders with non-IGAD members.[11] In addition, there is the possibility of a further border issue now that South Sudan has separated from Sudan in the referendum of 2011 as laid down in the IGAD-brokered CPA. Negotiations on that border proved very difficult and took far longer than scheduled.

IGAD's secretariat at least had become aware of the regional dimensions of border problems and had commissioned studies concerning both the problems and the organization's possible roles, but has yet to become directly involved. However, the unresolved border dispute between Ethiopia and Eritrea spilled over into Somalia where, as mentioned, IGAD committed itself to the TFG process and endorsed Ethiopia's armed intervention in 2006. That episode not only produced increased conflict in Somalia but also led to the stepping up of Eritrea's involvement in the Somali quagmire, turning what had been a border war between two IGAD members into a proxy conflict in a third country in which one of the parties, Ethiopia, had the backing of IGAD. That situation, and the international condemnation and sanctions on Eritrea for allegedly supporting terrorism, contributed to Eritrea's decision to withdraw from the organization amid accusations that it had become simply a tool of Ethiopia. Be that as it may it has nevertheless proved possible to make IGAD a starting point for positions that have won the support of the African Union (AU), conveniently headquartered in Ethiopia's capital, Addis Ababa, and moved on to secure the active engagement of the UN. Indeed, in November 2004 the UN Security Council even took the unusual step of leaving New York to hold a special session on Sudan in Nairobi.[12]

At the same time IGAD set up its own system, the Conflict Early Warning and Response Mechanism (CEWARN), in 2002 based in Addis Ababa. On paper it has good intentions, but in theory and practice it is seeking to operate in a minefield. Early warning is at best a hazardous venture and if it is goes wrong could serve to worsen a situation. Doubtless Ethiopia thought it was preventing Islamist conflict in Ethiopia itself when it launched its invasion of Somalia in 2006, but the result has heightened conflict there, and to judge from the subsequent talk of a growing presence of al-Qaeda in Somalia has had the reverse of the intention. In Darfur there was clearly a deteriorating situation at the time CEWARN was created, however the latter's mandate restricted it to border areas between IGAD members and conflicts between pastoralists so that its mandate did not extend to Darfur. In addition, IGAD was excluded from any involvement in Darfur since the Sudanese government and the international actors sought to keep separate the CPA and the issue of Darfur; instead it was the AU that tried initially to make its first foray into an ongoing conflict before calling on the UN for assistance, resulting in the hybrid United Nations–African Mission in Darfur (UNAMID).

ECONOMIC DEVELOPMENT

For some time, work on conflict in Africa has pointed to the economic dimensions of civil wars, including throwing out phrases such as 'greed or grievance' and 'resource curse' to suggest that these are underlying causes of what may often be presented as ethnic or cultural conflicts. Certainly there has been no shortage of such discussion with regard to IGAD member states since they provide so many cases of conflict for analysis and debate. It is equally clear that there is a significant regional economic dimension to many conflicts. The many cases of conflict have all involved a cross-border dimension that embraced the economic as well as the political and not just as a necessary supply route for the continuation of conflict but as a dimension of the economic benefits that may accrue to some combatants at least of sustaining their wars. Most if not all of this, of course, will not appear in the formal economic data on the countries involved but will be often well-known aspects of the informal economies which are so ubiquitous in Africa.

In addition, within the formal sector itself relations between neighbouring states may contribute to deteriorating relations, perhaps even to the point of conflict as the Horn has experienced. The Ethiopian–Eritrea war ostensibly has been about a border, but any analysis of the causes of that conflict has to include the continuing deterioration in economic relations between the two states following Eritrea's independence. As a landlocked state, Ethiopia was heavily dependent on access to the Eritrean port of Assab through which over 80 per cent of its trade passed. At the same time Eritrea was concerned at the terms of trade between the two countries, especially following the establishment of its own currency, the *nacfa*, at independence and its subsequent depreciation against the Ethiopian *burr*. The separation of South Sudan may bring comparable problems, since it too is landlocked while the bulk of Sudan's oil exports, the current driver of the country's economy and the largest reserves in any IGAD member, are mainly in the South (75 per cent of known reserves) but are exported by pipeline to the Red Sea through North Sudan. There is speculation about an alternative pipeline from South Sudan to the East African coast, but this would require a large new investment and take a considerable time.

＊ ＊ ＊

The brief review so far points to the efforts and limitations that IGAD has had in practice, but nobody could accuse its small staff in Djibouti of not trying. From its headquarters in the hot and isolated city state on the edge of its region of concern, IGAD has produced plenty of plans concerning many areas. IGAD may have not got far with its initial ideas with regard to economic development, but it has highlighted the problems at a regional level. It is common to point to the lack of complementary dimensions to African economies, structured as they have been historically either to local production for local consumption or in the imperial and post-independence eras for the provision of mainly raw materials to global markets. Yet within that there are areas in which there has been a growing need for at least the exploration of issues of integration. In the Horn infrastructure has been one of those areas, for while infrastructure is largely very poor it has also needed attention that requires some cooperation. The most obvious example is Ethiopia which, following the independence of Eritrea in 1993, has become the largest landlocked state in the world and for which the closure of the border with Eritrea has meant the need for new or improved alternatives. Power supplies and telecoms are other areas in which there has been cross-border cooperation.

There is also the extent to which there can be direct cooperation between states. One traditional sector has been pastoralists who are more numerous in the Horn than anywhere else in the world. Scarcely respecters of state boundaries their cross-border movements are a dimension of local and regional economies that will not disappear with 'modernization', as once assumed in some quarters, and which are relevant in social and political as well as economic terms, as the growth of conflict in Darfur over some 25 years has shown. On the other hand in the 'modern' sectors of the economies some of the resources developed primarily for global markets may contribute to regional integration. Sudan's oil has regional spin-off with regard to Ethiopia, and South Sudan's oil may well have links to East Africa in the future. A 2010 Chatham House paper pointed to a number of underlying themes across the region linking economic conditions to conflict.[13] In addition to access to ports and the pressures on pastoralism, energy issues, especially as the exploitation of oil and natural gas resources across the region increases, as well as the effects of drought and land rights, have all been linked to conflict with regional implications. The paper suggests three cross-border areas that have been or could become particularly problematic. One of these, the problems of Ethiopian–Eritrean economic issues, has already been mentioned. A second is the border area of southern Somalia–Kenya–Ethiopia where there are issues of landownership and riverine agriculture, as well as cross-border livestock trade. Third, livestock and port competition are a source of tensions in the area of Djibouti, Somaliland and north-east Ethiopia. Finally, resource rivalry has affected south-east Ethiopia and the neighbouring areas of southern Sudan and northern Uganda.

Some at least of these issues reflect the original intentions which gave rise to the establishment of IGADD, but apart from recognizing the problems and undertaking some research into the potential for cross-border economic cooperation, which it can be argued has some intrinsic value, there has been little that IGAD has been able to accomplish. It has found itself in something of a Catch-22. IGAD lacks the resources or capabilities to achieve anything on its own in the area of economic cooperation and has to turn instead to the international community and especially the IGAD Partners' Forum (IPF, often known as the 'Friends' of IGAD). Consisting of 16 states and four international organizations, it was established to give a boost to IGAD in 1997, but the Friends appear unconvinced of IGAD's abilities in this field. In so far as they do become involved in the issues raised, they generally look to their own governments or other international agencies, with the outcome that IGAD itself is seen as largely irrelevant in the field of economic development.

WATER

The need for the planned expansion of agriculture for both local and international consumption with burgeoning populations almost everywhere gives rise to water issues. The Nile has long been both the most discussed and most contentious source of water in the region and the growing difficulties between upstream and downstream states show the intensity and urgency of the subject. The most dependent country of all, Egypt, did not join IGAD, though it was granted observer status. Many put its exclusion down to the perceived long-running rivalry with Ethiopia, a situation that appeared to be continuing and intensifying in 2010. For a while it seemed that the two countries might engage with each other, but such efforts also showed the increasing tensions, with Ethiopia leading a group of seven upstream riparian countries while Egypt and Sudan, the only countries with a treaty on the Nile waters, signed in very different circumstances in 1959, appeared to work to maintain the status quo, a move underlined by Sudan's rejection of the Ethiopian-led Nile Basin Pact.[14] The nine states involved comprise the Nile Basin Initiative (NBI) established in 1999 as the pressures on the river became more intense, especially in Ethiopia and East Africa.[15] Thus while IGAD as an organization is not the responsible body for dealing with the question of the Nile waters, the subject clearly affects relations between IGAD members and, as indicated, that tends to mean that Sudan in particular is put in a difficult situation with its geographical position on the middle Nile, significant ambitions to develop its commercial agriculture alongside its mineral exploitation, and an historic agreement on water with Egypt. This situation is likely to become even more complicated now that South Sudan has become a separate state, which is a strong reason why Egypt and others in the Arab world have been actively courting the South's political leadership. In effect, on the water issue at least, Egypt's involvement with IGAD states looks more than being one simply of observer status. One possibly hopeful sign is that following the downfall of President Mubarak in Egypt in 2011, the new government there has taken a more conciliatory approach to Ethiopia in particular. While the Nile may be the most obvious river with regard to cooperation, it is far from being the only cross-border water issue in the region: as indicated, relations between Ethiopia and Somalia can also be influenced by issues relating to river basins in the eastern Horn.

TERRORISM

IGAD has also given thought to the subject of terrorism. It has been prevalent in the region since the early 1990s when Sudan welcomed

Osama bin Laden in 1991 and sheltered him as he built the al-Qaeda network.[16] From there it was involved in the confrontation with the US-led UN intervention in Somalia in 1993 as well as the attacks on the US embassies in Kenya and Tanzania in 1998. Islamist terrorists also operated in Ethiopia, especially in connection with opposition to the new regime, established in 1991. Developments in Somalia, especially the rise of the Islamic Courts' Union (ICU) in the mid-2000s and its destruction by Ethiopian forces with US backing, served to enhance a sense internationally of a growing threat from al-Shabaab and others, and particularly by Ethiopia which feels the most direct threat. In 2010 these fears were heightened by terrorist attacks in Kampala, apparently because of Uganda's willingness to commit troops to support the TFG in Mogadishu.

IGAD has responded by creating the IGAD Capacity Building Programme against Terrorism (ICPAT) which officially started in 2006 and like CEWARN is located in Addis Ababa and is also part of the general Peace and Security Strategy. Its aim is to try to coordinate counter-terrorism efforts by national governments across the region, and it too has an elaborate set of measures. Since it involves security agencies, it is difficult to evaluate its effectiveness, but the suspicion remains that such key areas as exchanging intelligence is much more likely to be undertaken bilaterally where there is perceived to be a mutual advantage than creating a common pool. (Eritrea showed its lack of interest from the first talks in 2002.)[17]

CONCLUSION

From this summary of IGAD's aims and limitations it is clear that a regional body has been set up for the Greater Horn which seeks in its own way to reflect comparable regional developments elsewhere in Africa, such as ECOWAS and SADC. It is also possible to argue that in spite of its limitations it is now recognized as an international organization working alongside the AU, the EU and the UN.[18] Indeed, within the hierarchy of these organizations it is to be seen as making a 'bottom-up' regional contribution to 'African solutions to African problems', which is so frequently sought: anything less than this can be seen as 'Afro-pessimism'.[19]

However, there is a need to probe beyond assertion into the regional and international forces at work within the Horn that have both influenced and limited the realistic expectations of IGAD. Given the level of conflict across the region, and the interconnected-ness of those conflicts, it is easy to see that, viewed internationally, there are common security issues. Indeed it is possible to see them in classic Buzan terms as forming a security complex: 'A group of states whose primary security concerns link together sufficiently closely that their national securities cannot realistically be considered apart from one another.'[20] The logic of that is that they cooperate to reduce the security concerns. But suppose those concerns at the level of the respective regimes work against each other reflecting their limitations as nation states. Not only have Eritrea and Ethiopia gone from being bedfellows against Mengistu (even if they occasionally kicked each other), they are now facing each other in hostile camps on either side of the still disputed border, with one of them at least prepared to withstand the international mediation of the supposed cause of their dispute.[21] And it is suggested that in the classic ways of finding external enemies to justify domestic coercion, these camps are being manipulated by both regimes to strengthen their domestic control to the point. Meanwhile Ethiopia judged it in its interest to fight for the imposition of the IGAD-backed TFG in Somalia rather than seeking an accommodation with the ICU, the most successful effort at the restoration of government in Somalia since the fall of Siad Barre. In Sudan the unfolding of 'marginalization' on all its border areas under successive governments over half a century has enriched the ruling elites of the centre even though it has created issues for its neighbours resulting from impoverishment, refugees and the overflow of domestic conflict. IGAD may have 'owned' the process that produced the CPA, but would it have been possible without wider internationalization, especially the involvement of the United States? And would it even have taken the shape it did without the United States, for it was the United States that checked the Egyptian–Libyan initiative of 2000 for a broader form of political participation than just the two armed camps of the NCP and the SPLA, an omission which continued through to the decision by other major political parties to boycott the 2010 elections.

The suspicion has been that IGAD and regionalism have not been a necessary step for the regimes of the Horn so much as the fulfilment of an agenda encouraged from outside at several levels of the international community. As indicated, IGAD's voice from the bottom has added to the legitimacy of outside international actors; at the same time it is noteworthy that IGAD members have scarcely put their money where their mouths are, since virtually all its activities have to be funded from outside beyond the salaries of the small staff of the secretariat. There is indeed a dependency in IGAD that has encouraged it to trim its activities to the wind.

Its concern with terrorism is an obvious example, for while there appear to be some links between Somali Islamists and international Islamism (that is, al-Qaeda) these are small compared with the overwhelmingly domestic agendas of all armed actors in the Horn, at least since Osama bin Laden quit Sudan in 1996. Yet brandishing the threat of Islamist terrorism becomes a ploy in international politics and brings responses, especially from the United States, as a number of recent studies have recounted.[22]

IGAD has been seen as heavily dependent on the international community not only for its establishment and operating costs, but also as a reflection of the post-Cold War era. The US-led West had been victorious in that long struggle and could now lead in the creation of what President George Bush Sr. called the New World Order. (The term swiftly became unfashionable, but the sentiment was to linger on in the 'Washington Consensus'.) However, the West's dominance in international relations has been in decline not least in the Horn, while the role of China and other Asian actors has strengthened. The realization of the importance of China gives rise to new problems, for its international relations role has largely to be inferred. While seeking to raise its game economically across much of the region, it remains taciturn in the way it operates politically. Yet for its economic strategy to continue to grow China has an interest in seeing the development of stability. With no clear ideological direction, how that will happen appears often to consist of going with the local political flow with a quiet word in the ear of those who appear to hold the tiller as it has been doing in Darfur.[23] In addition, China's economic involvement in the region will be strengthened by greater regional cooperation, a theme to which IGAD has returned in recent years, though not quite in the same way as the earliest IGADD efforts. Regional trade is a growing interest, with a major example being Ethiopia's over 80 per cent reliance on oil imports from Sudan, with plans for a reverse provision of electricity. These links are in turn related to China's support for infrastructure projects, such as an improved road link between the two countries and new dams on the Blue Nile in Ethiopia.

It is also the case that though a small organization exists to run IGAD, and there are governmental meetings as required by the rules, there is very little public perception of IGAD, which has a lower profile in the region than even the Arab League, let alone the AU and of course the UN. As such it has limited institutionalization, and while it has become a small part of the region's international furniture and unlikely to go away, it has hardly proved capable of making a sustained mark in its own right, rather than as the partner of other international and/or regional actors. IGAD has already lost one member, Eritrea, which has suspended its membership, and one wonders how much it matters to those that remain. Certainly, as indicated above, there are a number of issues in which the IGAD officials have hoped to play a part but in which IGAD's input is limited, and which themselves impact on regional relations. As such those issues in turn influence relations between the IGAD member states affecting the capabilities of the organization itself.

NOTES

1. Francis, D. J. (2006). *Uniting Africa: Building Peace and Security Systems*, Aldershot: Ashgate.
2. De Waal, A. (1997). *Famine that Kills: Darfur, Sudan* (revised edition), New York: Oxford University Press.
3. Woodward, P. (2003). *The Horn of Africa: Politics and International Relations* (revised edition), London: I. B. Tauris.
4. Johnson, D. H. (2003). *The Root Causes of Sudan's Civil Wars*, Oxford: James Currey; Lesch, A. (1998). *The Sudan: Contested National Identities*, Bloomington, IN: Indiana University Press.
5. Cohen, H. (2000). *Intervening in Africa: Superpower Peacemaking in a Troubled Continent*, Basingstoke: Palgrave Macmillan.
6. Woodward, P. (2006). *US Foreign Policy and the Horn of Africa*, Aldershot: Ashgate.
7. International Crisis Group (2010). *Sudan: Regional Perspectives on the Prospect of Southern Independence*, Africa Report 159. The report adds that Sudan's national government tried to avoid IGAD as a forum, seeing it as biased in favour of the South, and also sought to have the meeting postponed until after the elections (pp. 18–21).
8. *Sudan Tribune*, 30 June 2010.
9. Woodward, P. (2004). 'Somalia and Sudan: A Tale of Two Peace Processes', *Roundtable: The Commonwealth Journal of International Affairs*, vol. 93, no. 375.
10. Neuberger, B. (1986). *National Self-Determination in Postcolonial Africa*, Boulder, CO: Lynne Rienner.
11. These include the dispute between Egypt and Sudan over the region of Halayab and that between Eritrea and Djibouti over Doumeira.
12. It was no coincidence that John Danforth, formerly of US envoy to Sudan, was then US ambassador to the UN.
13. Love, R. (2009). *Economic Drivers of Conflict and Cooperation in the Horn of Africa*, Briefing Paper, London: Chatham House.
14. *Sudan Vision*, 10 May 2010. In April 2010 Ethiopia, Uganda, Tanzania, Rwanda and Kenya signed, while the Democratic Republic of Congo and Burundi had one year in which to sign: Egypt then lobbied them not to do so.
15. The nine members of the Nile Basin Initiative are Burundi, DR Congo, Egypt, Ethiopia, Kenya, Rwanda, Sudan, Tanzania and Uganda.

16. Gallab, A. (2008). *The First Islamist Republic: Development and Disintegration of Islamism in the Sudan*, Aldershot: Ashgate; Burr, J. M. and Collins, R. O. (2009). *Sudan in Turmoil: Hasan alTurabi and the Islamist State*, Princeton, NJ: Markus Wienner.

17. In 2004 IGAD also convened a meeting to discuss the establishment of an East African force which would form part of the AU's plan for an African Standby Force. However, in the light of the AU's shortcomings in its first peacekeeping operation in Darfur, little real progress has been achieved.

18. It was notable that when the EU launched its policy paper on the Horn of Africa in 2009 it specifically referred to the Horn as synonymous with the IGAD member states.

19. Francis, *Uniting Africa*, pp. 239-40.

20. Hamad, M. (2005). 'Regional Security Complex Theory and IGAD's Regime', doctoral thesis. University of Reading (unpublished).

21. Healy, S. (2008). *Lost Opportunities in the Horn of Africa: How Conflicts Connect and Peace Agreements Unravel*, London: Chatham House.

22. Rotberg, R. (ed.) (2005). *Battling Terrorism in the Horn of Africa*, Baltimore, MD: Brookings Institution; Davis, J. (ed.) (2007). *Africa and the War on Terrorism*, Aldershot: Ashgate.

23. It was interesting to note that in 2009 the US Special Envoy to Sudan saw the importance of visiting his Chinese counterpart in Beijing.

8
The Production of Somali Conflict and the Role of Internal and External Actors

Abdi Ismail Samatar

For nearly two decades much of the scholarship on Somalia has focused on the pathology of the failed state and the centrality of 'ethnic' cleavages in inducing political instability and violence in the country (Heinrich 1997; UNDO 1997; Kivimaki 2001; International Crisis Group 2003; Lewis 2004). The central argument of this literature is that loyalty to the clan and ethnic sentiment override other forms of belonging and this has led to political leaders favouring their genealogical groups in government appointments and the distribution of public resources. It has been argued that such clanism subverted the legitimacy of the government, fuelled the civil war and continues to stoke conflict. Another recent contribution to the Somali literature deals with terrorism and the claim that Somalia has become a transit route for terrorists or that local terrorists might have networked with al-Qaeda (Rotberg 2005; Shay 2005; Pirio 2007). While the theoretical frames and the objects of these studies are different, these seemingly divergent streams come to similar conclusions regarding the ways in which political stability and governmental institutions could be restored to the country. Both advocate formal tribalization of the nation's institutions as that will bring into the open the relationships among genealogical groups. They conjecture that such a strategy will prevent disproportionate access to state resources by favoured tribal groups (Lewis 1995, 2004). Superficially, the proposed strategy appears logical, but it also dovetails with the political agenda of warlords and sectarian elements of the elite. Below the surface, the approach is deeply contradictory and would deepen the exclusionary boundaries among the population such that the proposed remedy would undo common national belonging and enfeeble national institutions (Samatar and Samatar 2004).

This chapter takes a different tack and posits that the politicization of cultural identity from colonial times to the Cold War and the war on terror eras has led to the development of an uncivic political alliance between sectarian local actors and Cold War and terror warriors. The interplay between these forces in the country and in the region has been responsible for the demise of Somalia rather than parochial tribal sentiments. This does not mean that cultural values are not important politically; instead it is my argument that translating minor cultural difference among the population into state political projects creates counterproductive political barriers between communities, which in turn fuels conflict.

In a pioneering article Archie Mafeje argued that Africa's political trouble was not due to cultural differences among the population but the transformation of those differences by the state and the political elite into a political ideology (Mafeje 1971). On the other hand the modernization literature of the 1960s proposed that nation state-building in post-colonial Africa had no space for traditional practices and values (by which was meant tribal practices), while Marxist scholarship thought such cultural traditions akin to pre-capitalist values would impede social transformation. Recent articulations of the post-colonial left and neo-modernizationists (Barkan 2008) have come to terms with 'ethnicity' and now consider related cultural practices as compatible with the nation state. In tandem with these developments at least one African state, Ethiopia, transformed its administrative regions into ethnic ones in the hope that this would resolve political tensions in the country (Samatar 2004). But redrawing the country's provincial boundaries along ethnic lines and formal ethnicization of politics has not generated communal peace and an accountable system of government at the centre.

Mafeje's analysis remains as relevant today as it was nearly 40 years ago. More recently, Mamdani challenged revisionist ideas regarding culture and politics and unearthed the archaeology of contemporary ethnic politics. He argued that it is not possible to comprehend ethnic politics outside the parameters of the colonial era (Mamdani 2004: 6).

We surmise that the transformation of cultural values into political identities (Parekh 2008), and the use of these as instruments by the political elite to mobilize clients, has been divisive and often led to violence, as was the case in Rwanda in 1994 and in Kenya in 2007–8. My argument in this chapter is that the Somali case is one such transformation in which segments of the Somali political elite inspired by political genealogy linked up with Cold War/terror warriors and Ethiopia. The result of this association turned the country into a living hell.

The chapter is divided into six sections. The first narrates the development of modern Somali democracy and the ways in which the combination of sectarian local political entrepreneurs and their international and regional patrons led to the demise of the democratic decade. It describes the long military dictatorship which corroded the social fabric of Somali society. The second section examines the political and social consequences of national disintegration and the rule of warlords which has terrorized the population for two decades. In the third section we compare two Somali reconciliation conferences held in Djibouti and Kenya to demonstrate the claim that the international community and some IGAD countries are least interested in a Somali-owned project which might restore the Somali state and which might not easily succumb to the dictates of the war on terror and those of its regional allies. The fourth section focuses on the most successful local effort, led by the Union of Islamic Courts (UICs), to restore peace to Somalia and rebuild a common citizenship, and how this effort was wrecked by the US government in pursuit of its ideological war on terror and by Ethiopia. The fifth section narrates the return of violence to Mogadishu and southern Somalia since the US-supported Ethiopian intervention. The final section reflects on the implications of such internal and external alliances for Somalia's chances of recovery and for the region and the world.

DEMOCRACY, THE COLD WAR AND DICTATORSHIP

The Somali peninsula was carved up into five colonial territories at the Berlin Conference of 1884 (Omar 2001). Britain took over two areas (British Somaliland and the Northern Frontier Districts –NFD – of the Kenya Colony), the third went to France (French Somaliland), Southern Somalia became an Italian colony (Italian Somaliland) and Ethiopia seized western Somaliland – Haud and Reserve Area, and Ogaden (Drysdale 1964) Three of these territories gained independence to form two countries, the Somali Republic (British and Italian Somalilands) in 1960, and the French colony became the Republic of Djibouti in 1977. As for the NFD, the British government conducted a plebiscite in the region in 1961 in which 63 per cent of the population voted to unite with the Somali Republic (Drysdale 1964; Turton 1972; Healy 1981). However,

Britain ignored the democratic wishes of the population and kept them within the Kenyan colony. The people in the western reaches of Somali territory (the Somali region of Ethiopia) have been treated as subjects by all Ethiopian regimes (Khalif, and Doornbos 2002; *New York Times* 2007; Human Rights Watch 2008).

Somalia's pioneering political party, the Somali Youth League (SYL), was created in Mogadishu in 1943. Three core elements of SYL's principles were: a common Somali citizen based on equality among citizens; an accountable system of government anchored in Islamic doctrine; and a united country for the Somali people. One of the lasting legacies of the party has been the agreement among the majority of the population that the party's leaders were far-sighted and the country could have avoided the mayhem of the last 30 years had various governments upheld those ideas of accountability and equality. What went wrong and why did the party fail to hold to its post-colonial programme?

There is little historically grounded political analysis of this question and none of the established works deals with SYL, except Touval (1963). Oral and other sources indicate that though SYL was the biggest political party in the Somali world since its establishment, it failed to gain hegemony, except for a brief period in the 1950s. The party had to fight internal and external efforts designed to fragment the nation's civic unity by opportunistically exploiting marginal genealogical differences among the population. It seems that the principles of SYL and those of the opposition represented two divergent political tendencies. One embodied civic belonging anchored in equality among citizens and shared common traditions and values, while the other espoused genealogical political identity, which meant that a Somali's political affiliation was only with those of the same genealogical descent. In essence the latter replicated the old colonial project of turning genealogical differences into divergent political divisions. Illustrative of this is what the United Nations' Advisory Council said about the Italian administration in Southern Somalia in the 1950s and its attempts to turn genealogy into politics in order to undermine SYL's nationalist project (United Nations Trusteeship Council 1952: 18).

To forestall the movement's struggle towards the nationalist goal, Italian military forces engaged in a reign of terror against SYL's members and its supporters in which many lost their lives, while thousands of others were terrorized, imprisoned or deported to remote areas. However, the party leaders held their nerve and were able to defeat Italy's attempts to divide Somalis in order to prolong its rule by winning municipal and territorial assembly elections in 1953 and 1954 respectively.

The promise of independence which beckoned only temporarily side-lined the colonial project of divide and rule. A significant minority of aspirant politicians remained committed to political genealogy as the only instrument with the greatest potential of giving them a seat at the national table. For the time being it seemed that the sectarian project was hemmed in by independence euphoria, the quality of SYL leadership and its allied parties, and a majority of Somalis willing to endorse a sense of common political belonging (Samatar 1997). This mind-set reinforced SYL's image as the only party whose membership cut across regional and genealogical groups. But the war of manoeuvre was not over as a considerable number of SYL deputies would only hold to civic principles if that was in their own interests. Many personalities turned to tribalism to mobilize their constituency when personal gains did not come via the civic route. This is exactly how tribal politics was 'manufactured', to use Mafeje's (1971) insightful analysis.

Expediency via political genealogy progressively gained support among many MPs in the four post-colonial elections of 1961, 1964, 1967 and 1969. Clanist politics' first major breakthrough occurred during the constitutional referendum of 1961 when two major political leaders who were cabinet members of the government of national unity decided to oppose the draft constitution in the 1961 plebiscite. Sh. Ali Jimale, then Minister of Health, was incensed when the Provincial President of the Republic did not appoint his fellow 'clansman' and former prime minister of the Trusteeship territory as the republic's Premier. By contrast, Mohamed Ibrahim Egal, who was the Defence Minister, was enraged not because he made the 'wrong' political alliance with the losing candidate, but because he felt belittled by being given the defence portfolio since he considered himself to be the political leader of the former British Somaliland. Although these two ministers have never identified issues in the constitution which they disagreed with, they campaigned against its approval and quietly mobilized some of their genealogical groups to reject it. It is ironic that Jimale was a key member of the group who worked on drafting the constitution (Hussen 2002), while Egal had an opportunity to amend any article when members of the legislative council of the former British Somaliland were asked to review the document. British Somaliland legislatures added two articles (Somali Republic 1961). In spite of this history, the majority of the population in the two regions from which these men hailed unquestioningly accepted their ideas about political genealogy and voted against the draft constitution. Somalis in the rest of the country and a substantial minority in the two regions supported it. Why did these two men work so hard to defeat the very constitution they helped to draft? Sources close to the events indicate that they calculated that the defeat of the constitution would discredit the provincial president and his premier and that would give them or their allies the opportunity to stand for those posts (Hussen 2002). Jimale took the lead by mobilizing an opposition bloc in parliament whose only common denominator was the desire to get rid of the incumbent president. Even so he lost the presidential election by just one vote (Department of State, Foreign Service Dispatch 1961). Sharmarke, the reappointed prime minister, took the high moral ground and appointed members of the opposition, including Jimale and Egal, as ministers. These attempts to create a government that included all the major political camps were insufficient to appease these men and their political stratagems ensured that the government would limp from one vote of confidence to another.

In addition to the opposition's destabilizing tactics, the United States severely criticized Sharmarke's government for accepting the Soviets' offer to arm and train its military (Department of State 1964). Thereafter, US officials considered Sharmarke to be a pro-communist leader despite the fact that he assured them of Somalia's non-alignment.

Despite these internal and external difficulties the government was able to win a majority of the seats (69 out of 121) in the parliamentary election of 1964. But because some members of the party were not loyal to its principles the actual number of SYL supporters in parliament was less than 60. As a result, the party lacked a majority to govern the country with any confidence, but President Osman remained an anchor of stability for the government. Just when everyone thought that Premier Sharmarke had led the party to a major victory, President Osman took a different view. He maintained that the difficulties the country had experienced over the previous four years required a bolder leadership. Surprisingly, he appointed Abdirazak H. Hussen, who had established himself as the most effective minister in the previous cabinet (Africa Report 1964: 6). Hussen's appointment was a political watershed as he abandoned the idea of a government of national unity and pursued a hard-line nationalist/development agenda (Samatar and Samatar 2002). Over the course of the first year of his premiership the reform process led to post-colonial Africa's first mass dismissal of top bureaucrats for incompetence and corruption. Further, with this reform came the dominance of northerners in key civil service posts. Finally, this government's anti-corruption drive was the most systematic and sustained the country had ever known (Africa Report 1964: 22). However, this campaign to professionalize the civil service also became an opportunity for those who were opposed to it to mobilize their followers for a counter-attack. They made many attempts to destabilize the government (Department of State, Airgram from American Embassy, Mogadishu 1964). When all of these failed to bring down the government, they set their sights on the 1967 presidential election as a strategic opportunity to oust the president and appoint one of their own.

Sharmarke championed this cause and became their leader. The first signal came when the central committee of SYL voted in April 1967 to nominate President Osman as the party's candidate although Osman had not asked the party to nominate him. The party's difficulty was exacerbated by the fact that Osman was not keen to remain president and was unwilling to pay MPs or promise them posts in return for their support. By contrast, Sharmarke exploited every opportunity to win the presidency. He was concerned that he might be opposed by the West given his reputation as pro-Soviet during his term in office as Prime Minister. To ease these concerns he reached out to his political nemesis, Mohamed Ibrahim Egal. Sharmarke promised Egal the premiership if he would join his campaign and mobilize his allies in parliament. Egal was considered a safe pair of hands by Western diplomats and he approached the American mission for support (Lemarchand 1979).

Egal and Sharmarke were joined by others, such as the former Secretary General of SYL, Yassin Nur Hassan. These three men ran the campaign and used the power of the purse or the promise of government posts to win over MPs. Their chances were boosted further by the un-strategic and untimely pronouncement that the government's Foreign Minister had promised a visiting North Korean delegation in April 1967 that Somalia would consider establishing diplomatic relations with that country. Premier Hussen and his cabinet did not agree to North Korean's claim, but US diplomats took offence to the visit and apparently made their displeasure known (Hussen 2002).

Osman reluctantly accepted his nomination in April, just two months before the election, but he remained resolute about not campaigning as he persistently told many who wished to support him that they should vote with their conscience (Osman May

1967). The responsibility for organizing the president's supporters in parliament fell to Premier Hussen who spent much effort to win backing for Osman. Although Hussen's effort was eclipsed by the well-funded machine of their opponent, he and civic-minded MPs gave Sharmarke's group a strong challenge. Hussen held fast to the foundational principles of SYL, upheld Osman's own standards and honoured his government's record of accountability and commitment to democracy. However, in the end their efforts fell short of the target. What broke Osman's candidacy was the defection of several ministers who abandoned their side because of promises made by the other side. In addition, Sharmarke gained the votes of three former ministers and one former deputy minister, who had been dismissed by Hussen for corruption, by promising to drop the charges. These individuals were protected from prosecution by the President of the Assembly who resisted demands to bring their case to the floor (Sh. Mukhtar June 2005). In spite of these deceptions Sharmarke won the presidency by one vote only.

The election of a new Somali president and the transfer of power marked a major political benchmark in the country and the continent. It marked the third legitimate change of government in the Somali Republic since independence. It was also the first peaceful and democratic transfer of presidential power in the country and the continent. Such a democratic milestone belied the forces which produced it and their long-term effects on the Somali Republic and the fate of the Somali people.

This regime change had several ramifications that undermined the long-term stability and viability of the country. First, the new regime abandoned the anti-corruption agenda which the previous government came to be known and respected for. The hallmark of this shift was signalled by corruption at the highest level when Premier Egal authorized the use of public money for the construction of his private villa in Mogadishu (Araaleh 2001). Second, the slow but systematic marginalization of the merit- and process-based civil service system corroded the integrity of public service and undermined public confidence in the system. This meant that appointments could be made to the service without regard to the established professional order. One of the most critical interventions was the promotion of the Governor of Upper Juba who had denied the former Minister of Interior, Abdulkadir Mohamed Aden, the right to register his candidacy in Buur Hakab in 1969, to Chief Judge of the Supreme Court. For his part in this affair the Governor was given the dubious name Buur Liqe (Devour the Mountain). The new government's strategy served its purpose when many candidates who felt that the 1969 election was rigged petitioned the Supreme Court, only for Buur Liqe to throw out their appeals. Third, it made the purchase of parliamentarians' votes more common than it has ever been. Finally, the regime attempted to stay in power by using the national police force as its party's instrument during the 1969 election. It forced out the respected chief of police and replaced him with someone sympathetic to the government's wishes (Qalib 2004). The cumulative effects of these developments became apparent after the parliamentary election of 1969.

Despite the fact that it was open season for corruption under this regime the West, and particularly the United States, never criticized the government.[1] In fact, The West's endorsement of the regime, level of corruption and the erosion of democratic practice provided ample ammunition for the Soviet-trained military whose nationalist credentials most Somalis did not question. Sensing the population's disillusionment, the military, which had been drawing up plans for a coup, now waited for the opportune time.

The political crisis that erupted after President Sharmarke was murdered by one of his police bodyguards in October 1969 while on a state visit to Las Anood provided an opening for the military. Parliamentarians went into frenzy to sell their votes for the presidential election, and Somalia's political elite took the practice to a new height even before the President's funeral. The military swiftly moved in the dead of night a few hours before parliament was able to elect a new President.

The combined effects of two forces made the demise of Somali democracy possible. Sectarian Somali leaders outlawed pluralist politics since its practice meant systemic corruption. In addition, US–Soviet rivalry in the Horn of Africa meant that the superpowers paid least attention to the consequences their policies had on local populations. Instead, each superpower supported whichever local political group would do their bidding. Groups that best suited this agenda were either those that subscribed to political genealogy or the military which was eager to have a superpower patron.

MILITARY DICTATORSHIP, SUPERPOWER RIVALRY AND STATE FAILURE

Somalia's democratic political tradition came to an abrupt end with the coup. The Supreme Revolutionary Council (SRC) declared that it intended to eliminate corruption, restore justice and develop the country. Most Somalis were relieved that the corrupt order had been overthrown and supported the coup, although a few understood that the coup was a political calamity in spite of the need to oust the corrupt regime. Former President Osman, who was a national democratic symbol, and Prime Minister Hussen, who set the national standard against political corruption, were the first victims when they were arrested without a legitimate cause. Leaders of the deposed regime were also apprehended and held in the same location. Osman and Hussen were incarcerated for nearly four years, while former Prime Minister Egal remained in jail for much longer (Hussen 2003). The coup plotters also annulled the constitution and all the attendant democratic principles. They went further and announced the adoption of a socialist programme whose essence they barely understood (Samatar 1993). This marked the first clear indication that their Soviet 'advisers' had most influence (Payton 1980).

For the first few years the military authority enacted three progressive social programmes which sustained its popular legitimacy until 1975. First, previous Somali governments had developed a Latin script for the Somali language but hesitated to adopt it as they were apprehensive about the backlash that religious leaders, who preferred Arabic, might mount. The military swiftly adopted the script and embarked on a national literacy campaign. Further, the government decreed Somali as the country's lingua franca and the medium of instruction in primary and secondary schools. Second, the military authority significantly expanded access to education and established a national university. Finally, it expanded the transport infrastructure of the country by building a road network that linked the northern and southern regions.

All this took place in tandem with major political interventions which destroyed the regime's legitimacy and the capacity of the country's political and security institutions, and the livelihoods of millions. Among these were the destruction of the civil service, distortion of justice, perversion of communal relations and the criminalization of dissent.

Among the military's first policy directives was to bring public services administration completely under its purview. Senior military officers took over the ministries and directed their operations. Civil servants in these departments lost nearly all of their professional autonomy. Public servants' professional insulation from unprofessional political interventions, which the administrations of the first and second Republics nurtured and that the last civilian administration abused, was in disarray. A strategic causality of this was the military itself and the process started at the very top. Two former members of the SRC reported that General Barre systematically diverted their energies to non-military issues while he retained military command himself.[2] The changes evolved over the first six years of the regime and were accelerated after the Ethiopian–Somali war of 1977–78.

The military regime's opportunistic allegiance to the socialist project unravelled with the war. Somalis claim the Somali-inhabited territories which were either colonized by the imperial regimes in Ethiopia or ceded to them by the British (Drysdale, 1964). Political instability in Ethiopia as a result of the collapse of the monarchy and the loss of US military support once the Ethiopian coup-makers accepted Soviet help presented the Somali regime with an opportunity to reclaim those territories (Legum and Lee 1977; Farer 1979). However, the Soviets saw Ethiopia as a bigger prize than Somalia and attempted to keep both countries within its sphere of influence by providing support for the regime in Addis Ababa while maintaining a foothold in Somalia. They dispatched Fidel Castro to cajole Somali and Ethiopian leaders into some type of federation but that failed in the context of open warfare between the countries. Somalia's military rulers subsequently expelled their Soviet military advisers who conveniently went across the border to aid the Ethiopian response to the Somali intervention. The Soviets airlifted massive military hardware to Ethiopia and the Cubans sent several thousand troops to stand against, and then reverse, Somali successes on the battlefield. The United States was anxious about the success of the Soviets and immediately offered support to the Somali regime. Such assistance continued despite the regime's atrocious human rights record and deep corruption.

Several middle-ranking officers attempted a coup to overthrow the regime for managing the war badly and the government responded ruthlessly by using the army and security forces not only to deal with the culprits, but also with their genealogical groups. Use of the military to punish entire communities for the actions of individuals opposed to the regime brought back memories of the colonial practice of collective punishments (Africa Watch 1990). Collective punishment as a governance strategy forced many people to seek protection within their genealogical groups, and genealogizing politics had two lasting repercussions for the country. It undermined the population's common identity by fragmenting citizens into exclusivist camps and weakened the opposition to authoritarian rule as they could not mount a united front. The opposition's fragmentation was partly engineered by Ethiopia, which provided separate military bases for each group. The regime staggered on despite the withdrawal of US aid in the late 1980s as some Middle East oil states continued to provide modest financial assistance to Somalia. It collapsed as many of its members of the military drifted into different sectarian camps and as its central command became discredited. Without a legitimate central authority to hold the country those in the opposition who championed political genealogy finally achieved the logical consequence of their sectarian dreams and Somalia became the first country in modern history to have no government.

WARLORDS AND SECTARIAN NIGHTMARE

Somalis had waited for 15 years to see the end of the tyrannical regime but their hopes turned into a nightmare on January 1991 when the fragmented opposition forces routed what was left of the regime's military force. The anticipated respite did not materialize and the faction that took control of the capital declared one of its members as president without consulting other opposition groups. Another element of the same faction disputed the claim of leadership and the wrangle descended into a terrifying civil war which killed several thousand people and split the capital into two zones. General Aideed who controlled south Mogadishu and his militia preyed on the city's population, but the most pernicious treatment was meted out to residents of the Bay region. Militias used food as a weapon against defenceless civilians and imposed the most devastating man-made famine in the country's history, which claimed at least 300,000 lives. The scenes of this human tragedy were so ghastly that President Bush felt compelled to send a strong military force to Mogadishu to open the roads so food aid could reach the victims.

Operation Restore Hope, as the American intervention was known, was successful in its immediate objective of feeding starving people, but failed to tame the warlords and assist the population to rebuild their political institutions. Two factors accounted for this. First, the attention of the US commanders was diverted when the militias of the dominant warlord in South Mogadishu killed several UN troops and the US commander ordered his arrest. General Aideed's militias ambushed US marines in the process and killed 18 soldiers in what became known as 'Black Hawk Down'. The American counter-attacks slaughtered hundreds of Somalis. Aideed's militia retaliated by desecrating the bodies of some of the US soldiers by dragging their bodies through the streets of Mogadishu. These appalling scenes led to the withdrawal of US and UN troops. Second, the UN and the US leaders on the ground worked from the wrong political assumption which simply reinforced the old theme of political genealogy (Sahnoun 1994). These actors uncritically accepted that the political conflict was between genealogical groups and consequently their effort was sucked into the black hole of sectarian politics. As such, they concentrated on warlords and tribal leaders instead of working with civilians who were keen to have a rule-governed political authority.

The combination of the substantial amount of money, close to $2 billion, the intervention injected into Mogadishu and vast quantities of weapons looted from the armoury of the Somali military created fertile ground for a vicious civil war. Warlordism became the logical end point of sectarian and genealogical politics. Warlords' brutal practices exposed the myth that political genealogy would protect the interest of the 'group' and be a vehicle for more accountable governance. Civics and ordinary people lived through this terror for over a decade and the quality of life of the majority of the population declined precipitously, particularly in the south of the country.

Sectarian political agendas which inspired many civilian politicians late in the democratic era and the divisive mechanisms which they used as vehicles to realize their personal ambitions undermined the democratic project. The military regime, whose pretext for overthrowing the elected government was to restore accountability, adopted the same strategy to remain in power, and consequently deepened and institutionalized divisions among the population and recklessly destroyed all national institutions. Warlords who are the products of the old regime's dysfunctional political machinations have driven sectarianism to its logical conclusion. Thus, sectarian political agenda in its various guises – civilian, military and warlord – uprooted civic life, normalized brute violence and has turned one of Africa's most democratic cultures and societies into a living hell.

FRUITLESS PEACE CONFERENCES

Regional and international actors have organized nearly a dozen peace and reconciliation conferences since the UN and US troops withdrew in 1994. All but one of the congresses was dominated by warlords, who, not surprisingly, were unable to agree on a common agenda for resolving the country's political conflict. It was the convention organized by Djibouti in 2000 that showed the most promise. Djibouti's government invited all those who claimed to be political leaders, members of civil society and community groups, as well as warlords, but unlike previous congresses the warlords were invited as individual participants rather than agenda-setters, something that offended many of them who consequently refused to attend. The absence of these merchants of violence made the deliberations more congenial as participants had to engage in political compromises, although a significant number of sectarian politicians gerrymandered the agenda and chose to use genealogical division as the basis of political representation. Instituting political genealogy as the foundation of power-sharing turned sectarianism into the formal political ideology that would govern Somali political and public affairs. Though many of the participants were troubled by this turn of events they stayed with the trend in the hope that once peace was restored and government institutions established an opportunity would arise to overcome this strategy.

The Arta conference produced the first political agreement to involve all civil stakeholders. It created a national transitional charter, a parliament and a transitional government (TNG). War-weary Somalis were delighted at the prospect that the long nightmare might finally be over; however, two major pitfalls lay ahead. First, the Ethiopian government was not happy with the outcome of the convention as its client warlords who refused to take part were excluded from the new dispensation. Immediately after the conference was concluded the Ethiopian Prime Minister began to voice his dissent by arguing that the process was incomplete and Somalia's regional neighbours should work together to bring the warlords into the fold. Ethiopia then called for a meeting of its client warlords and helped create a warlord alliance, the Somalia Reconciliation and Restoration Council (SRRC). The group then began to dismiss the TNG as another faction, while the regime in Addis Ababa began to lobby the African Union and, more importantly, the IGAD to sponsor yet another conference. In the end, such a conference was convened. Somalia's 14th reconciliation conference was held in Kenya in 2002–4. It soon became clear that the agenda for this conference was not to reconcile the TNG with the Ethiopian-backed warlords, but to start from scratch in order to unseat the TNG and empower the warlords (Samatar 2002). The international community endorsed this effort and argued that all representation had to be based on the insidious genealogical formula (4.5) despite the fact that the warlords appointed nearly four-fifths of the delegates.

Gerrymandering the process continued until it delivered a national charter anchored in tribal political identity and the triumph of the warlords affiliated with Ethiopia as Somalia's new government (TFG). Somalis once more welcomed the development in the hope that the warlords would be sobered by the burden of their new responsibility. The EU, which was the principal financial backer of the conference, continued to provide some resources for the new regime, but the United States adopted a wait-and-see approach and did not recognize the TFG immediately.[3] However, long before the establishment of the TFG the US government, through its various intelligence agencies, had engaged some of Mogadishu's warlords – now members of the TFG – to hunt down what it considered to be terrorists and their radical Islamic supporters. Consequently, the warlords created an organization known as the Somali Alliance for the Restoration of Peace and Counter-Terrorism, which was funded by the Central Intelligence Agency (Mazzetti 2006).

The TFG floundered as the warlords squabbled for two years over who had what authority. As the stalemate continued, the US-funded warlord alliance launched fierce attacks on religious groups and targeted others. Religious leaders in Mogadishu felt the heat and they mobilized the population against the attacks. Before long the majority of the city's residents closed ranks with them. The people and religious leaders had triumphed by mid-2006.

THE UNION OF ISLAMIC COURTS AND RESTORATION OF PEACE

Shortly after the warlords were driven out of town the creation of a new force, the Union of Islamic Courts (UICs), was announced. UICs' militias formally took control of the capital and peace was restored to the city for the first time in 18 years. It is astonishing that the UICs were able to restore peace to the city and surrounding regions in such a short time with very few resources.

Unlike other political associations driven by self-aggrandizing warlords or lust for loot, the Courts were brought together by their commitment to Islamic values and rule of law anchored in their interpretation of the faith. Their message found resonance with the public to support their attempts to reinvigorate a sense of common national belonging. The influence and respect which the UICs garnered from across Somalia unnerved the warlords, the Ethiopian-backed TFG and other regional administration in the country. Regional tribal administrations in the north-west and north-east were so anxious about the growing influence of the UICs that the heads of the two administrations declared that they would institute shari'a law as the basis of governance in their areas. These administrations' about-face testified to the appeal of Islam and the nationalist goals which the Courts articulated.

Commerce and public life regained a degree of normality and the UICs began to engage in restoring public buildings and infrastructure. Mogadishu's airport and seaport, which the warlords had kept locked for nearly a decade, were opened for business. Commerce returned to these venues and national and international air travel became possible. All the road blocks were removed from city streets and the public and businesses were relieved of the enormous surcharges warlord militias used to exact.

By far the most important effect the UICs had on the city and surrounding regions was the introduction of a force that put an end to theft and looting as a way of garnering resources for those in authority. Moderately disciplined Courts militias temporarily changed the predator–prey relationship into one of respect and admiration. This is not to say that there were no teething problems since some of the militias occasionally took it on themselves to 'make' laws in some of the neighbourhoods for which they were responsible. These uncoordinated infractions were a major source of irritation to the leadership and were widely reported in the Western media. Some of these reports depicted such minor incidents as the hallmarks of the fundamentalist orientation of the Courts. Unfortunately, members of the Courts, including the most senior, lacked any meaningful experience in geo-politics and the ideologically charged nature of the war on terror. Moreover, the Courts were badly organized and did not have a tight and disciplined command and control, and so were unable to develop a political strategy that would defuse the paranoia of those who propagated Islamophobia. As a result, they fell into the traps which their enemies set. In addition, the absence of a clear line of command meant that the Courts did not have a coherent military strategy. Thus, field commanders acted as they saw fit in the absence of a dominant, agenda-setting central command. Finally, the rapid success of the Courts' militias in defeating the warlords and the population's enthusiasm gave many in the Courts a false sense of inviolability which ultimately undid the hope which their rise spawned.

By October 2006 the whole country was buzzing with excitement about more areas falling to the Courts, and the TFG which was isolated in the regional centre of Baidoa seemed destined to disappear. What the Courts and most Somalis did not know was that the United States and its proxy, Ethiopia, were determined to bring down the Courts.[4] The United States insisted that three terrorists accused of taking part in the bombing of its embassies in Kenya and Tanzania were safe in Mogadishu under the protection of the Courts. Meanwhile, US and British forces were engaged in logistical planning for the Ethiopians to intervene in Somalia under the pretext of assisting the internationally recognized TFG (Copson 2007; Rice and Goldenber 2007). More Ethiopian forces were sent to Baidoa and this convinced some elements of the Courts that they should pre-empt further Ethiopian incursions. These individuals declared a jihad against Ethiopia if its troops did not withdraw from Somalia.[5] US and Ethiopian propaganda machinery used this declaration as evidence that the Courts were part of the 'international jihadist camp' and had to be forcefully eradicated before the danger engulfed the whole region (UN Security Council 2006). Courts militias encircled Baidoa as more Ethiopian forces streamed into Somalia. Two weeks after the UN Security Council passed Resolution 1725, sponsored by the United States, Ethiopia initiated a full-scale invasion of Somalia. Ironically, Mogadishu fell to the Ethiopians on Christmas Day. The revival of the nationalist spirit which the Courts engendered and the short and peaceful six months came to an abrupt end. The international community which failed to come to the aid of the Somali people during almost two decades of warlord terror was relieved that 'Meles has saved their asses in Somalia'.

RESISTANCE TO OCCUPATION AND THE RETURN OF VIOLENCE

Prime Minister Zenawi declared – in a manner reminiscent of George Bush's claim about the invasion of Iraq – that the UICs had been smashed and that his troops would withdraw from Somalia in a matter of weeks. Some commentators took this assertion at face value, while others were more sceptical. Nearly all analysts indicated that most Somalis were opposed to the invasion and that Ethiopia would not withdraw its troops unless it was forced out (Samatar 2007). A few disorganized demonstrations against the Ethiopian occupation took place during the first month. However, formal resistance only began in earnest in early March 2007. Small Somali units began to engage in hit-and-run operations in the capital. Ethiopian troops retaliated with massive and indiscriminate aerial and artillery bombardments of urban areas as resistance intensified. This led to the destruction of entire districts, the death of some 10,000 people and the displacement of over one million. By April a third of the city's buildings were in ruins and the modest economic infrastructure which the population had rebuilt during the previous decade was wrecked. In addition, the Ethiopian forces and their TFG allies denied the displaced population access to humanitarian aid while the international community feebly attempted to nudge the TFG to permit UN agencies to deliver emergency relief.

The United States, which has been the staunchest supporter of the invasion and the TFG, was untroubled by the humanitarian crisis, which the UN Human Rights Commissioner described as the 'worst humanitarian catastrophe in Africa' (Human Rights Watch 2007; Duplat and Weir 2008). It simply repeated its support for the TFG and the Ethiopian invasion in the name of seeking to apprehend *three terrorists*. As the US and Ethiopian plans to crush the resistance stalled, the former provided funds and persuaded the TFG to organize a reconciliation conference, which failed (National Reconciliation Committee 2007).[6] Daily news reports demonstrated that military operations by the resistance had increased and had spread to areas of the country that were previously unscathed. By the autumn of 2008 guerrillas controlled more than 80 per cent of the country.

As it increasingly became apparent that the Ethiopian occupation was doomed and that the TFG had little chance of surviving, the international community engineered another conference that would 'reconcile' the TFG with members of the UICs deemed 'moderate' by the West. Once these members accepted the genealogical political formula (4.5) as the basis of power-sharing with members of the TFG, the process moved quickly and culminated in the formation of another transitional government. A new team of TFG leaders was appointed immediately but this process and the way it was managed only deepened the divisions among the forces that resisted the Ethiopian occupation. Once the dust settled it became clear that most of southern Somalia was controlled by those who rejected the new dispensation and who are affiliated with violent extremists. The consequence has been a nasty and violent political project between these extremists the TFG and AU force. By August 2010 nearly all of south-central Somalia was controlled by the opposition and the latter had projected their violent reach into Uganda.

THE IMPLICATIONS OF SECTARIAN POLITICS AND INTERVENTIONS

Two decades of tyranny by the military preceded the wars that have terrorized Somalis since 1991. These cruel conditions are the result of the interplay of internal and international/regional actors. The interests of Cold War and terror warriors and their regional allies dovetailed with those of sectarian elements of the Somali elite and this collaboration has shaped the political climate which fostered corruption, undermined civic life and produced catastrophe. Local political elites have been unable to get out of their sectarian straitjacket in order to restore the state project, and IGAD, Ethiopia and the international community's intervention have derailed Somalis' attempts to establish peace and political authority.

The confluence of external interventions and sectarian Somali operations not only continues to exacerbate conflict in Somalia but also has six serious consequences for the region and the wider world. First, unless there is a qualitative shift in the nature of international and regional intervention Somalia will remain the source of instability in the region, and the humanitarian conditions which are already dire will become unbearable. Second, efforts by the international community, IGAD and Ethiopia to hamstring Somali political order by empowering sectarian groups will not help Ethiopia or the international community. On the contrary, the more opportunistic the international/regional intervention is the more likely it is that a significant proportion of the Somali people will be alienated, which will only embolden the extremists. Third, Ethiopia's occupation of Somalia and its persistent meddling in the country's affairs for over two decades has also diverted resources away from development in that country while intensifying hostility between the two countries. Without seriously rethinking this strategy both the Ethiopian and Somali people will continue to suffer from underdevelopment due to the misuse of their meagre resources. Fourth, IGAD's close association with the Ethiopian agenda has not served the region and has undermined the organization's impartiality and hence legitimacy in the eyes of the Somali people. The use of IGAD's platform to push this agenda through the AU and the UN tarnished these organizations' credibility and has become a powerful recruiting tool for the extremists while at the same time discouraging Somali civic nationalists from organizing. Fifth, the West's terror strategy in Somalia and their support for political clients like the TFG continues to reinforce divisive and destructive politics which disheartens civilians and provides fertile ground for extremists.

Sixth, at the heart of the Somali calamity has been the absence of an organized and vibrant civic force since the late 1960s which could champion the people's cause. At a minimum, without an organized Somali civic movement which can take on the challenge, the problem will fester. But the rise of a Somali civic movement will need qualitatively different support from the international community to maximize the prospects for peace and democracy in Somalia and whole region.

Finally, the dominant scholarship on the Somali question has generated a lot of smoke but has shed very little light on the problem. It has advocated the institutionalization of a sectarian political project in Somalia without reflecting on how such an approach would reverse the prevailing catastrophe. Further, this literature, mainly produced by consultants and NGOs, is driven by political expediency rather than a practical and ethical quest for justice and peace. Hence, there is a pressing need for a concerted intellectual effort whose aim is to provide a scholarly grounding for a national civic programme anchored in inclusive politics and an accountable system of government. Such an intellectual agenda will dovetail with similar programmes in the region and the world at large and is the only way out of the nightmare.

NOTES

1. Vice President Humphrey came to Mogadishu for 12 hours to provide moral support for Egal in 1968.
2. Minneapolis and Mogadishu, interviews, 1997 and 2001.
3. Conversation with State Department officials, October 2004.
4. The author's conversation with Assistant Secretary of State Frazer revealed this. Washington, DC, September 2006.
5. Among the many now discredited official sources that claimed that the Courts were radical internationalists is the UN Committee on Arms Sanction on Somalia. See UN Security Council, *Report of the Monitoring Group on Somalia Pursuant to Security Council Resolution 1676*, New York, November 2006. This report claimed that the UICs 'sent an approximately 720-person strong military force to Lebanon to fight alongside Hizbollah against the Israel military' (p. 23).
6. Conversation with Assistant Secretary of State for African Affairs, Washington, DC, 29 June 2007.

REFERENCES

Abdillahi SultanTimacade (1968). Poem. Mogadishu.
Abdulkadir, F. (2005). Interview, Nairobi.
Africa Report (1964). August, p. 22.
Africa Report (1964). November, p. 6.

Africa Watch (1990). *Somalia: A Government at War with its Own People*, London: Africa Watch.

Araaleh, Ali S. (2001). Interview, Nairobi, March.

Araaleh, Ali S. (2001). Interview, Nairobi, July.

Barkan, J. (2008). 'Kenya's Great Rift', *Foreign Affairs*, vol. 87: 1, www.foreignaffairs.org.

Copson, R. (2007). *The United States in Africa*, New York: Zed Books.

Department of State (1964). Airgram from US Embassy, Mogadishu, 27 February.

Department of State (1964). Airgram from US Embassy, Mogadishu, 27 June.

Department of State (1966). Foreign Service Dispatch from US Embassy Mogadishu, 10 July.

Drysdale, J. (1964). *The Somali Dispute*. London: Pall Mall Press.

Duplat, P. and Weir, E. (2008). 'Somalia: Proceed with Caution', *Refugees International Bulletin*, 31 March.

Farer, T. (1979). *War Clouds on the Horn of Africa: Crisis of Détente*, New York: Carnegie Endowment for International Peace.

Field notes (2003). Nairobi, 11 March.

Healy, S. (1981). 'The Principle of Self-Determination: Still Alive and Well', *Millennium: Journal of International Studies*, vol. 10, no. 1: 14–28.

Heinrich, W. (1997). *Building the Peace: Experiences of Collaborative Peace Building in Somalia 1993–1996*. Uppsala: Life and Peace.

Human Rights Watch (2007). *Shell-Shocked: Civilians under Siege in Mogadishu*. Washington, DC.

Human Rights Watch (2008). *Collective Punishment: War Crimes and Crimes against Humanity in the Ogaden Area of Ethiopia's Somali Regional State*, Washington, DC.

Hussen, Abdirazak H. (2002). Interview, Minneapolis, November.

Hussen, Abdirazak H. (2003). Interview, Minneapolis, April.

International Crisis Group (2003). *Somaliland: Democratization and its Discontents*, Washington, DC.

Khalif, M. and Doornbos, M. (2002). 'The Somali Region in Ethiopia: A Neglected Human Rights Tragedy', *Review of African Political Economy*, vol. 91: 73–94.

Kivimaki, T. (2001). *Explaining Violence in Somalia*, Helsinki: CTI Conflict Transformation Service.

Legum, C. and Lee, B. (1977). *Conflict in the Horn of Africa*, New York: Africana Publishing Company.

Lemarchand, R. (1979). 'The CIA in Africa: How Central? How Intelligent?' in E. Ray, K. van meter Schaap, and L. Wolf (eds.), *Dirty Work 2: The CIA in Africa*. Secaucus, NJ: C. I. Publication.

Lewis, I. M. (1995). 'A Study of Decentralized Political Structures for Somalia: A Menu of Options', London: unpublished report commissioned by the EU, EC Somali Unit.

Lewis, I. M. (2004). 'Visible and Invisible Differences: The Somali Paradox', *Africa*, vol. 74, no. 4: 489–515.

Mafeje, A. (1971). 'The Ideology of 'Tribalism'', *Journal of Modern African Studies*, vol. 9, no. 2: 253–61.

Mamdani, M. (2004). 'Race and Ethnicity as Political Identities in the African Context', in N. Tazi (ed.), *Keywords: Identity*, New York: Other Press.

Mazzetti, M. (2006). 'Efforts by CIA Fail in Somalia, Officials Charge', *New York Times*, 8 June, www.nytimes.com/2006/06/08/world/africa/08intel.html.

National Reconciliation Committee (2007). *Somali National Reconciliation Congress*, Mogadishu.

New York Times (2007). 'Ethiopia: Crackdown in the East Punishes Civilians', 4 July.

Omar, M. O. (2001). *The Scramble in the Horn of Africa: History of Somalia 1827–1977*, New Delhi: Somali Publications.

Osman, Aden Abdulle (1967). Diary, June.

Parekh, B. (2008). *A New Politics of Identity: Political Principles for an Interdependent World*. New York: Macmillan.

Payton, G. (1980). 'The Somali Coup of 1969: The Case of Soviet Complicity', *Journal of Modern African Studies*, vol. 18, no. 3: 493–508.

Pirio, G.A. (2007). *The Africa Jihad: Bin Laden's Quest for the Horn of Africa*. Lawrence, NJ: Red Sea Press.

Qalib, Jama M. (2004). Interview, Nairobi.

Rice, X. and Goldenberg, S. (2007). 'How the US Forged an Alliance with Ethiopia over Invasion', *The Guardian*, www.guardian.co.uk/world/2007/jan/13/alqaida.usa.

Rotberg, R. (2005). *Battling Terrorism in the Horn of Africa*. Washington, DC: Brookings Institution.

Sahnoun, M. (1994). *Somalia: The Missed Opportunities*. Washington, DC: US Peace Institute.

Samatar, A. I. (1993). 'Structural Adjustment as Development Strategy? Bananas, Boom and Poverty in Somalia', *Economic Geography*, vol. 69, no. 1: 25–44.

Samatar, A. I. (1997). 'Leadership and Ethnicity in the Making of African State Models', *Third World Quarterly*, vol. 18,no. 4: 687–708.

Samatar, A. I. (2002). 'Empowering Warlords and Enfeebling Civics', *Hiiraan Online*, December.

Samatar, A. I. (2004). 'Ethiopian Federalism: Autonomy versus Control in the Somali Region', *Third World Quarterly*, vol. 25, no. 6: 1131–54.

Samatar, A. I. (2007). 'Ethiopian Invasion of Somalia, US Warlordism and AU Shame', *Review of African Political Economy*, vol. 34, no. 111: 155–65.

Samatar, A. I. and Samatar, A. (2002). 'Somalis as Africa's First Democrats', *Bildhaan: International Journal of Somali Studies*, vol. 2: 1–64.

Samatar, A. I. and Samatar, A. (2004). 'International Crisis Group Report on Somaliland: An Alternative Somali Response', *Bildhaan: International Journal of Somali Studies*, vol. 3: 3–22.

Sh. Mukhtar, 2005. Interview, Mogadishu.

Shay, S. (2005). *Somalia between Jihad and Restoration*. New Brunswick, NJ: Transaction Publishers.

Somali Republic (1960). *The Constitution of the Somali Republic*. Mogadishu.

Touval, S. (1963). *Somali Nationalism: International Politics and the Drive for Unity in the Horn of Africa*, Cambridge, MA: Harvard University Press.

Turton, E. R. (1972). 'Somali Resistance to Colonial Rule and the Development of Somali Political Activity in Kenya, 1893–1960', *Journal of African History*, vol. 13, no. 1: 119–43.

UN Security Council (2006). *Report of the Monitoring Group on Somalia Pursuant to Security Council Resolution 167*. New York.

UNDO (1977), *Clan Map of Somalia*. Nairobi: United Nations Development Organization.

United Nations Trusteeship Council (1952). Official Record, 11th Session, 415th meeting, 9 June: 18.

9
Militia and Piracy in the Horn of Africa: External Responses

Bjørn Møller

INTRODUCTION

After a long period of neglect, the Horn of Africa has again become the focus of the West and to some extent the rest of the international community. However commendable this might seem, judged by previous experience it may not really be a good thing, both because the motives behind the involvement of the West are predominantly selfish and because its understanding of the region leaves much to be desired. This explains why the involvement of external players in tbe past has typically exacerbated the region's problems rather than contributing to their solution. In this chapter the focus is Somalia and especially two phenomena: terrorism and piracy. As a preliminary, however, a very brief account will be given of the region, conceived of as a sub-regional security complex, and attention given to its 'patterns of amity and enmity'.

THE (GREATER) HORN OF AFRICA AS A SECURITY COMPLEX

Both the name and the delimitation of the sub-region are contested. The names which are most often encountered are the Horn of Africa, the Greater Horn and East and North-east Africa, to which I might add the IGAD region, the delimitations of which are listed in Table 9.1.

Table 9.1 shows an uncontested core and a somewhat open-ended periphery, the former comprising Somalia, Ethiopia, Eritrea and Djibouti, and an outer ring of countries which may or may not be included.

The region arguably constitutes a security complex in the sense of a group of countries whose national securities cannot realistically be considered apart from one another, partly because of 'ties of amity and enmity'.[1] Even if the Horn is not yet a fully-fledged security complex, at the very least it constitutes a 'proto-' or 'pre-complex', according to Buzan and Wæver.[2] As we shall see, there is a sense of regionness, manifested in the sub-regional organization IGAD, but not really any hegemonic power to lead the region. Even though Ethiopia probably has the ambitions and to some extent the size to take on such a role,[3] it has played a part in too many of the region's conflicts to possess the requisite 'detachment' and legitimacy to fulfil it.

Table 9.1 Sub-Regional Delimitations

Djibouti	x	x	x	x	x
Egypt	–	x	x	–	–
Eritrea	x	x	x	x	(x)
Ethiopia	x	x	x	x	x
Kenya	(x)	x	(x)	x	x
Somalia	x	x	x	x	x
Sudan	(x)	x	x	x	x
Tanzania	–	x	–	x	–
Uganda	–	x	–	x	x

As far as the 'ties of amity and enmity' are concerned there are more of the latter than of the former and even the existing ties of amity have often been based on the logic that 'my enemy's enemy is my friend' rather than on genuine affinity.[4] Three relations of enmity have been particularly venomous.

- Ethiopia and Somalia are each other's arch-enemies, mainly because of Somalia's irridentist ambitions of uniting all Somali nationals in one state, which entails claims on Ethiopian territory. Not only has this produced one full-scale war between the two countries – the Ogaden war (1977–78)[5] – it has also involved the continuous involvement of each in the internal affairs of the other. Somalia has thus supported first the Western Somali Liberation Front (WSLF) and then the Ogaden National Liberation Front (ONLF) as well as the little known United Western Somali Liberation Front (UWSLF) and for a short period in 2006 the Oromo Liberation Front (OLF), which claims to represent the largest ethnic group in Ethiopia.[6] As we shall see, Ethiopia has responded in kind by supporting various Somali rebel movements and even (so-called) governments, the only requirement being that their goals were compatabile with those of Addis Ababa.

- Ethiopia and Eritrea likewise have a long tradition of enmity, dating back to the protracted struggle by the Eritrean People's Liberation Front (EPLF) for independence, which began shortly after the forced incorporation of the former Italian colony into Ethiopia.[7] The fact that the two incumbent presidents were close allies and comrades-in-arms in their struggle against the Dergue regime in Ethiopia produced no more than a brief honeymoon period after their victory[8] and the growing mutual hostility culminated in a full-scale war (1998–2000).[9] Ever since, they have been waging a proxy war against each other by supporting opposing (government or insurgent) armed groups, not least in Somalia.[10]
- Sudan and Uganda have also long been at loggerheads, partly manifested in a protracted proxy war – Uganda supporting the SPLA in south Sudan (replacing Ethiopia as foreign patron)[11] and Sudan supporting the Lord's Resistance Army (LRA) in northern Uganda.[12]

Not only has there thus been strained relations between several states in the Horn of Africa, but all states are afflicted by domestic conflict, ranging from predominantly political ones with only sporadic or low-key resort to violence in, for instance, Ethiopia and Kenya[13] to fully-fledged civil wars in Somalia and Sudan.[14] Needless to say, while this has increased the demand for regional efforts at conflict resolution, it has simultaneously reduced the supply of such efforts in the sense of incapacitating the regional organization, the Inter-Governmental Authority on Development (IGAD).[15] This organization is handicapped by not quite corresponding to the confines of the security complex as well as by the fact that one of the most problematic actors, Eritrea, has suspended its membership. A more profound problem is that few of the member states have much military or other capacity to help solve other countries' problems before they have solved their own. Should they nevertheless try, they would immediately be suspected of having a hidden agenda – often rightly so. This has not least been the case with regard to Somalia, to which we shall now turn.

SOMALIA: STATE FAILURE, WARLORDISM AND TERRORISM

The Somali state collapsed completely in 1991 when the regime of Siad Barre was overthrown without any of the competing rebel groups being strong enough to replace it.[16] It has remained stateless ever since, thus representing the world's most obvious case of complete state collapse.

Statelessness

In fact the Somali state has collapsed in more than one sense. First, south-central Somalia has remained without any government since 1991, even though more than a dozen externally sponsored attempts have been made to restore some form of statehood.[17] A couple of these have brought into being political structures that have been granted at least partial international recognition, tantamount to formal or external statehood, but none has come close to possessing empirical or internal statehood in the sense of actually governing anything.[18]

Second, the north-western part of the country, the former British colonial territory of Somaliland, seceded from the rest, the former Italian Somaliland, in 1991 and has remained de facto independent ever since. Even though it has managed to create an 'empirical state' it lacks international recognition,[19] implying that the quasi-government of the quasi-state of 'Somalia' also claims to represent and govern this part of what used to be Somalia, which might in fact have sufficed for it to meet the failed state criterion. A third part of the country, Puntland, remains in kind of limbo, as it declared itself autonomous in 1998 and has remained so ever since, without formally proclaiming independence.[20] Should it decide to do so, there will probably be nothing 'rump Somalia' can do to prevent this from happening, except perhaps to hamper its international diplomatic recognition. Quite a strong case might thus be made for Somalia being trifurcated or even a state system *in statu nascendi*.[21]

Not only the West but also most of the 'international community' have grown accustomed to viewing statelessness as a serious defect in need of repair. Rather than investigating matters on the ground in the stateless territory, politicians and most of the academic community have simply equated statelessness with disorder, anarchy and chaos, and on this basis embarked on state-building attempts, even when these were almost certain to fail. At best external actors could serve as midwives for 'governments without governance capacity' rather than providing scope for territories exhibiting what has aptly been called 'governance without government'.[22]

After the departure in 1995 of the last troops from the exceptionally ineffective combined United Nations–United States peacekeeping mission (UNOSOM I-II and UNITAF)[23] Somalia was largely left to its own devices until around 2005. In this period, the country did pretty well in terms of day-to-day security and economically as traditional and other non-state authorities stepped into fill the vacuum created by the absence of a state. The all-pervasive clan structure with its rules for *diya* (compensation) payments provided both a modicum of deterrence and mechanisms for conflict resolution; the business community and others who could afford it hired former militia members as security guards; a blend of shari'a and customary law provided a legal framework; and local and/ or clan-affiliated courts sprang up throughout the country, often accompanied by court militias providing some informal 'policing'.[24] Not only did the domestic economy fare reasonably well, but foreign trade also flourished and, perhaps most surprisingly, the country did not relapse into a barter economy even when the last authentic banknotes had disappeared, but managed to maintain a monetary economy based on various forms of counterfeit paper money.[25]

State-Building?

Even though the country was thus evidently able to manage without them, two would-be governments were nevertheless appointed in the new millennium. First came the Transitional National Government (TNG), which was established in 2000 as the outcome of an internationally sponsored conference in Arta, Djibouti. Besides severe internal disputes, the TNG also proved utterly incapable of governing the country – indeed, it did not even bother to pretend that it was trying. Its actual control extended to only half of the capital plus various small enclaves in the interior, and it was never able to ensure even the personal security of its members, as several members of the TNG were assassinated. By 2003 the TNG had collapsed completely in all but name, having received some formal recognition by the UN, the Organization for African Unity (OAU), IGAD, the Arab League, the Organization of the Islamic Conference (OIC) and a few other international actors.[26]

Next came the Traditional Federal Government (TFG), which was created in 2004 under the auspices of IGAD as a product of the so-called Eldoret process, involving Somali 'political leaders' who were, for the most part, self-appointed.[27] Regional rivalry between Ethiopia on the one side, sponsoring the Somali Reconciliation and Reconstruction Council (SRRC), and Djibouti and various Arab countries on the other side, supporting the TNG, did not help at all. Nevertheless, a 'draft transitional federal charter' was formally adopted, followed by the establishment of various 'transitional federal institutions' (TFI), the most important being the Transitional

Federal Parliament (TFP) and the Transitional Federal Government (TFG) and a Transitional Federal President.

This might in fact describe the political structure of almost any country, except for two minor details. First was the fact that the parliament empowered to appoint the rest of the TFI was not to be actually elected, but appointed by the various clans. While a number of clans were indeed co-opted into the agreement, others were excluded, and from the very beginning the TFI were dominated by the SRRC and Ethiopia's closest ally in Somalia, Abdullahi Yusuf Ahmed from Puntland whom Addis Ababa managed to have elected as President.[28] Second, and even more seriously, the TFI have never really governed anything, and the TFG did not find the situation in Somalia safe enough for it to dare relocate from Kenya to Somalia without foreign protection.

Having appealed in vain to both the UN and the AU for a protection force of 20,000, it eventually settled for Ethiopian armed protection, allowing it to move its headquarters to Somalia in January 2006, albeit not to the capital, Mogadishu, but to Baidoa, while still denying the presence of any Ethiopian troops. Only after a full-fledged Ethiopian invasion in December 2006 did the TFG dare relocate to Mogadishu, yet still sorely lacked governance capacity as the country plunged into chaos, by which time the TFG's alliance with Addis Ababa had deprived it of whatever little legitimacy it might previously have enjoyed.

2006 proved to be a veritable *annus horribilis*, when everything that could go wrong did, partly because of external interference.[29] It all began with a clandestine US mission in February to create an Alliance for the Restoration of Peace and Counter-Terrorism (ARPCT) through a handsome distribution of dollar bills to various warlords in Mogadishu and elsewhere.[30] This operation backfired even more than most other clandestine missions, as it provoked the various shari'a courts (which had already formed a loose coordination body) to unite in the Union of Islamic Courts (UIC, also known by various other acronyms) with a coordinated command of the various court militias.

The US motives for this singularly ill-fated meddling in domestic affairs in a country they had deliberately ignored since their rather undignified departure in 1994 had to do with its fears of terrorism. In concrete terms, the United States seems to have suspected at least one of the alleged planners of the two embassy bombings in Nairobi and Dar-es-Salaam in August 1998[31] might be hiding in Somalia; and more abstractly Washington feared that Somalia as a 'failed state' would serve as a safe haven for terrorists. Even though virtually everybody has eventually come to believe in this link between state failure and terrorism, a closer look at the figures shows there to be no correlation between the two regardless of how one defines the hypothesized link – the failed state as a battlefield of terrorism, a breeding ground for terrorists or a transit area for international terrorists en route to their target.[32] Interestingly, in the early 1990s al-Qaeda had also erroneously believed that a Somali state collapse would provide the network with an ideal setting, but the correspondence between the operative they dispatched to Somalia during the civil war clearly shows that the terrorists found the environment at least as challenging and inhospitable as other, more respectable foreign actors.[33]

The UIC quickly defeated the ARPCT and had by June 2006 established control over most of south-central Somalia, including all of Mogadishu, thus coming much closer to actual statehood than any of the moribund and de facto externally imposed 'governments' before them.[34] However, they never managed to establish a clear and hierarchical governing structure, which allowed partly self-proclaimed spokesmen for minor groups to come to prominence. Among these rising stars was Sheik Aways, a former military commander of the Al-Ittihad Al-Islamiya (AIAI), which had enjoyed some success in the early 1990s, only to be defeated,[35] following which they receded into near-oblivion, also because their ideological foundation in a Wahhabist version of Islam had little resonance among the Somali population, who were accustomed to much more liberal and undogmatic forms of Islam.[36]

The rise to prominence of a former AIAI commander sounded alarm bells both in Ethiopia – where the AIAI had been, perhaps rightly, accused of a couple of terrorist attacks in the mid-1990s – and in the United States, which had included Sheikh Aways and his organization in its list of foreign terrorists and terror organizations. When the UIC also began flirting with the various rebel groups in Ethiopia – not only those claiming to represent the ethnic Somalis, but also the Oromos – Ethiopia began planning for a military invasion. Having apparently consulted Washington and obtained its approval, in late December 2006 it launched a large-scale military invasion, albeit officially acting on behalf of the TFG. The UIC in turn almost immediately dispersed, only to continue the struggle in a very disorganized fashion, blending small-scale guerrilla warfare with acts of terrorism, in which they received support from al-Qaeda, which declared Somalia a new battleground in its global jihad against the infidel, now personified in Ethiopia, the United States and virtually all the expatriates living in Somalia.[37] Following the invasion and the ensuing re-ignition of the civil war, the TFG became increasingly isolated nationally, notwithstanding its unwavering support from abroad. Following negotiations in Djibouti the TFG had by the end of 2008 decided to extend its own mandate, which had expired, and it had undergone a rather profound transformation by co-opting one faction of the former UIC, now renamed the Alliance for the Re-Liberation of Somalia (ARS, created in September 2007) into an enlarged TFP and a 'unity' TFG and appointed one of its leaders as president. It therefore seems more appropriate to refer to this as 'TFG-2' rather than keeping up the pretence that it is the original TFG. Indeed, the main feature shared by TFG-1 and TFG-2 was that neither has possessed any governance capacity whatsoever.[38]

Whereas Somalia had not previously been a hotbed of terrorism, it now became one as a result of the 'war on terror'. Not only did it now attract foreign fighters, but new armed groups also sprang up across the country with an ideological affinity to Osama bin Laden's notorious network and with a particularly nasty disposition and an unfortunate preference for attacking humanitarians. Most prominently among these nefarious forces was the al-Shabaab ('youth') militia, which had links to the AIAI, but soon superseded it in all respects.[39] The fact that the country had been invaded by an infidel (Christian) neighbour whose counter-insurgency warfare was very brutal[40] allowed them to skilfully blend a patriotic with their own religious political agenda.

Realizing that its presence was unwelcome, Ethiopia from the very beginning was looking for an exit option, leaving it to find other external actors willing and able to support the TFG. Fortunately for Addis Ababa, but otherwise very unwisely, the AU offered to send a peacekeeping force to replace the Ethiopian occupation forces, but only two member states, Uganda and Burundi, agreed to send troops. This left the African Union Mission to Somalia (AMISOM), which had been projected to comprise around 6,000 troops, seriously understaffed and unable to do much more than protect itself. The requests by the AU to the UN to dispatch a UN mission were rejected. At the time of writing (June 2011) neither the TFG-2 nor AMISOM had made any headway and the solemn proclamation by an AU summit meeting on the need to strengthen its peacekeeping mission seemed as unlikely to be implemented as previous declarations to the same effect.[41]

In summary, a wide range of external actors have played important roles in bringing about the seemingly hopeless situation still prevailing in mid-2011, ranging from non-state actors such as the al-Qaeda network via neighbouring states and great powers such as the United States to a panoply of international organizations. An overview of who supports whom is shown in Figure 9.1. Unfortunately, most of these external players are there mainly for disparate, selfish reasons, which goes a long way towards explaining why they seem to have done more harm than good. The same is the case for the additional external actors who are involved in counter-piracy operations off the coast of Somalia without getting involved on the ground.

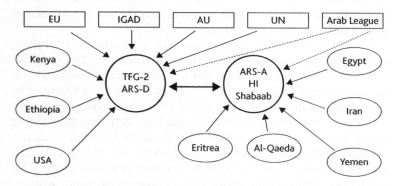

Legend: AU: African Union; ARS-A: Alliance for the Reliberation of Somalia-Asmara; ARS-D: Alliance for the Reliberation of Somalia-Djibouti; HI: Hizb al-Islam; IGAD: Intergovernmental Authority on Development; EU: European Union; UN: United Nations; USA: United States of America. Single arrows signify support and double arrows antagonism

Figure 9.1   Alignments and Antagonisms in Somalia c. 2010

MILITIAS, TERRORISTS AND PIRATES

At the time of writing the picture is one of a rather bizarre sovereignty game played by the various states as well as international organizations, ranging from IGAD via the AU, NATO and the EU to the UN, all of which keep up the pretence that there is a fragile, but nevertheless genuine state in Somalia which is worth supporting, even though it is obvious to everybody else that there is not.[42] Had it not been for AMISOM the TFG-2 would have left Mogadishu a long time ago, as have most of its members, who are concerned about their personal safety than the fate of their country. While quasi-states such as Somaliland and Puntland exercise some meaningful control over their respective territories, south-central Somalia completely lacks any Weberian 'monopoly on the legitimate use of force'[43] and various other armed actors are the real power-holders.

On land we find various militias, including the notorious al-Shabaab and the armed wing of another Wahhabist group, the Hizb al-Islam. The fact that both have been labelled as terrorists by the United States and others (not without reason, it must be said) makes it complicated to deal with them, which is highly problematic considering that they control most of south-central Somalia. Their control may, however, be more precarious than one might think. First of all, despite their ideological affinity and common origins (both descending from AIAI) they do not form a solid alliance, and their relationship has alternated between collaboration and rivalry, and occasionally armed struggle.[44] Second, quite a few of the various militias ostensibly operating under the auspices of al-Shabaab or Hizb al-Islam seem to do so for opportunistic reasons rather than out of religious fervour, implying that they may well switch their alignment if this is seen as in their interests in economic or security terms.[45] Besides these 'homegrown religious loonies' an unknown number of religious fanatics from abroad have apparently followed the call by al-Qaeda leader Al-Zawahiri to join their Islamist brethren in the jihad against the infidel invaders.[46]

In addition to these (at least ostensibly) religious militias, there are several gangster-like militias preying on both the local population and, even more so, what is left of the expatriate community, who are affiliated to the various international organizations. Finally, and mainly in response to the aggregate 'militia problem', there are quite a lot of armed private security company staff in Somalia, mainly serving as bodyguards for the expatriates or involved in the training of Somali security personnel.[47]

At sea (but of course home-based on land) we find various pirate gangs and syndicates preying on both the shipping intended for Somalia or other countries in the region (mainly on the east coast) and international shipping sailing from Asia and the Middle East to Europe and North America via the Gulf of Aden–Suez Canal route.[48] Unsurprisingly, it is primarily the latter which has attracted international attention in the form of national and multinational naval forces patrolling a corridor through the Gulf of Aden as well as parts of the adjacent seas.[49]

One should not, of course, trivialize the piracy problem, which incurs substantial economic costs, mainly in the form of exorbitant and rising ransom payments,[50] which were estimated at between $4.9 billion and $8.3 billion in 2010.[51] However, the fact that the vast majority of shipping companies still prefer the short Suez route to the safer, but longer and more expensive route round the Cape seems to indicate that the average costs are far from prohibitive. In addition to the economic costs, there are, of course, serious human costs. Even though the Somali pirates are statistically less likely than their 'colleagues' in Asia to kill their captives (which would indeed be bad for business),[52] being held hostage for a protracted period is surely far from enjoyable.[53]

Table 9.2   Somali Piracy, 2003–9

Location	2003	2004	2005	2006	2007	2008	2009	2010
Somalia East Coast	3	2	35	10	31	19	80	139
Gulf of Aden	18	8	10	10	13	92	117	53
Red Sea	–	–	–	–	–	–	15	25
Somalia Total	21	10	45	20	44	111	197	217
World	445	329	276	239	263	293	410	445

There has been considerable speculation about the reasons for the sharp rise in Somali piracy, especially since 2005 (see Table 9.2).[54] Some have attributed this to the deteriorating economic situation which has 'pushed' unemployed Somalis into piracy. In this view the pirates are seen more as victims than as perpetrators and criminals.[55] There is certainly some truth to this as the long period of statelessness – manifested in the absence of any law enforcement capacity and especially of any functioning coastguard – left Somalia's territorial waters and its exclusive economic zone (EEZ) vulnerable to maritime poaching by foreign trawler fleets as well as to the dumping of toxic waste. Referring to these activities as 'resource piracy' some analysts have depicted the pirates as engaged in 'defensive piracy'.[56] Some of the first pirate gangs did, indeed, describe themselves as 'voluntary coastguards'[57] and some may even be viewed by other Somalis as 'social bandits' in the Hobsbawmian sense,[58] but the pirates do not behave like 'saltwater Robin Hoods' by taking from the rich in order to give to the poor. At most they take ransom monies from the filthy rich of the world and, by spending at least some of the proceeds locally, benefit, however indirectly, some of the dirt poor of the world. Considering that the annual income per pirate has been loosely estimated at $33,000–79,000, compared to the next best guess of US$500,[59] the lure of easy money seems a satisfactory explanation of how former fishermen or militia members have been drawn into piracy and the reason why piracy began to rise when it did may simply be that the Somali pirates found a way to attack the big and valuable prey and have been adept at learning the lessons ever since.[60]

A supplementary explanation is, of course, that there has been nothing to stop them. Even though a legal case can be made for the duty of Somalia to contain piracy,[61] such a duty does not create the ability to do so. A report published by Jack Lang, the UN Secretary-General's special adviser on Somali piracy (especially legal issues pertaining to it), in January 2011[62] was thus certainly right in pointing to the need for a comprehensive approach which should both give pirates something better to do than robbing ships, by creating jobs ashore and/or restoring the fishery of Somalia and strengthening the ability of 'Somalia' to enforce the law and thus honour its international obligations. This is easier said than done, however, and the experience with external interventions in the past gives few grounds for optimism. The only institutional setup so far that has had any success with containing piracy was the Islamic courts in 2006, as shown by the figures for the east coast of Somalia in Table 9.2.

CONCLUSION

What this chapter has shown is that the Horn of Africa is a troubled sub-region with numerous conflicts within as well as between countries, and with very little institutional capacity to handle them. Those countries which might have the capacity lack the legitimacy, and vice versa. This has touched all the region's countries, but not to the same extent. Somalia stands out as by far the most afflicted and is now home to some of the most intense fighting between some of the most atrocious armed groups in the region, and partly as a result the worst humanitarian crisis in the entire continent.

While this might sound like a strong argument for determined extra-regional engagement, it is not. Judging by the experience so far, ever since the first intervention in the early 1990s – not to mention the Cold War – the involvement of external players tends to exacerbate problems rather than solve them, partly because the humanitarian motives are mixed with selfish ones and partly because of a total inability to understand the situation on the ground. However cynical and/or defeatist this may sound, the Somali population may thus best be served by the disengagement of the international community, with one significant exception. There is still, and will undoubtedly for quite some time remain, a desperate need for emergency relief in the form of food supplies, medical support and the like.

NOTES

1. Buzan, Barry (1991). *People, States and Fear. An Agenda for International Security Studies in the Post–Cold War Era* (2nd edition), Hemel Hempstead: Harvester Wheatsheaf, pp. 186–229, quotation from p. 190.
2. Buzan, Barry and Wæver, Ole (2003). *Regions and Power. The Structure of International Security*, Cambridge: Cambridge University Press, p. 64. On the Horn see pp. 230–1 and 241–3.
3. Iyob, Ruth (1993). 'Regional Hegemony: Domination and Resistance in the Horn of Africa', *Journal of Modern African Studies*, vol. 31, no. 2: 257–76.
4. Good overviews include Lyons, Terrence B. (1992). 'The Horn of Africa Regional Politics: A Hobbesian World', in Howard Wriggins (ed.), *Dynamics of Regional Politics. Four Systems on the Indian Ocean Rim*, New York: Columbia University Press, pp. 153–209; Selassie, Bereket Habte (1980). *Conflict and Intervention in the Horn of Africa*, New York: Monthly Review Press; Woodward, Peter (2003). *The Horn of Africa. Politics and International Relations*, London: I. B. Tauris; Clapham, Christopher (1995). 'The Horn of Africa: A Conflict Zone', in Oliver Furley (ed.), *Conflict in Africa*, London: I. B. Tauris, pp. 72–91; Cliffe, Lionel (1999). 'Regional Dimensions of Conflict in the Horn of Africa', *Third World Quarterly*, vol. 20, no. 1: 89–112.
5. Farer, Tom J. (1979). *War Clouds on the Horn of Africa: The Widening Storm* (2nd edition), New York: Carnegie Endowment for International Peace; Gorman, Robert F. (1981). *Political Conflict on the Horn of Africa*, New York: Praeger; Tareke, Gebru (2000). 'The Ethiopia–Somalia War 1977 Revisited', *International Journal of African Historical Studies*, vol. 33, no. 3: 635–67.
6. Kyama, Reuben (2006). 'Ethnic Somalis Threaten to Destabilize Ethiopia', *Terrorism Focus*, vol. 3, no. 46. On the 'Oromo problem', see Gudina, Merera (2007). 'Ethnicity, Democratization and Decentralization in Ethiopia: The Case of Oromina', *Eastern Africa Social Science Research Review*, vol. 23, no. 1: 81–106.
7. Negash, Tekeste (1997). *Eritrea and Ethiopia. The Federal Experience*, New Brunswick, NJ: Transaction Publishers, *passim*; Iyob, Ruth (1995). *The Eritrean Struggle for Independence. Domination, Resistance, Nationalism, 1941–1993*, Cambridge: Cambridge University Press; Pool, David (2001). *From Guerrillas to Government. The Eritrean People's Liberation Front*, Oxford: James Currey, *passim*.
8. Ottaway, Marina (1995). 'Eritrea and Ethiopia: Negotiations in a Transitional Conflict', in I. William Zartman (ed.), *Elusive Peace. Negotiating an End to Civil Wars*, Washington, DC: Brookings Institution, pp. 103–19.
9. Negash, Tekeste and Tronvol, Kjetil (2000). *Brothers at War. Making Sense of the Eritrean–Ethiopian War*, Oxford: James Currey; Lata, Leenco (2003). 'The Ethiopia–Eritrea War', in Jane Boulden (ed.), *Dealing with Conflict in Africa. The United Nations and Regional Organizations*, Basingstoke: Palgrave Macmillan, pp. 153–84; Abbink, Jon (1998). 'Briefing: The Eritrean–Ethiopian

Border Dispute', *African Affairs*, vol. 97, no. 389: 551–65; Iyob, Ruth (2000). 'The Ethiopian–Eritrean Conflict: Diasporic vs. Hegemonic States in the Horn of Africa, 1991–2000', *Journal of Modern African Studies*, vol. 38, no. 4: 659–82; Tronvoll, Kjetil (1999). 'Borders of Violence – Boundaries of Identity: Demarcating the Eritrean Nation-State', *Ethnic and Racial Studies*, vol. 22, no. 6: 1037–60; Reid, Richard (2003). 'Old Problems in New Conflicts: Some Observations on Eritrea and Its Relations with Tigray, from Liberation Struggle to Inter-State War', *Africa*, vol. 73, no. 3: 369–401.

10. Abbink, Jon (2003). 'Ethiopia–Eritrea: Proxy Wars and Prospects for Peace in the Horn of Africa', *Journal of Contemporary African Studies*, vol. 21, no. 3: 407–25.

11. Woodward, *The Horn of Africa*, pp. 50–1, 123 and *passim*; Johnson, Douglas H. (2003). *The Root Causes of Sudan's Civil War*, Oxford: James Currey, pp. 88–9.

12. Prunier, Gérard (2004). 'Rebel Movements and Proxy Warfare: Uganda, Sudan and the Congo (1986–1999)', *African Affairs*, vol. 103 no. 412: 359–83.

13. On Ethiopia, see Hagmann, Tobias (2005). 'Beyond Clanishness and Colonialism: Understanding Political Disorder in Ethiopia's Somali Region, 1991–2004', *Journal of Modern African Studies*, vol. 43, no. 4: 509–36; Samatar, Abdi Ismail (2004). 'Ethiopian Federalism: Autonomy versus Control in the Somali Region', *Third World Quarterly*, vol. 25, no. 6: 1131–54. On the disturbances in Kenya, see International Crisis Group (2008). 'Kenya in Crisis', *Africa Report*, no. 137, Brussels: ICG; Branch, Daniel and Cheeseman, Nic (2008). 'Democratization, Sequencing, and State Failure in Africa: Lessons from Kenya', *African Affairs*, vol. 108, no. 430: 1–26.

14. On the North–South civil war, see Johnson, *The Root Causes of Sudan's Civil War*, *passim*; Deng, Francis M. (1995). *War of Visions. Conflict of Identities in the Sudan*, Washington, DC: Brookings Institution, *passim*; Lesch, Ann Mosely (1998). *The Sudan. Contested Identities*, Oxford: James Currey. On Darfur, see Prunier, Gérard (2005): *Darfur. The Ambiguous Genocide*, Ithaca, NY: Cornell University Press; de Waal, Alex (ed.) (2007). *War in Darfur and the Search for Peace*, London: Justice Africa; Flint, Julie and de Waal, Alex (2005). *Darfur: A Short History of a Long War*, London: Zed Books, *passim*; Daly, M. W. (2007). *Darfur's Sorrow. A History of Destruction and Genocide*, Cambridge: Cambridge University Press, *passim*.

15. Juma, Monica Kathina (2003). 'The Inter-Governmental Authority on Development and the East African Community', in Mwesiga Baregu and Christopher Landsberg (eds.), *From Cape to Congo. Southern Africa's Evolving Security Challenges*, Boulder, CO: Lynne Rienner, pp. 225–52; Apuuli, Kasaija Philip (2004). 'IGAD's Protocol on Conflict Early Warning and Response Mechanism (CEWARN). A Ray of Hope in Conflict Prevention', in Alfred G. Nehma (ed.), *The Quest for Peace in Africa. Transformations, Democracy and Public Policy*, Utrecht: International Books, pp. 173–87; Mwaüra, Cirû and Schmeidl, Susanne (eds.) (2002). *Early Warning and Conflict Management in the Horn of Africa*, Lawrenceville, NJ: Red Sea Press, *passim*.

16. Adam, Hussein M. (1995). 'Somalia: A Terrible Beauty Being Born?' in I. William Zartman (ed.), *Collapsed States. The Disintegration and Restoration of Legitimate Authority*, Boulder, CO: Lynne Rienner, pp. 69–90.

17. Menkhaus, Kent (2006). 'Governance without Government in Somalia: Spoilers, State Building, and the Politics of Coping', *International Security*, vol. 31,

no. 3: 74–106. For a much more extreme version of the same basic idea, see Van Notten, Michael (2005). *The Law of the Somalis. A Stable Foundation for Economic Development in the Horn of Africa*, Trenton, NJ: Red Sea Press, *passim*.

18. On the terminology, see Jackson, Robert (1987). 'Quasi-States, Dual Regimes, and Neoclassical Theory', *International Organization*, vol. 41, no. 4: 519–49; Jackson, Robert (1990). *Quasi-States, Sovereignty, International Relations, and the Third World*, Cambridge: Cambridge University Press, *passim*.

19. Bradbury, Mark (2008). *Becoming Somaliland*, Oxford: James Currey; Kibble, Steve (2001). 'Somaliland: Surviving without Recognition; Somalia: Recognized but Failing?' *International Relations*, vol. 15, no. 5: 5–25; Hansen, Stig Jarle and Kibble, Steve (2007). 'Somaliland: A New Democracy in the Horn of Africa', *Review of African Political Economy*, vol. 34, no. 113: 461–76; Eggers, Alison K. (2007). 'When is a State a State? The Case for Recognition of Somaliland', *Boston College International and Comparative Law Review*, vol. 30: 211–22.

20. Höhne, Markus V. (2006). 'Political Identity, Emerging State Structures and Conflict in Northern Somalia', *Journal of Modern African Studies*, vol. 44, no. 3: 397–414; Höhne, Markus V. (2009). 'Mimesis and Mimicry in Dynamics of State and Identity Formation in Northern Somalia', *Africa*, vol. 79, no. 2: 252–81; Doornbos, Martin (2000). 'When is a State a State? Exploring Puntland', in Piet Konings, Wim van Binsbergen and Gerti Hesseling (eds.), *Trajectoires de libération en Afrique contemporaine*, Paris: Karthala, pp. 125–39.

21. Haldén, Peter (2008). 'Somalia: Failed State or Nascent States–System?' *FOI Somali Papers*, no. 1, Stockholm: Swedish Defence Research Agency, pp. 53–6.

22. Menkhaus, 'Governance without Government in Somalia'.

23. On the interventions(s), see Lyons, Terrence and Samatar, Ahmed I. (1995). *Somalia. State Collapse, Multilateral Intervention, and Strategies for Political Reconstruction*, Washington, DC: Brookings Institution; Sahnoun, Mohamed (1994). *Somalia. The Missed Opportunities*, Washington, DC: United States Institute for Peace, *passim*; Hirsch, John L. and Oakley, Robert B. (1995). *Somalia and Operation Restore Hope. Reflections on Peacemaking and Peacekeeping*, Washington, DC: United States Institute for Peace Press, *passim*; Lewis, Ioan and Mayall, James (1996). 'Somalia', in James Mayall (ed.), *The New Interventionism 1991–1994. United Nations' Experience in Cambodia, Former Yugoslavia and Somalia*, Cambridge: Cambridge University Press, pp. 94–126; Findlay, Trevor (2002). *The Use of Force in Peace Operations*, Oxford: Oxford University Press, pp. 142–8 and 166–218; Wheeler, Nicholas J. (2000). *Saving Strangers: Humanitarian Intervention in International Society*, Oxford: Oxford University Press, pp. 172–207.

24. Menkhaus, 'Governance without Government in Somalia'; Menkhaus, Ken (2007). 'Local Security Systems in Somali East Africa', in Louise Andersen, Bjørn Møller and Finn Stepputat (eds.), *Fragile States and Insecure People? Violence, Security, and Statehood in the Twenty–First Century*, Basingstoke: Palgrave Macmillan, pp. 67–97; Hagmann, Tobias and Hoehne, Markus (2009). 'Failures of the State Failure Debate: Evidence from the Somali Territories', *Journal of International Development*, vol. 21, no. 1: 42–57; Le Sage, Andre (2005). *Stateless Justice in Somalia. Formal and Informal Rule of Law Initiatives*, Geneva: Centre for Humanitarian Dialogue; Osimbajo, Yemi (1996). 'Legality

in a Collapsed State: The Somali Experience', *International and Comparative Law Quarterly*, vol. 45, no. 4: 910–23.

25. Little, Peter D. (2003). *Somalia: Economy Without State*, Oxford: James Currey, *passim*; Mubarak, Jamil A. (2003). 'A Case of Private Supply of Money in Stateless Somalia', *Journal of African Economies*, vol. 11, no. 3: 309–25; Leeson, Peter T. (2007). 'Better off Stateless: Somalia Before and After Government Collapse', *Journal of Comparative Economics*, vol. 35, no. 4, pp. 689–710; Webersik, Christian (2006). 'Mogadishu: An Economy without a State', *Third World Quarterly*, vol. 27, no. 8: 1463–80.

26. Jan, Amin (2001). 'Somalia: Building Sovereignty or Restoring Peace', in Elizabeth M. Cousens and Chetan Kumar (eds.), *Peacebuilding as Politics. Cultivating Peace in Fragile Societies*, Boulder, CO: Lynne Rienner, pp. 53–88; Lortan, Fiona (2000). 'Africa Watch. Rebuilding the Somali State', *African Security Review*, vol. 9, nos. 5–6: 94–103; Anonymous (2002). 'Government Recognition in Somalia and Regional Political Stability in the Horn of Africa', *Journal of Modern African Studies*, vol. 49, no. 2: 247–72, esp. pp. 252–4; Streleau, Susanne and Ngesi, S'Fiso (2003). 'Somalia: Beginning the Journey from Anarchy to Order', in Erik Doxtader and Charles Villa-Vicencio (eds.), *Through Fire with Water. The Roots of Division and the Potential for Reconciliation in Africa*, Cape Town: David Philips, pp. 154–85, esp. pp. 155–6; International Crisis Group (2002). 'Somalia: Countering Terrorism in a Failed State', *Africa Report*, no. 45, Brussels: ICG, pp. 5–7; International Crisis Group (2003). 'A Blueprint for Peace in Somalia', *Africa Report*, no. 59: 3; Doornbos, Martin (2002). 'Somalia: Alternative Scenarios for Political Reconstruction', *African Affairs*, no. 101: 93–107.

27. International Crisis Group, 'A Blueprint for Peace'; Eno, Mohamed A. (2007). 'Inclusive but Unequal: The Enigma of the SNRC and the Four-Point–Five (4.5) Factor', in Abdulahi A. Osman and Issaka K. Souare (eds.), *Somalia at the Crossroads. Challenges and Perspectives on Reconstituting a Failed State*, London: Adonis & Abbey, pp. 58–81; Lewis, Ioan M. (2010). 'Mogadishu Scrap Merchants Form a Gangster Government: An EU Contribution', in Ioan M. Lewis, *Making and Breaking States in Africa: The Somali Experiment*, Trenton, NJ: Red Sea Press, pp. 179–94.

28. International Crisis Group (2004). 'Biting the Somali Bullet', *Africa Reports*, no. 79, Brussels: ICG; International Crisis Group (2004). 'Somalia: Continuation of War by Other Means', *Africa Reports*, no. 88.

29. Menkhaus, Ken (2007). 'The Crisis in Somalia: Tragedy in Five Acts', *African Affairs*, vol. 100, no. 204: 357–90.

30. Prunier, Gerard (2006). 'A World of Conflict since 9/11: The CIA Coup in Somalia', *Review of African Political Economy*, vol. 33, no. 110: 749–52; McGregor, Andrew (2006). 'Warlords or Counter-Terrorists: U.S. Intervention in Somalia', *Terrorism Focus*, vol. 3, no. 21.

31. On the 1998 attacks, see Champagne, Becky (lead ed.) (2005). *Anatomy of a Terrorist Attack. An In-depth Investigation into the 1998 Bombings of the U.S. Embassies in Kenya and Tanzania*, Pittsburg, PA: Matthew B. Ridgway Center.

32. For the actual figures and correlation analysis, see Møller, Bjørn (2007). 'Terror Prevention and Development Aid: What We Know and Don't Know', DIIS Report, no. 2007:3, Copenhagen: DIIS, www.diis.dk/graphics/ Publications/ Reports2006/diisreport–2007–3.pdf.

33. Harmony Project (2007). *Al Qaeda's (Mis)Adventures in the Horn of Africa*, Westpoint, NY: Combating Terrorism Center, United States Military Academy, *passim*.

34. Bryden, Matt (2006). 'Can Somalia Salvage Itself?' *Current History*, vol. 105, no. 691: 225–8; Stevenson, Jonathan (2007). 'Risks and Opportunities in Somalia', *Survival*, vol. 49, no. 2: 5–20; Shay, Shaul (2008). *Somalia between Jihad and Restoration*, Edison, NJ: Transaction Publishers, pp. 93–128 and *passim*; Spencer, Robert (2007). 'Somalia: Rise and Fall of an Islamist Regime', *Journal of International Security Affairs*, no. 13: 31–7.

35. Tadesse, Medhane (2002). *Al–Ittihad. Political Islam and Black Economy in Somalia*, Addis Ababa: Meag; Le Sage, Andre (2001). 'Prospects for al Itihad and Islamist Radicalism in Somalia', *Review of African Political Economy*, vol. 28, no. 89: 472–7.

36. Marchal, Roland (2004). 'Islamic Political Dynamics in the Somali Civil War', in Alex de Waal (ed.), *Islamism and Its Enemies in the Horn of Africa*, London: Hurst & Co, pp. 114–45; Adam, Hussein (2010). 'Political Islam in Somali History', in Markus Hoehn and Virginia Luling (eds.), *Milk and Peace, Drought and War. Somali Culture, Society and Politics. Essays in Honour of I. M. Lewis*, London: Hurst, pp. 119–35; Elmi, Afyare Abdi (2010). *Understanding the Somalia Conflagration. Identity, Political Islam and Peacebuilding*, London: Pluto Press, pp. 48–72.

37. Ayman Al-Zawahiri, quoted in Blanchard, Christopher (2007). 'Al Qaeda: Statements and Evolving Ideology', *CRS Reports for Congress*, no. RL32759, Washington, DC: Congressional Research Service, pp. 13–14.

38. International Crisis Group (2008). 'Somalia: To Move Beyond the Failed State', *Africa Report*, no. 147, Brussels: ICG, pp. 10–11; Bruton, Bronwyn (2009). 'In the Quicksands of Somalia', *Foreign Affairs*, vol. 88, no. 6: 79–94; Dagne, Ted (2009). 'Somalia: Prospects for a Lasting Peace', *Mediterranean Quarterly*, vol. 20, no. 2: 95–112.

39. Hansen, Stig Jarle (2008). 'Misspent Youth. Somalia's Shabab Insurgents', *Jane's Intelligence Review*, September: 16–20; Marchal, Roland (2009). 'A Tentative Assessment of the Somali *Harakat Al–Shabaab*', *Journal of Eastern African Studies*, vol. 3, no. 3: 381–404; Bruton, Bronwyn E. (2010). 'Somalia: A New Approach', *Council Special Report*, no. 52, New York: Council on Foreign Relations.

40. Human Rights Watch (2007). 'Shell-Shocked: Civilians under Siege in Mogadishu', *Human Rights Watch*, vol. 19, no. 12A; Human Rights Watch (2008). '"So Much to Fear": War Crimes and Devastation in Somalia', *HRW Report*, no. 1-56432-415-x.

41. Feldman, Robert L. (2008). 'Problems Plaguing the African Union Peacekeeping Forces', *Defense and Security Analysis*, vol. 24, no. 3: 267–79; Williams, Paul D. (2009). 'Into the Mogadishu Maelstrom: The African Union Mission to Somalia', *International Peacekeeping*, vol. 16, no. 4: 514–30; International Crisis Group (2011). 'Somalia: The Transitional Government on Life Support', *Africa Report*, vol. 170, Brussels: ICG, pp. 17–19 and *passim*.

42. On the term, see Jackson, 'Quasi-States, Dual Regimes, and Neoclassical Theory, pp. 32–49; and Adler-Nissen, Rebecca and Gammeltoft-Hansen, Thomas (eds.) (2008). *Sovereignty Games. Instrumentalizing State Sovereignty in Europe and Beyond*, New York: Palgrave Macmillan, *passim*.

43. Weber, Max (1946). 'Politics as Vocation', in H. H. Gerth and C. Wright Mills (eds.), *From Max Weber: Essays in Sociology*, New York: Galaxy Books, pp. 77–128, quote from p. 78.

44. International Crisis Group (2010). 'Somalia's Divided Islamists', *Africa Briefing*, no. 74, Brussels: ICG.

45. See Hansen, 'Misspent Youth', pp. 16–20; Hansen, Stig Jarle (2008). 'Private Security and Local Politics in Somalia', *Review of African Political Economy*, vol. 35, no. 1, pp. 585–98; Marchal, 'A Tentative Assessment of the Somali *Harakat Al–Shabaab*'; Bruton, 'Somalia: A New Approach'.

46. See Ayman Al–Zawahiri, quoted in Blanchard, Christopher (2007). 'Al Qaeda: Statements and Evolving Ideology', *CRS Reports for Congress*, no. RL32759, Washington, DC: Congressional Research Service, pp. 13–14; Ibrahim, Mohamed (2010). 'Somalia and Global Terrorism: A Growing Connection?' *Journal of Contemporary African Studies*, vol. 28, no. 3: 283–95; Vidino, Lorenzo, Pantucci, Raffaello and Kohlmann, Evan (2010). 'Bringing Global Jihad to the Horn of Africa: al Shabaab, Western Fighters, and the Sacralization of the Somali Conflict', *African Security*, vol. 2, no. 4: 216–38.

47. Kinsey, Christopher Paul, Hansen, Stig Jarle and Franklin, George (2009). 'The Impact of Private Security Companies on Somalia's Governance Networks', *Cambridge Review of International Affairs*, vol. 22, no. 1: 147–61.

48. Kraska, James and Wilson, Brian (2009). 'Maritime Piracy in East Africa', *Journal of International Affairs*, vol. 62, no. 2: 55–68; Murphy, Martin N. (2008). *Small Boats, Weak States, Dirty Money. Piracy and Maritime Terrorism in the Modern World*, London: Hurst, pp. 101–10; Murphy, Martin N. (2011). *Somalia: The New Barbary? Piracy and Islam in the Horn of Africa*, London: Hurst, *passim*.

49. Kraska, James (2009). 'Coalition Strategy and the Pirates of the Gulf of Aden and the Red Sea', *Comparative Strategy*, vol. 28, no. 3: 197–216.

50. Lansing, Paul and Petersen, Michael (2011). 'Ship-Owners and the Twenty-First Century Somali Pirates: The Business Ethics of Ransom Payments', *Journal of Business Ethics*, vol. 3: 507–16.

51. Bowden, Ann et al. (2011). 'The Economic Cost of Maritime Piracy', Working Paper, One Earth Future, December; Bowden, Ann et al. (2011). 'The Economics of Piracy. Pirate Ransoms and Livelihoods off the Coast of Somalia', *Geopolicity*, May See also Xiaowen Fu, Ng, Adolf K.Y. and Lau, Yui–Yip (2010). 'The Impacts of Maritime Piracy on Global Economic Development: the Case of Somalia', *Maritime Policy and Management*, vol. 37, no. 7: 677–97; Sullivan, Alexa K. (2010). 'Piracy in the Horn of Africa and Its Effects on the Global Supply Chain', *Journal of Transportation Security*, vol. 3, no. 4: 231–43.

52. An excellent analysis of the economics of piracy is Leeson, Peter T. (2009). *The Invisible Hook: The Hidden Economics of Pirates*, Princeton, NJ: Princeton University Press. Even though it focuses on the 'golden age' its findings seem applicable to modern piracy.

53. Hurlburt, Kaija (2011). *The Human Cost of Somali Piracy*, Oceans Beyond Piracy, www.oceansbeyondpiracy.org.

54. Based on data from Table 9.1 (listing actual and attempted attacks) in the 2009 and 2010 ICC International Maritime Bureau's Annual Reports (2010 and 2011). *Piracy and Armed Robbery against Ships*, London: ICC. The figures for 2009 differ slightly between the two reports, but the most recent ones have been used.

55. Kisiangani, Emmanuel (2010). 'Somali Pirates: Villains or Victims?' *South African Journal of International Affairs*, vol. 17, no. 3: 361–374; Marchal, Roland (2011). 'Somali Piracy: The Local Context of an International Obsession', *Humanity. An International Journal of Human Rights, Humanitarianism and Development*, vol. 2, no. 1: 31–50.

56. Samatar, Abdi Ismail, Lindberg, Mark and Mahayni, Basil (2010). 'The Dialectics of Piracy in Somalia: the Rich versus the Poor', *Third World Quarterly*, vol. 31, no. 8: 1377–94. An even more elaborate typology is found in Huang, Hun-Lun (2010). 'Who Are Sea Cutthroats? A Typological Analysis of Pirates', *Crime, Law and Social Change*, vol. 53, no. 3: 277–98.

57. 'Somali Coastguard', *Shiptalk*, 17 February 2006; 'Off the Coast of Somalia: "We Are Not Pirates. These Are Our Waters, Not Theirs"', *The Independent*, 14 November 2008; 'On the Lawless East African Coast, Piracy is the Only Business that Pays', *Guardian News and Media*, 10 April 2008; '"We Consider Ourselves Heroes" – a Somali Pirate Speaks', *The Guardian*, 22 November 2008.

58. Hobsbawm, Eric (1969). *Bandits*, London: Delacorte Press, *passim*.

59. Bowden et al., 'The Economic Cost of Maritime Piracy'.

60. Psarros, George Ad., Christensen, Alexander F., Skjong, Rolf and Gravir, Gjermund (2011). 'On the Success Rates of Maritime Piracy Attacks', *Journal of Transportation Security*, vol. 4, no. 7: 309.

61. Abeyratne, Ruwantissa (2009). 'The Responsibility of Somalia for the Acts of the Somali Pirates', *Journal of Transportation Security*, vol. 2, no. 3: 63–76.

62. 'Report of the Special Adviser to the Secretary-General on Legal Issues Pertaining to Piracy off the Coast of Somalia', UN Documents, no. S/2011/3025, January 2011.

Notes on the Contributors

Seifudein Adem has taught at Addis Ababa University, Ethiopia and at the University of Tsukuba, Japan. He is currently research associate professor of political science at Binghamton University, New York, and is president-emeritus of the New York African Studies Association. Among several other books, he is a co-editor of *Politics of War and Culture of Violence* (Africa World Press, 2008).

Redie Bereketeab holds a PhD in Sociology from Uppsala University, Sweden. Currently he is working at the Nordic Africa Institute as a researcher on conflict and state building in the Horn of Africa. He also teaches, part-time, African development and conflicts, state crisis and development in the Horn of Africa at the Department of Government at Uppsala University (Development Studies). His research interests include state, nation, nationalism, identity, conflict, democratization and governance. He is the author of several articles, book chapters and books. His latest publication is *State Building in Post-Liberation Eritrea: Challenges, Achievements and Potentials* (2009).

Kassahun Berhanu is currently Chair and Associate Professor, Department of Political Science and International Relations, Addis Ababa University. He was a IGAD nominee as a member of the Panel of Experts in the Abyei Boundary Commission from April to July 2005 and resident Vice President of the Organization of Social Science Research in Eastern and Southern Africa from December 2005 to January 2007.

Hassan Mahadallah is a Somali living in the United States. He holds a PhD in Political Science from Tulane University, New Orleans, LA and an MA in International Relations from Baylor University, Waco, TX. Currently, he is a full professor at Nelson Mandela School of Public Policy and Urban Affairs at Southern University, Baton Rouge, LA. His research interests include the US administration and foreign policy, and politics and governments in the Horn of Africa. His publications on these topics appear in academic journals and edited books.

Kidane Mengisteab is Professor of African Studies and Political Science at Pennsylvania State University. His research interests encompass the relevance of African 'traditional' institutions of governance and traditional judicial systems, conflict resolution and democratization in contemporary Africa, and the socioeconomic implications of the expansion of extractive industries and commercial farming in Africa. He is author or editor of several books on Africa. His most recent book, with Okbazghi Yohannes, is *Anatomy of an African Tragedy: Political, Economic and Foreign Policy Crisis in Post-Independence Eritrea* (2005). Mengisteab is currently completing a book entitled *The Horn of Africa: A Hot Spot on the Global System*, in which he examines the key internal and external factors that have rendered the Horn of Africa prone to chronic conflicts.

Bjørn Møller holds an MA in History and a PhD in Political Science. From 1985 to 2011 he was senior researcher, first at the Copenhagen Peace Research Institute and then the Danish Institute for International Studies. Since 2011 he has been Professor of International Politics at the Department of Political Science of the University of Aalborg, Copenhagen. He is also an external lecturer at the Institute of Political Science as well as at the Centre of African Studies at the University of Copenhagen.

Abdalbasit Saeed is a socio-cultural anthropologist currently working as an independent private consultant. He graduated at the Faculty of Economic and Social Studies, University of Khartoum (1971), and obtained an MA (1978) at the Institute of African and Asian Studies, University of Khartoum and a PhD in Socio-cultural Anthropology, at the Faculty of Liberal Arts, University of Connecticut. He is actively involved in civic community life through his elected positions as Chairman of the Board of Trustees for the Network of Nuba-based National Non-Governmental Organizations (NUBANET) operating in South Kordofan State. Deputy Chairman, the Sudan National Civic Forum, and Secretary General, The National Justice Party–Sudan.

Abdi Ismail Samatar is Professor of Geography at the University of Minnesota and Research Fellow at the University of Pretoria. He is the author of several books and over sixty articles and essays. Among his books is *An African Miracle: State and Class Leadership and Colonial Legacy in Botswana Development* (1999).

Peter Woodward is Professor Emeritus, University of Reading, UK; and formerly Lecturer in Political Science at the University of Khartoum, Sudan. He is author of various books and articles on north-east Africa, most recently *US Foreign Policy and the Horn of Africa* (2006); and was editor of *African Affairs*, the Journal of the Royal African Society, from 1986 to 1997.

Index

Compiled by Sue Carlton

Printed and bound by CPI Group (UK) Ltd, Croydon, CR0 4YY

16/04/2025

14658481-0002